How Humans Learn

HOW HUMANS LEARN

THE SCIENCE AND STORIES BEHIND EFFECTIVE COLLEGE TEACHING

Joshua R. Eyler

WEST VIRGINIA UNIVERSITY PRESS
MORGANTOWN 2018

ISBN:
Cloth 978-1-946684-65-3
Paper 978-1-946684-64-6
Ebook 978-1-946684-66-0

Library of Congress Cataloging-in-Publication Data
Names: Eyler, Joshua, author.
Title: How humans learn : the science and stories behind effective college
    teaching / Joshua R. Eyler.
Description: First edition. | Morgantown : West Virginia University Press,
    2018. | Series: Teaching and learning in higher education | Includes
    bibliographical references and index.
Identifiers: LCCN 2018025280| ISBN 9781946684653 (cloth) | ISBN
    9781946684646 (pbk.) | ISBN 9781946684660 (ebook)
Subjects: LCSH: College teaching--Methodology. | College teaching--Psycho-
    logical aspects. | Learning, Psychology of. | Cognitive learning. |
    Cognitive neuroscience. | Brain research.
Classification: LCC LB2331 .E98 2018 | DDC 378.1/25--dc23
LC record available at https://lccn.loc.gov/2018025280

Cover and book design by Than Saffel / WVU Press

For Christopher Fee and Thomas Scheivert,
two extraordinary teachers.

and

For Kariann and Lucy,
who have taught me everything that matters.

CONTENTS

—

ACKNOWLEDGMENTS

—

I have wanted to be a teacher since I was five years old, and I've been fortunate to be able to stand in front of a classroom and to work with amazing students and colleagues for much of my adult life. This book is a testament to the powerful lessons I have learned from them through the years. Higher education has often been the subject of fierce attacks by politicians, pundits, and outspoken writers who have never actually taught a course, but when I think of the many people at our colleges and universities who work tirelessly for our students I remain optimistic about our future.

For supporting my work on this book in so many ways, I have many people to thank.

Part of my research was funded by the Program in Writing and Communication and the Humanities Research Center at Rice University. I am grateful for their financial support, which allowed me to visit colleagues at institutions across the country to talk about effective teaching practices.

The amazing staff at Rice's Fondren Library never skipped a beat with my numerous requests for interlibrary loans and other off-site materials.

I am lucky to work with Betsy Barre and Robin Paige at the Center for Teaching Excellence. They push me daily to think about teaching and the research on teaching in new ways. In particular, I owe Robin, a sociologist, a great deal of gratitude for our conversations about the importance of the social world in our understanding of education. Betsy, too, has tolerated frequent interruptions to her work as I ran into her office to try out one idea after another. She has always been characteristically patient and insightful and they are both model colleagues and friends. Beth

Castillo, Elaine Chang, and Danielle Tilillie have also been instrumental in the work we do at the CTE and, thus, have helped me to sharpen my focus for this project.

Others who have been influential in shaping the ideas found in this book include: Lisa Balabanlilar, Kelly Baker, Beth Beason-Abmayr, Temma Berg, Jason Berger, Lee Skallerup Bessette, Fred Biggs, Derek Bruff, Alex Byrd, Sarah Rose Cavanagh, Laurie Cella, Matthew Cella, Jeffrey Jerome Cohen, Adrienne Correa, Paul Corrigan, Steve Cox, Catherine Denial, James Donahue, Kimberly Eby, Will Eggers, Sarah Ehlers, Liz Eich, Jennie-Rebecca Falcetta, Kevin Gannon, Brian Gibson, Kathleen Gibson, Marcus Gobrecht, Len Goldberg, Bridget Gorman, Michael Gustin, Bob Hasenfratz, Mikki Hebl, Matthias Henze, Susan Hrach, Jonathan Hsy, Mariko Izumi, Steve Jenkins, Jason Jones, Dorothy Kim, Rachel Kimbro, Gene Kraus, Noreen Lape, Chris Lunardi, Jon Malesic, Kathleen Matthews, Dave Mazella, Caleb McDaniel, Elizabeth McFalls, Michael McFalls, Pat McHenry, Michelle Miller, Sean Michael Morris, Frank Napolitano, John O'Connor, Jim Owen, Sandy Parsons, Chuck Pearson, Ian Petrie, Andrew Pfrenger, Wendy Pfrenger, Thomas Recchio, Emily Redding, Joshua Redding, Shelley Reid, Kimberly Reichel, Stephanie Roach, Daniel Ross, Mark Sample, Aaron Sanders, E. Virginia Sanders, Gregory Semenza, John Sexton, Allison Singley, Liana Silva, Scott Solomon, Bonni Stachowiak, George Stanton, Jesse Stommel, Robert Talbert, Kisha Tracy, Bethany Usher, Tracy Volz, John Warner, and Jaimin Weets.

I had the opportunity to present versions of some of these chapters at Columbus State University, Grand View University, the University of Michigan-Flint, Radford University, the University of Texas School of Dentistry, and Rice. I am grateful for the comments and questions I received from those who attended these talks.

I thank the incredible and dedicated students who helped me with some of my research—Ujalashah Dhanani, Hanna Downing, Alexander Lam, and Lucy Matveeva.

The staff at West Virginia University Press and the two discerning readers the press chose to review the book have improved it tremendously.

Stephanie Fuqua read a draft of the entire manuscript and gave me very valuable feedback.

Donna Boyd, Susan Engel, Kathleen Gibson, Emily Hendryx, Dennis Huston, John Hutchinson, Jessica Lahey, Lesa Tran Lu, Gretchen Kreahling McKay, Cameron Hunt McNabb, Peter Newbury, Ann Saterbak, Donald Saari, Kimberly Shaw, Patricia Taylor, and Matthew Wettergreen graciously allowed me to interview them or observe their teaching so that I could provide concrete examples of outstanding practices to support the arguments I make in the book.

James Lang and Derek Krissoff have been steadfast, wise, and encouraging editors. Their enthusiasm for this project has been unwavering and I am thankful to have worked with them.

I have dedicated this book, in part, to the two teachers who have meant the most to me. First is Tom Scheivert, who was my English teacher in eleventh and twelfth grades. His classes were rigorous, and he had very high standards, but he was also kind and generous with his time. He saw my potential before I did, and he encouraged me to pursue lofty goals. The other is Chris Fee, who has been my teacher, friend, and mentor since I first took his classes at Gettysburg College. Other than my family, no one has had more influence on the person I have become than Chris. (Try not to blame him too much for this.) I am very lucky to have met both of them and to have been their student.

My parents, Betsy and Rick Eyler, were my first teachers, and I am still learning from them. Other members of my family—

including Sarah Eyler, Amy Eyler, Jon Fuqua, Sydney Fuqua, Andrew Little, Jim Little, Karen Little, Sue Little, Doriann Shuler, and Carrie Wilson—have been incredibly supportive throughout the process as well.

At present, my daughter Lucy is five years old. Watching her grow and learn as a baby, then as a toddler, and now as a smart, inquisitive, and kind little girl helped me to develop some of the questions that led to this book. Being her dad has opened up my world in countless other ways.

My wife, Kariann Fuqua, has always been the biggest advocate for this project and my most outspoken supporter. Every single idea in these pages has been made better by her advice, constructive criticism, and creative perspective as an artist. Beyond all of this, Kariann is also a phenomenal teacher in her own right, and I have learned much from her in that regard. In the end, I wrote this book for her, and I hope it lives up to the faith she has always had in it and in me.

———

How Human Beings Learn

The new developmental research suggests that our unique evolutionary trick, our central adaptation, our greatest weapon in the struggle for survival, is precisely our dazzling ability to learn when we are babies and to teach when we are grown-ups.

—Alison Gopnik, Andrew N. Meltzoff, and Patricia K. Kuhl,
The Scientist in the Crib

WHEN I BEGAN my freshman year at Gettysburg College, I knew two things with the absolute certainty that only an eighteen-year-old can possess: 1) I was someday going to write the Great American Novel; and 2) I was going to get a degree that would allow me to go back to my hometown of Hanover, Pennsylvania—a rural, blue-collar borough best known for the snack foods made in its factories—to be a teacher and a coach. Although I am still holding out hope for that novel, the second goal ultimately changed on an August morning in 1997. I was a sophomore by that point, filing into a classroom in Glatfelter Hall with about twenty or more of my fellow English majors. We had all enrolled in a required course on the history of the English language and had relatively low expectations, to say the least. The course did not enjoy a stellar reputation with students: we valued it in the same way one might prize calisthenics for its character-building qualities. Through the grapevine, however, we had heard that the course would be taught by one of the department's new hires—a medievalist who had just finished his degree at the University of Glasgow.

Sure enough, at precisely nine o'clock, the classroom door burst open and Chris Fee (one of the people to whom this book is dedicated) jumped inside shouting "Hwæt!" It's probably worth refreshing all of our memories that "Hwæt" was often used at the beginning of Old English poems, including everyone's favorite *Beowulf.* The meaning of the word is hotly contested, but it usually signifies something to the effect of "Hey! Listen up! I need to tell you a story!" And what a story it turned out to be.

Chris's enthusiasm, his emphasis on student engagement, and his ability to make the Middle Ages connect vibrantly to the modern world were unlike anything I had ever seen in the classroom. He led discussions with humor, and he asked insightful questions about very old texts that fascinated me. He has this way of expecting that all of his students are going to do brilliant work, and he makes them believe it too. A paper covered in comments from him is a sign of respect, and he tells this to students. Under his guidance, I began to have confidence in my ideas because he treated me as if my voice were important and my thoughts mattered. In those moments when I fell short of the lofty bar he had set, he gave me thorough and wise feedback and pushed me to do better in the way only the best mentors can. When I sat in Chris's classes, I never laughed so hard, nor learned so much.

I particularly remember his Medieval Drama course. Although he had never taught the course before, he had a grand plan that we were all going to stage a medieval religious play at the end of the semester. We spent the first part of the term doing more traditional textual analysis, and then we broke up into teams to put on the production. I landed in a group tasked with translating the Middle English of the Wakefield "Noah" play into a modern idiom, but other students were working on props, making directorial decisions, and even building an actual pageant wagon for us to perform upon. For me, the biggest surprise of the semester was the directors' decision to cast me as Noah himself. I had no acting experience whatsoever, but I relished the role and had a lot of fun. I also acquired a much deeper understanding of drama, both medieval and modern. Chris's pedagogical experiment had worked, and the experience taught us more than any other approach to the subject could have.

Before I graduated, I took many courses with Chris, talked with him over lunches, and learned much from his example. When I told him I wanted to go to graduate school for medieval literature, he gave me some sage advice about the realities of an academic career and then worked his hardest to help me get into a good program. One evening, before I left to begin my PhD program at the University of Connecticut, I had dinner with Chris and asked him why he had helped me so much during my time as a student. Was there any way, I wondered, that I could repay him for his teaching and his kindness? He simply said that he hoped I would do the same thing for a student if I were ever in a position similar to his. I told him I would, and it is not an exaggeration to say that this promise is the foundation on which I have built my career.

We know a great deal about the kind of transformative teaching practiced by instructors like Chris Fee. Thousands of books and articles have been published over the last few decades that have clarified for us the techniques we can use in the classroom to help students learn more successfully. Remarkably, some of these studies actually agree with each other. They point to many of the practices that I saw modeled in Chris's courses and that you'll be reading about in this book. For example, the experiential nature of the Medieval Drama course has been shown to help students make great strides in their learning. Similarly, Chris's engagement and connection with students as well as his well-crafted discussions are strategies backed by a wealth of evidence supporting their efficacy.

We even know, to a significant degree, how these kinds of effective teaching methods work. From inquiry-based approaches to educational games and beyond, there are handbooks and other published guides to help us learn, step by step, how to implement these techniques in our classes. While I have found all of this work extremely valuable, both as a faculty member and as someone who works with instructors on university-wide teaching initiatives, something still continues to gnaw at me. It is one thing to have evidence that a strategy works, but it is another thing entirely to know *why* students learn more when certain techniques are used over others. What is it about the fundamental way human beings learn that makes some teaching strategies successful and others fall short? I wrote this book because I wanted to dip below the surface of educational research to explore these bigger questions that we often assume we have already answered. As I discovered, we may have been assuming too much in this regard. Before I began my research, I thought these answers would be easy to find, but this proved not to be the case. Pieces of the puzzle were isolated in fields that do not talk to each other very often, and even once I had located some of them, the picture was still less than complete. I had to dig into subfields of subfields that I wasn't aware of prior to embarking on this rollercoaster ride. What you are reading now is a synthesis of all that I discovered throughout what has been for me a truly wondrous process.

To be sure, there has been work, even very recently, that has explored the learning processes of students as well as the ways in which instructors can maximize learning by employing evidence-based strategies in the classroom. Some researchers have looked very carefully at the role played by memory in learning,[1] while others have predominantly used the lens of cognitive psychology.[2]

4

I have certainly benefited much from the findings of these writers, but this book takes a different perspective, a bird's-eye view if you will. My basic premise is that we cannot understand how modern college students learn if we do not first place them into a much larger narrative. The story of human learning is a beautiful tale woven into the tapestry of our distant, our recent, and—indeed—our own personal past. To know anything significant about the learning of our students, we must first be able to grasp those deeply rooted mechanisms by which people have always learned and that are vital to the way we understand the world. In other words, human beings approach new ideas, dissect them, and reconstruct them into knowledge in ways that are not just similar, but are part of our very fiber as a species. I focus primarily on our core foundational commonalities as humans before turning to the variety of means that we use as teachers to account for differences among our students. In taking this approach, I do not mean to suggest that attention to diversity in all of its many dimensions is not important. To the contrary, once we understand the fundamental principles of human learning it then becomes easier, not more difficult, to change course for individual learners who are not responding to one strategy or another.

What Is Learning?

First things first: what do we mean when we talk about learning? Although learning is certainly the goal of education, it is not confined to the walls of a classroom. We constantly learn things every day about our lives, our world, ourselves. It turns out, though, that trying to get a handle on the meaning of a term like "learning" is roughly akin to the act of squeezing Jell-O. As you start to put pressure on it, it begins to slip out of your grasp and eventually fires out in many different directions.

Is learning an intentional process? Sometimes. The wealth of studies on implicit learning demonstrates that we can learn even when we are not aware that we trying to do so.[3] Like Pavlov's dogs, we can also learn behaviors through conditioning, although this is certainly not the same thing as constructing knowledge. I do not develop more insights into quantum mechanics every time the dinner bell rings. On the whole, whether or not we need to be active participants for learning to occur depends entirely on the type of learning that is desired.

Additionally, many disciplines have somewhat different definitions of learning. While it is easy to suggest, for example, that we learn through our own observations, social scientists would be quick to point out that we need critical schema by which to assess these experiences in order to truly learn from them. Another take on the subject comes from scientists, who have shown that learning occurs when the brain changes physiologically in some critical way and that these changes, which are often referred to using the term "plasticity," are happening all the time. As Cedar Riener, a cognitive psychologist at Randolph-Macon College, recently noted:

> Your brain is changing right now as you read this sentence, such that if you read this exact sentence again tomorrow, you would recognize exactly when and where you read it, if you read it next week, you would probably remember that you had read it somewhere recently, and if you read this exact sentence again next year, you would probably get a sense of déjà vu. But it would seem silly to claim that I just rewired your brain, even though reading that sentence has absolutely changed the biology of your brain in a durable way.[4]

Note that Riener is quick to point out that our brains are not machines that get wired or programmed, but they are living organisms that are ever changing because we are always learning.

Still further, for the humanities, learning is contextually dependent and often happens through a process of questioning, answering, and designing new questions. Learning in these disciplines is more often about using texts (written, visual, etc.) to build a framework of knowledge and about developing the ability to wrestle successfully with ambiguity, as I did in Chris's class as a student and now try to help my own students do in my literature classes. It is clear, then, that learning is tricky business, but—above all—it is a process whose component mechanisms we all share as members of the same species.

What Do We Have in Common?

Much attention has been paid to our differences when it comes to learning. The notion of learning styles was in vogue for a while, though educational psychologists have worked hard to demonstrate that none of us neatly fall into one particular category or another. It is better to think of our approach to learning as drawing on multiple strategies depending on the context.[5] All of this research focuses on how we are different from each other, but I want to shine some light on our similarities. This is very much a book about the deep-seated commonalities that human beings share with respect to learning. Without question, these shared traits eventually give rise to individual differences, many of which have to do with sociocultural forces, but we cannot fully understand the latter without first looking at the former.

As Daniel Willingham has explained, "Children are more alike than different in terms of how they think and learn."[6] This straightforward claim provides an underpinning for my argument. However, I would like to push Willingham's idea even further. When we look closely, we begin to see clearly that the ways in which we learn as adults are directly connected to how we learn when we are very young and that the learning processes of infants and children are deeply rooted in our evolution as a species. Juan Carlos Gómez has done some important work in this area and suggests that the "argument is simple: our minds are part of a wider evolutionary pattern discernible in the minds of other primates. Its most characteristic feature is development as an adaptive strategy."[7] For Gómez, humans share cognitive patterns not just with each other, but with other primates as well. This suggests how deeply ingrained our mechanisms for learning are. The lynchpin in joining our evolutionary history with our understanding of modern humans, as Gómez notes, can be found in the development—especially cognitive development—of children. The interest in this wide-lens perspective on human beings can be traced back to the 1980s and the founding of a field now known as evolutionary developmental biology (or evo-devo as practitioners call it, though this to me sounds like the name of a bad alt-rock band from the 90s).[8] The research in this relatively new discipline is important for a variety of reasons, not least of which is its emphasis on continuity rather than disjuncture.

But the emphasis on continuity does not stop with bridging the divide between ancient and modern humans. Other researchers have found important links between the learning processes of children and adults. For example, Susan Carey has found the "same signatures of [cognitive] processing in adulthood and childhood" and adds that this "continuity through the life span is an important property of core cognition, for several reasons."[9] It is Alison Gopnik, along with her collaborators, who has done some of the most influential work in this area, though. In an important article called "The Scientist as Child," Gopnik contends that "once the child has engaged in the theorizing necessary to specify the features of its world, most of us, most of the time, may simply go on to the central evolutionary business of feeding and reproducing. But these powerful theory formation abilities continue to allow all of us at some times, and some of us, namely professional scientists, much of the time to continue to discover more and more stuff about the world around us. On this view, science is a kind of spandrel, an epiphenomenon of childhood."[10] This is a powerful claim. Throughout the article she flips convention on its head by suggesting not just that children can make scientific discoveries of their own, but that scientists themselves can make discoveries because their learning mechanisms have not significantly changed since childhood. Along with Andrew Meltzoff and Patricia Kuhl, Gopnik reinforces this position in *The Scientist in the Crib*, explaining that "scientists are such successful learners because they use cognitive abilities that evolution designed for the use of children."[11] I would like to broaden these views to include people other than scientists, as their claim is applicable to all adults who pursue inquiry and discovery in some way. The building blocks of human learning are put into place when we are very young and continue to influence the way we make sense of the world throughout our lives. The brain may mature and develop, but the ways in which we learn remain largely the same. Recent research has begun to show that this is true for all kinds of learning, even mathematics.[12]

Crossing Disciplines

The notion that we share so much as a species can certainly help to keep things in perspective (like department meetings or Yelp reviews), but what does it have to do with our day-to-day practices as teachers in higher education? In truth, we will need to journey carefully through a variety of different disciplines before it is possible to gain a more complete picture of the complexities of human learning, in general, and the learning processes of college students in particular. The most obvious place to begin our quest is the field of cognitive psychology, and—as I noted above—many others have done so. But if we focus only on insights from this domain, we limit ourselves. While I use studies from cognitive psychology to support my claims, I also delve deeply into a neighboring field: developmental psychology. I argue that understanding how cognition develops in infants and young children will also tell us much about the ways in which an eighteen-year-old learns, say, introductory chemistry. I admit that this is something of a novel approach. The literature on teaching and learning in higher education rarely glances backward toward our early years in an attempt to figure out what is happening in our college classrooms. The research I have done for this book, however, suggests that such an approach not only is revealing, but also might be necessary if we ever hope to generate a more nuanced picture of our students as learners.

As we have seen, though, even turning to child development for insight, promising though it may be, brings us into the story near its conclusion. If we do this, we miss the opening chapters, and endings tend to make little sense without beginnings. So I have paired my research in psychology with some attention to evolutionary biology and biological anthropology, two related disciplines that have been interested in cognition, intelligence, and learning for a long time. Taking an evolutionary perspective on learning is filled with much potential, but it is not without its pitfalls either. For one thing, there are a wide variety of explanations for a whole host of evolutionary phenomena, including many of the elements I'll be discussing in this book, like brain size and the influence of social interactions. About the development of brain size in *Homo sapiens*, in fact, one researcher has said, "Every possible mode, type, and level of selection has been identified as a possible cause of human brain expansion by someone, somewhere."[13] And that's just one example. From delightful statements like this, I've learned an important lesson: tread carefully.

We also need to be cautious to avoid what Marlene Zuk, and Leslie Aiello before her, have called "paleofantasies." For Zuk, a paleofantasy is any theory that assumes the process of evolution stopped thousands of years ago and that we are, as she puts it, "stuck in a world to which we are not adapted."[14] In other words, many popular ideas that bring evolution to bear on the way we behave in the modern world seem not to understand that humans have continued to evolve through the millennia and, indeed, will continue to evolve. The notion that we are exactly like our distant ancestors, then, can be a dangerous trap.[15] This is not to say that we shouldn't use evolutionary biology and anthropology to help us think about learning and behavior. Rather, we simply must acknowledge that while evolution has influenced human responses to the world, we are also different from our ancestors.

The field that has unquestionably received most of the recent attention for its possible revelations about education has been neuroscience. For a number of reasons, discussions about the applicability of findings in neuroscience to research on learning have been fraught with controversy. In their recent book *Make it Stick*, Peter C. Brown, Henry L. Roediger III, and Mark A. McDaniel caution that "we're still a very long way from knowing what neuroscience will tell us about how to improve education."[16] Educators have a propensity to see wide-ranging panaceas in very specific scientific studies. Too many have jumped too quickly on isolated studies and tried to argue for the complete overhaul of pedagogies and educational systems from limited data.

However, there is much that is known and has been proven time and again on a large scale about the functions of the brain that can illuminate important ideas about human learning. I doubt I could find a neuroscientist who would tell me that the brain does not change when it learns something, and therefore it is logical to investigate the significance of neuroscientific findings for education. In her book *The New Science of Teaching and Learning: Using the Best of Mind, Brain, and Education Science in the Classroom*, Tracey Tokuhama-Espinosa helps us to decipher which areas of neuroscience might be fruitful for this kind of exploration, particularly because she has substantiated what is known about the brain with enough certainty to apply to research on education, what might be applicable, and also what we should consider to be "neuromyths" that would be disingenuous if applied to education.[17] With informed, authoritative guidance like this, it becomes possible to see links between teaching and neuroscience.

These disciplines have significantly contributed within their domains to our understanding of the learning process. It stands to reason, then, that if we notice similar patterns emerging from psychology, evolutionary biology, and neuroscience, then they might together help us to understand how human beings learn. The particular patterns I noticed from the literature in these fields turned out to be curiosity, sociality, emotion, authenticity, and failure. There may, of course, be others, but together these form a good starting point. I devote one chapter to each of these topics, giving special attention to the ways in which the subject under investigation is tied to our students' cognition. Likewise, every chapter follows a similar template: I begin with a survey of the scientific research before moving into a discussion of the ways in which this research can inform our teaching practices. Interspersed throughout each chapter, I offer some suggestions for small steps you might take right away if you were interested in implementing these techniques. I then conclude with a short section on "Key Takeaways" for instructors, departments, and institutions.

One reason for structuring the book in this way is to cultivate a mode of inquiry that places science in conversation with recent educational research and actual classroom practices. My goal is to use this knowledge of learning as a kind of litmus test for which pedagogical strategies will be effective and as a tool for explaining *why* such techniques work. To that end, I have interviewed or observed outstanding, innovative instructors from across the country who teach in a wide variety of institutions in order to match theory with pragmatic application. This is, or should be, a driving motive for all educational research.

It is worth noting that all of my examples of classroom practice come from the Western model of higher education. I do think that the theories I outline here are more broadly applicable, including to K–12 classrooms, but I have confined myself to what I am most familiar with for the pedagogical illustrations. Many of the instructors profiled in what follows are award-winning teachers (some at the national level), but I have not attempted to be scientific in the choices I made about whom to select. Instead, I wanted to be illustrative, capturing examples from a range of disciplines and institutions. With that in mind, I used the website for the Carnegie Foundation's US Professor of the Year Program along with resources on listservs to which I belong and scholarly journals on teaching and learning to make my choices. Admittedly, teaching awards are only one indication of outstanding classroom practice, but they are highly publicized, which helped me to choose a range of instructors. I interviewed and observed a hearty number of faculty at a variety of colleges and universities, but I also decided to use models for great teaching from the place I know best (and the place to which it was easiest to travel): my home base of Rice University.

I have one small disclaimer before we move along: I am not a scientist. Though hardly shocking to anyone who has read my CV, or even the back of this book, it is important to make this clear at the outset. I have a PhD in medieval studies, and—while I would argue that the scientific method should not solely belong to STEM disciplines—it would be rare to see a medievalist doing research in a physics lab.[18] More relevant to the current project is my role as director of the Center for Teaching Excellence at Rice, where I study how college students learn and, therefore, the most effective teaching practices for helping them achieve success. In the course of this work, I have noticed a particular kind of disconnect. Scholars who study postsecondary teaching and learning rarely look to science (especially the biological sciences) for answers, and scientists are often wary of educators using their work to make claims about student learning. Of course, I'm painting with a broad brush here, but this is generally true in practice as well as in the literature, and I will address why this divide is understandable. Still, as a generalist, it is clear to me that science can add immeasurably to our knowledge about how students learn and the attendant implications for improving teaching. While being careful not to extrapolate too wildly from individual experiments or to claim a unified theory for education, I also want to avoid ignoring the forest because we're all so transfixed on the trees. That is, if we are able to glean, accurately assess, and integrate information from scientific research that will help us know more about student learning, then it is neglectful not to do so.

Designing curricula and courses that pay little heed to the fundamental ways in which human beings learn leads to knowledge gains that are less deep and complete. We may see evidence of memorization and even some conceptual development, but we will not have employed our most valuable resources to achieve learning that is sustainable. Perhaps most importantly, when we utilize the science of learning, it becomes easier to see teaching as something that every instructor can do well. The principles I discuss in this book are tools we can use to help our students to be successful and all of us to become effective, even exemplary teachers. This claim—that we can all be great teachers—may seem bold, but I really do think that everyone who stands in front of a college classroom has the potential to be the kind of instructor Chris Fee was for me all those years ago. We may not fling open the doors of our classrooms bellowing Anglo-Saxon greetings, but we can all have a similar effect on our students' educational journeys, provided we care about who they are and pay close attention to how they learn.

CHAPTER 1

Curiosity

We ascended as a species through incandescent curiosity—that hallmark of scientists in every century—at play in the world.

—Barbara Kiser, "Learning Through Doing," *Nature*

Curiosity is nearly universal in babies, and, in our culture at least, continues to propel children, intellectually, through early childhood. Beyond early childhood, however, its fate rests in great part on the people and experiences that surround and shape a child's daily life. While there are some situations where it would not be good to ask too many questions, or to investigate too persistently, there is a clear empirical link between the hungry mind and the educated mind.

—Susan Engel, *The Hungry Mind*

I only began drinking coffee shortly after my daughter Lucy was born. That may be hard for some to believe, but it is true. Oh, I was no caffeine-saint, but diet soda had always been my poison. When the sleep deprivation that accompanies parenthood set in, I realized I needed something that had a little bit more octane in it, and I finally switched to coffee, much to my wife's delight. Why am I telling you, dear readers, about coffee? Because of our red coffee cups, that's why. We had, at that time, two red coffee cups that were bigger than all the others. Given the amount of sleep that had abandoned me, I often used these cups in the vain hopes that some amount of coffee might restore me to my previous levels of wake-fulness. Sadly, this experiment failed, but another one quickly began.

At about six months of age, I noticed that Lucy became deeply curious about these red cups. She would stare at them, reach her hand out to touch them, rub them (when they were not hot), and try to grab them. She did this with many things around the house, frequently attempting to put them in her mouth as well. For her, learning was about necessity: "That's an interesting looking cup. I need to touch it RIGHT NOW." It was about relevance: "I wonder if that funny red cup is important for my daily needs." It was about trial and error: "I have judged this cup and determined that it is not of immediate significance." I could see all of this being played out concretely each time I drank from one of the cups.

What was revelatory for me, however, was the completely unbri-dled curiosity I witnessed from her in those moments. I began to wonder how, as a teacher, I could spark the same kind of intellec-tual curiosity in my students—about the Middle Ages as opposed to, say, red cups. We were all children once, so what happens to this curiosity that was once the driving force of our daily lives?[1] This key question sent me on the quest for information that I document in this chapter. The more I looked, the more I noticed that many of the arrows began to point in one direction: curiosity is an essential part of the way human beings learn, and it always has been. In order to learn something, we must first wonder about it. This was true of our distant ancestors, and it is true of all of us. Somewhere between the time when children are very young and when they make their way to our college classrooms, however, some of this curiosity gets lost.

Let's go find it.

What Is Curiosity?

Any discussion of curiosity must first begin with the thorny question of definitions. Nearly every article I read about curiosity while conducting research for this project contained some version of the question, "How can we possibly talk about curiosity if we cannot specifically define it?" In fact, perhaps the best place to start my discussion is with the recent declaration by Min Jeong Kang and her coauthors that "despite the importance of curiosity, its psychological and neural underpinnings remain poorly understood."[2] As a biological response, or even as an intellectual construct, curiosity is so complex and nuanced that the only thing scholars can really agree on is its importance. George Loewenstein, one of the foremost researchers on curiosity, has summarized this point of consensus nicely: "Curiosity has been consistently recognized as a critical motive that influences human behavior in both positive and negative ways at all stages of the life cycle. It has been identified as a driving force in child development . . . and as one of the most important spurs to educational attainment."[3] Loewenstein's depiction of the trait's significance cuts across many spheres here, demonstrating both the breadth of the field with respect to the study of curiosity, as well as the reasons for the disparate approaches to the subject. Researchers are bringing to the table a host of methodologies from a variety of disciplines. This is never a bad thing, of course, and the outcome has been important discoveries and multiple lenses through which to view curiosity.

Once we move past the recognized importance of curiosity, though, the multidisciplinary nature of the subject makes things a bit muddy. I'm okay with muddiness as long as we are eventually able to see through to the object itself, and this is the case with curiosity, though its shape and size may look different from what we would expect. Curiosity has been sliced and diced, categorized and recategorized, divided and subdivided, all in an attempt to figure out what it is and whether distinct types of it are at play at various times. Some studies tackle the nature of curiosity head on, while others try to avoid this quagmire by reframing the concept into something else closely related. Interest, novelty, and wonder are all analogous ideas that have been studied in order to isolate a particular aspect of curiosity that could yield verifiable insights. For similar reasons, some have posited that curiosity is a kind of exploration or have linked it to creativity.[4]

Those who study curiosity on its own terms, though, have taken a number of approaches to defining it. In the landmark article from which his earlier comments were taken, Loewenstein sought to cull through the many descriptions and explanations of curiosity in order to derive a definition that could readily be tested. To do so, he first analyzed the dominant theories that governed our understanding of curiosity for much of the twentieth century. Two approaches emerged as being foundational to our early conceptualization of curiosity, both of which fit under the umbrella of behaviorism—a school of thought that was very much in vogue in the early part of the twentieth century. One of these approaches saw curiosity as being a series of behavioral responses to stimuli. The other largely stemmed from the work of Daniel Berlyne, who diverged from this earlier view and began to suggest in the 1950s and 60s that curiosity was a biological drive stemming from an arousal brought on by novelty.[5] In Berlyne's view, it is this drive-arousal pairing that steers our behavior.[6]

What bothered Loewenstein about these definitions was the inability to test any of them. Above all else, he felt that the study of curiosity was in desperate need of this kind of operational definition. As a result, Loewenstein proposed that curiosity is an "information gap," which he explains as the distance between "what one knows and what one wants to know." Explaining a bit further, he notes that "curiosity, in this view arises when one's informational reference point in a particular domain becomes elevated above one's current level of knowledge." Unlike other researchers before him, Loewenstein was very clear that he was not addressing questions about the "cause" of curiosity, which he deemed to be "inherently unanswerable."[7] He was also clear that his information gap theory was developed specifically for the purpose of designing experiments to test for levels of curiosity. It is easy to get the impression from recent work on the subject of curiosity,[8] though, that Loewenstein's approach has become the dominant lens for exploring the subject. There is nothing inherently wrong with this. Loewenstein's work has been influential and has led to tremendous insights on curiosity. However, we must always remember the limitations he himself set out for his theory, and Emily M. Grossnickle acknowledges these constraints in a paper where she attempts to construct a working definition of curiosity to complement Loewenstein's operational one. Hers goes the farthest to capture the many facets of curiosity: "At its core, curiosity is the desire for new knowledge, information, experiences, or stimulation to resolve gaps or experience the unknown."[9] Like Loewenstein's definition, Grossnickle's is derived from a methodical reading of the voluminous literature on curiosity. Though the debt to Loewenstein is clear by the use of the term "gaps," this definition is designed to allow for broad exploration of the concept more generally.

Recently, neuroscientists have also sought to understand curiosity in terms of the brain's activity and, in particular, the role played by curiosity in motivation and reward. M. T. Bardo and his colleagues have gone as far as to suggest that humans appear to have an "innate biological need for novelty" and has linked this need directly to our curiosity.[10] But what happens in our brains when we are curious? To move toward answers to this question, several labs have designed experiments that centered on asking participants trivia questions both while undergoing an fMRI and without the use of this technology.[11] Min Jeong Kang has led the way with this approach. Her widely cited paper describes the process of asking participants questions of a quality not unlike those one might find at a local pub quiz night. The questions varied in their degree of difficulty, and participants rated both their level of curiosity about the answers and their confidence in their answers. Kang and her coauthors discovered that when participants rated their curiosity about an answer as being high, their brains showed more activity in areas like the caudate, which is linked to "reward anticipation, or reward learning, across a wide variety of primary and secondary reinforcers."[12] High ratings of curiosity were also linked to activity in areas of the brain responsible for memory, particularly when the first guess had been wrong (more on this later in the chapter).

In a subsequent study, Matthias J. Gruber, Bernard D. Gelman, and Charan Ranganath achieved similar results and added two important elements to the mix. They found an increase in participants' levels of dopamine when curiosity was high. Dopamine is a neurochemical that has been linked to pleasure activation and addiction, among many other things, and plays a number of important roles in our brains. Its connection to curiosity here is therefore quite fascinating. Gruber and his colleagues also discovered that participants were more likely to remember incidental information (in the case of this experiment, details about human faces) when curiosity was activated.[13] Neuroscientifically speaking, then, we might say curiosity is a mechanism by which we anticipate a reward of information and then remember this acquired knowledge later when we need to access it.[14] In some ways, these new findings loop us back to Berlyne's much earlier discussion of

22

curiosity as a biological drive connected to arousal. The combination of his older work and the information we are learning from neuroscientists adds important facets to the definitions constructed by Loewenstein and Grossnickle.

If we move beyond these attempts to define curiosity, though, we will find that some researchers have addressed our subject's gargantuan nature by identifying different varieties of curiosity and exploring the nuances of each type.[15] Of these different categories, one in particular (epistemic curiosity) is the most relevant for a study of education because it is so closely tied to cognition and the acquisition of knowledge. It should be noted that this is the type of curiosity on which Loewenstein focused. I don't think it can be entirely separated from the other ways in which people are curious, however. It is in part our brain's attraction to novelty that drives us more deeply into subjects that interest us.[16]

You'll notice that we haven't come to any conclusions here. There is no doubt that these studies, and many others like them, have allowed for a nuanced understanding of curiosity, but curiosity is so vast a subject that is it is difficult to favor one approach over another. I'm not sure we need to do that, however. Curiosity is perhaps best viewed as a combination of all of these perspectives. Now that we have a broad sense of the term's various meanings, we can turn to the question of why it is so essential for human learning. To answer that we will need to begin by looking millions of years into our past.

A Curious Species

Human beings aren't the only curious creatures, of course. Anyone who has ever seen a dog cock his head, staring quizzically, knows this to be the case. Apes, our closest relatives, are famously curious animals as well, but what distinguishes us is our ability to use the information we acquire to build knowledge and complex conceptual frameworks. Indeed, according to Juan Luis de Arsuaga, "we are distinguished from chimpanzees by only about 1.6 percent of our sixty to eighty thousand genes. In fact, no more than fifty to one hundred genes are responsible for the cognitive differences between us and them. A very small but very significant genetic change has given us a unique intelligence, making us radically different from all other species."[17] One important element of this intelligence is our profound curiosity. It might be said, in fact, that *Homo sapiens* is the species of curiosity. The medievalist in me thinks that we should dive right into etymology here. If we did, we would discover that the Latin word *sapiens* connotes wisdom and very literally means "knowing." But to truly know anything we must first ask questions, seeking to dig deeper. In other words, we need to be curious. We are a species characterized by our inquisitiveness and our desire to know.

The story of our deep-seated curiosity is a tangled one, especially because discussing the evolution of cognition and intelligence is a tricky business that combines highly technical considerations regarding changes in brain size over the course of millions of years with detailed analysis of the environmental factors that might have led to enhanced cognitive capacities over this same period of time. But it is possible to weave together a narrative from the evolutionary record. As we start to look more closely at the evidence, it turns out that everything begins with our extraordinarily big noggins. Well, not the noggins *per se*, but the actual brains inside of them. In fact, renowned anthropologist Dean Falk specifically attributes our innate curiosity to, as she puts it, the "unusually large brain" of human beings.[18]

Harry Jerison was one of the first researchers to study the evolution of our intelligence by attending to the question of brain size. His premise was "that the integrative functions of the brain, which will define intelligence for us, are limited by the amount of brain that is typical for an animal of a particular species."[19] Jerison believed that "by treating relative brain size as a measure of intelligence at the species level, a between-species measure, it is possible to develop a coherent story about the probable history of intelligence as a biological phenomenon. Like other biological processes, intelligence must have evolved under the influence of natural selection."[20] His research provides the foundation for much of the current work on the evolution of both brains and our intelligence, but what does it all mean? Let's look at his methods. Jerison developed a metric called the encephalization quotient, or *EQ*, as a way to study relative brain size. I'm sure many readers of this book already have a good handle on the intricacies of the encephalization quotient. Perhaps, though, you're like me: when I first encountered the term, I figured I'd better turn right around and go back to writing about medieval literature again. My trepidations were ultimately ill founded, since, as it happens, the concept is rather easy to understand and is particularly important as we look at the evolution of cognition. In Jerison's own words, the *EQ* is the "ratio of actual brain size to expected brain size. . . . Our brain is, thus, about 6 times as large as we should expect it to be were we typical mammals, which puts us with the dolphins, at the head of the living vertebrates, with respect to relative brain size."[21] This is a stunning finding! To call the difference between expected and actual brain size in our species an aberration of nature is too strong, but it is certainly almost unheard of, as Jerison noted. As we follow the breadcrumbs toward understanding the evolution of curiosity, it may be beneficial to pause for a moment and to consider why the brains of human beings are so big.

Some of the earliest evidence of our expanding brain can be found in endocasts of *Australopithecus rudolfensis*, an ancestor of our species that lived about 1.9 million years ago. Since then, the size of the human brain has increased nearly twofold.[22] Evolutionary biologists and biological anthropologists have developed a range of possibilities for explaining this increase. In fact, as Barbara L. Finlay has noted, there may be too many hypotheses to choose from: "Plausible adaptive scenarios designed to account for the evolution of large brains in humans do not just successfully account for it, they do so many times over. We have no shortage of hypotheses. Indeed, we have too many, and all are probably correct, at least in part. The problem of accounting for human brain evolution is not choosing which one of the many ways our behavior differs from our nearest relatives is the essential one, but developing an explanatory scheme that encompasses all of them."[23] Especially for a book like this one, where a main goal is to explore the overall effect of evolution on learning, it is dicey to emphasize one hypothesis over another. Social interactions among early members of our species may have accounted for it, but so could a lot of other things, and we needn't put all of our interpretive eggs into any one basket when the larger point is that our brains got a lot bigger and that the evolution of cognition is tied to this development. Kathleen Gibson, a leading researcher in this area, has gone as far as to say that "the increased information-processing capacity of the human brain allows humans to combine and recombine greater numbers of actions, perceptions, and concepts together to create higher-order conceptual or behavioral constructs than do apes. These constructions are often hierarchical in that new constructs are subordinated into still higher-order constructs. The recombinatory and hierarchical nature of human mental constructions, as well as the human ability to incorporate large amounts of information into varied constructs, appears to account for human creative abilities."[24] This is the first, and in some ways, the most important step toward understanding the role of curiosity as a deep-rooted mechanism for human learning because it would follow that curiosity is a necessary precondition for the kind of creativity Gibson describes here.

Simply being able to construct novel concepts, however, does not indicate the desire to do so or the questioning that leads to such creation. In a personal interview with Gibson, I asked her if these mental constructions led to the development of our curiosity.[25] She stressed that curiosity, in fact, would likely have preceded the constructions, since our closest primate relatives are intensely curious species as well. In other words, curiosity is fundamental to human beings, and the enlargement of our brains would have enhanced our curious disposition. Curiosity, then, seems to have evolved to help us seek out answers, sometimes in beautifully creative ways, and to build more accurate knowledge by processing and correcting faulty assumptions or hypotheses.

It is perhaps this crucial significance of curiosity that has led scholars such as Bo Gräslund to make remarks like this one:

> Curiosity is often seen as humanity's most typical trait, as the seed of our eagerness to explore the world and to try something new, of our attempts to understand the unknown and to ask the eternal questions. As the core of all creativity, curiosity may have been a decisive quality for all our subsequent cultural and social evolution. . . . Curiosity is particularly found in mammals and not least among apes and humans. Infants and children are in their turn more curious than adults, probably because curiosity and play are so important for the acquisition of social and cultural skills. For this reason Konrad Lorenz suggested that human curiosity was an evolutionary consequence of neoteny.[26]

What is neoteny? I'm glad you asked. Neoteny, in its strictest sense, denotes a large-scale retention by a species of its juvenile form and function, along with delayed developmental processes. Human beings, for example, mature at a much slower rate than other primates, and we maintain more of this immaturity in our appearance and actions as adults than is the case with these other species. In order to demonstrate the extent of our neoteny, some early biologists went as far as to create elaborate lists of the ways in which *Homo sapiens* is typified by juvenile characteristics that carry over into adulthood or, put another way, "fetal conditions that have become permanent."[27] For example, Louis Bolk, a researcher from the late nineteenth and early twentieth centuries, remarked upon a number of neotenous traits, including a decrease in our body hair and the small size of our teeth relative to other primates.[28] This kind of cataloguing is perhaps going a bit too far, as neoteny seems to be truer in the macro view than it is in the micro, but it is fascinating to note that the shape of an adult human skull diverges very little from the shape of a child's, which is different from other primates. Comparative images of infant and adult chimpanzee skulls show dramatic changes in shape indicating clear divergence brought on by maturation.[29] This simply isn't the case for human beings.

While the human brain began its long, beautiful journey toward complex cognition and creativity, it was paired with an increasingly extended developmental process that would allow such changes to take place. As individuals, we not only traverse these developmental stages for an exceedingly long amount of time (when compared to our primate relatives), but we bear the mark of this juvenile development for the breadth of our lives, both in our form and in our cognitive processes. So it is with the evolution of *Homo sapiens* as a whole, and our curiosity is the legacy by which we can connect our evolutionary history with ourselves. Though it may be latent for reasons I will explore later in the chapter, we retain the same sense of wonder about the world as adults that I observed in my infant daughter when she reached for my coffee cup. This is not a quirk of nature, but an evolutionary adaptation that has allowed us to discover, to invent, and to learn. Our species has been shaped by nature to be wide-eyed children approaching the world inquisitively from beginning to end, always striving to know more.

Children, Curiosity, and Inquiry

As a way to bring the evolutionary context I just outlined to bear on our understanding of human learning, we should turn now to children themselves and the role played by curiosity in their cognitive development. Indeed, psychologists have long been fascinated by children's curiosity and have sought to explore it through a wealth of experiments. But I think the description that most beautifully captures the dynamism of children's curiosity comes from Barbara Tizard and Martin Hughes, who conducted a large-scale study of children's conversations in the 1980s. As they listened to more and more children, all of whom were between three and four years of age, "[they] found [them]selves continually being surprised and impressed. . . . As [they] studied their conversations [they] were forced to admire their curiosity, their open, questioning minds, and, above all, the persistent and logical manner in which they struggled to make sense of their world."[30] Such a description fits right in with the evolutionary perspective I've previously discussed. If our curiosity is (at least partly) the result of neoteny, our retention of juvenile characteristics that are tied to a long developmental period, then it stands to reason that this curiosity would be most prominent at our earliest ages. Although this observation can seem theoretical on the page, it comes to life as we observe children in infancy and beyond.

Curiosity is such a fundamental aspect of a young child's cognitive development that it is easy to see why many researchers have argued that it is not simply a learning tool, but rather a need or even an instinct, as those early behaviorists suggested. Children seek to know about the world not because they want to, but because they *have* to. To a certain extent, their survival depends on it, but more broadly their social, intellectual, and emotional worlds are driven by curiosity. Learning then occurs when this innate curiosity leads the child to explore and test the world around her. Gopnik, Meltzoff, and Kuhl note that the "rapid and profound changes in children's understanding of the world seem related to the ways they explore and experiment. Children actively do things to promote their understanding of disappearances, causes, and categories."[31] This dynamic has been studied in children of all ages, including infants. As it happens, infant sucking and other kinds of behaviors that denote a fixation of their attention are keys to helping us understand how babies learn. Babies begin the process of exploration by displaying their curiosity in physical ways like sucking, then following through with grasping and touch.[32] In an important 2015 study, Aimee Stahl and Lisa Feigenson found that "when infants see an object defy their expectations, they learn about that object better, explore that object more, and test relevant hypotheses for that object's behavior. Seen through this lens, the decades of findings that infants look longer at surprising events suggest not only that infants are equipped with core knowledge about fundamental aspects of the world but also that this knowledge is harnessed to empower new learning even in infancy."[33] To arrive at these conclusions, Stahl and Feigenson used everyday objects such as balls, blocks, and toy cars to violate expectations. In one experiment, babies would see a ball or car roll behind a screen toward a wall. In some cases, the car or ball would be stopped by the wall when the screen was removed, and in other cases the object would seem to have passed through the wall and then come out on the other side. The experimenters then gave this same object to the babies to explore along with a "distractor" (either the ball or the car, whichever one wasn't used in the experiment). In the end, babies looked longer at and played more with only the object that defied the expectations—only the thing about which they were curious.

These ties between curiosity, exploration, and learning grow even stronger as children advance beyond infancy. A fascinating 2011 article details a series of experiments testing these links in eighty-five children between the ages of four and six. The studies were run by a team of psychologists and cognitive scientists from the University of Louisville, MIT, Stanford, Harvard, and the University of California, Berkeley. The children were divided into four groups, with each group experiencing a different experimental condition. Each condition involved the use of a specially designed toy. In the first group, "the experimenter said, 'Look at my toy! This is my toy. I'm going to show you how my toy works. Watch this!' The experimenter then pulled the yellow tube out from the purple tube to produce the squeak sound. She said, 'Wow, see that? This is how my toy works!' and demonstrated the same action again."[34]

In the second group, the experimenter began the same way but interrupted herself before the second, reinforcing demonstration of the squeaking function and left to attend to other matters. For the third group, the experimenter appeared to suddenly discover the toy, wondered aloud about how the toy worked, and "accidentally" discovered the squeaking. The reinforcement demonstration was completed in this condition. Finally, in the fourth group, the experimenter simply showed the toy to the children and walked away. As the researchers note, "In all conditions, the experimenter then said, 'Wow, isn't that cool? I'm going to let you play and see if you can figure out how this toy works. Let me know when you're done!'"[35] The first group—the one where the children were intentionally instructed as to the function of the toy—played with the toy for less time and did less with the toy than all of the other groups. They explored less and tried out fewer possibilities. The results, in fact, were not only statistically significant but impressively so.[36] The more curiosity was diminished through exposition and direct instruction here, the less exploration was initiated. Not only does this study reveal how fundamental curiosity is for human learning, but the implications of this research also have value for understanding effective teaching, a subject to which I will soon turn.[37]

I would be remiss if I did not briefly touch on the importance of Jean Piaget for this discussion. He looms large in any examination of curiosity within a developmental framework, not least because of the important role he felt curiosity played in the expansion of a child's cognitive capabilities. He identified an "interest in novelty" or "the search for the new" as arising in the fifth stage of sensorimotor development, one of what he poetically named a "tertiary circular reaction."[38] For Piaget, the key dynamic at play with curiosity fell in the transition from assimilation to accommodation (two of his most foundational concepts). In Piaget's schema, a child will try to assimilate all new information into current knowledge frameworks. If this is not possible, she will then need to accommodate to allow for the development of a new network of ideas. He saw curiosity as a bridge between the two. The failure to assimilate sparks an understanding that something is new and will need to be accommodated. The critical point for Piaget's conceptualization of curiosity here, though, is that to generate the interest in new things the information must appear to be closely related to other ideas that have already been assimilated. Curiosity is engaged when the child realizes the novel idea does not work like these others and must be accommodated.[39] He also believed that curiosity led to "inventions or at least real discoveries" for children.[40]

It has sometimes seemed to me that the reception of Piaget's work by others is like the Elvis/Beatles conundrum Quentin Tarantino lays out in *Pulp Fiction*: you can either love one or the other, but there's not really a middle ground. So it is with Piaget. Some psychologists have built their entire research programs on Piagetian models, while others recognize his importance while (rightly, I think) criticizing his focus on children's "egocentric" natures. That is, he problematically downplayed the importance of social interactions for cognitive development.

One shape these critiques have taken has been in the realm of children's questions. While researchers have long been interested in the kinds of questions children ask,[41] recent attention has been given to the act of asking questions as an engine for cognition. In particular, Michelle Chouinard's 2007 monograph "Children's Questions: A Mechanism for Cognitive Development" has been important for reframing the significance of the questioning process.[42] Chouinard's work focuses on children between the ages of one and five and, at one level, adds significantly to our knowledge about the sheer numbers of questions children ask at these ages (sometimes hundreds per day) and whether these questions are simply seeking facts or more expansive explanations. Although the number of questions children ask remains fairly consistent, especially between ages two and five,[43] the type of questions begin to shift from those that are solely focused on information to more conceptual, explanatory questions. Even a pre-verbal child at age one can ask questions by pointing to objects, for example, but more than 90 percent of these questions are rooted in a desire for facts rather than more complex explanations.[44] On another level, though, Chouinard's work suggests that questions and questioning behaviors serve as "Information Requesting Mechanism[s]"[45] that allow children to utilize their curiosity to make cognitive gains:

Unlike information that children might come across while engaged by something else, or information that other people offer when children are not ready for it (information that might be ignored or misinterpreted based on the children's current conceptual structures), in theory children's questions get answers exactly when the children can use them most, when they are open to the information, and when they are trying to resolve a state of disequilibrium. Also, information that the child is ready for or interested in may make the biggest impression in terms of memory and cognitive organization.[46]

The disequilibrium Chouinard describes here is very similar to Loewenstein's definition of curiosity as an information gap. Both frameworks see resolution of these states as essential for learning. When curiosity is piqued, children ask questions to satisfy it. Importantly, though, Chouinard also indicates that the curiosity caused by disequilibrium is necessary for children to learn about the world. Question asking is one of their most important tools for building this knowledge.

Chouinard goes on to suggest that question asking gains additional significance for children, because the "ability to ask questions to restore equilibrium may be especially helpful in building up initial and subsequent conceptual structures by eliciting guidance when children are not sure which way to go."[47] Previously, it seems that question asking was assumed to be only a strategy for adult learning, but this research tells another tale altogether. As Chouinard begins to weave the strands of her findings together, she ultimately strikes upon something that has the potential to affect the way we understand education at any level, including the work we do with students in colleges and universities.[48] In analyzing the data from the children in these studies, along with databases of recorded conversations, Chouinard uncovered something fascinating about the nature of question asking. Not only were children asking different types of questions over the course of the day, as we have already examined, but—regardless of their age—they would move from fact-based questions to exploratory questions *within the same conversational thread*: "Overall, then, the data strongly confirm the prediction that children start out an exchange asking for facts, and shift their focus towards explanatory information farther into the exchange. So, this progression of complexity occurs within an exchange as well as over the course of their development; these patterns bear out the predictions based on the shift seen as adult learners move from novice to more expert on a topic."[49] I will confess that when I first read this, I nearly jumped out of my chair in excitement. There are clear connections here between child learners and adult learners. First, children recruit facts and then they develop concepts from these facts. That they do this within the same exchange and at the earliest ages reveals an underexplored element of the way human beings learn. We often speak of education as something that happens to people and learning as the process by which people achieve these goals. But what if we already know how to educate ourselves? What if the process is a natural one that simply requires some attention, cultivation, and guidance to be fully utilized?

Educators have been striving for many decades to create the kind of courses that help older children and young adults to learn in just this way. We design inquiry-based assignments, we take great care to ask the right questions, and we make sure to scaffold everything properly. In other words, we have been operating under the assumption that we need to train people how to approach learning in this way. Chouinard, however, has provided evidence here that children may already know how to do all of this innately. The mechanisms by which we learn concepts may be a natural result of our development, and question asking would be the cognitive tool that allows us to kick these processes into gear. If this is true, it would suggest that the role of the teacher is a) to help students learn how to maximize this ability to use questions to learn, and b) to then get out of their way. I will concede that it is more complex than this, and I will go into some detail as to why, but an easily justifiable claim based on this evidence is that setting up educational environments that run counter to these processes is an exercise in futility because we are actively working against the very cognitive structures that have evolved to help us learn most effectively.

Given this research on the importance of curiosity and inquiry for learning and cognitive development, then, we might expect to see an increased emphasis placed on these elements in our educational system. Unfortunately, this does not seem to be the case as often as we would hope. In fact, some scholars who study education note both the absence of activities in classrooms that help to cultivate intellectual curiosity, on the one hand, and a diminishment of curiosity in the students themselves on the other. David Shernoff and Mihaly Csikszentmihalyi paint a rather bleak picture of the situation. "Educators," they note, "have often observed that children have limitless curiosity and thirst for knowledge before they enter school." This much—I hope—we knew, but the authors proceed by striking the chord of doom that was sure to follow such a leading statement: "Several years later, those same children can be found in school buildings with their minds wandering and attention straying. Suddenly, student motivation is a problem. Public schools are continually characterized by pervasive boredom."[50] Certainly, this is not the case in every school, but it is clearly enough of a problem for scholars to find it worth noting.[51]

In an effort to dig deeper, Susan Engel did a study on what she calls "episodes of curiosity" in kindergarten and fifth grade. She wanted to see whether our intuitions about diminishing curiosity were correct. What she found as she rigorously studied five kindergarten classrooms and five fifth grade classrooms was both dramatic and depressing. To be frank, there wasn't a lot of curiosity at either level. However, there was an average of 2.36 episodes of curiosity per two-hour observation period in kindergarten, but only .48 in fifth grade. She also notes that "nine of the ten classrooms had at least one two-hour stretch where there were no expressions of curiosity" and that two of the fifth grade classrooms never had a single episode of curiosity in any of the observations.[52] Engel concludes her discussion of the study by stating that "observations as well as interviews and surveys suggest that though children are curious, students are not."[53]

This, to put it mildly, is troublesome. All the more so because Engel also reveals that "between the ages of three and eleven . . . children seem to either develop an appetite for knowledge and the habit of inquiry, or they don't."[54] What happens to children during their years in school that serves to quell the natural, vital curiosity that had been such a powerful force for learning when they were very young? What effect does this waning of curiosity have on their learning once they reach college? I don't think we can place blame upon only one thing here. The answer must be found in a complex system of factors that, taken together, work against our natural resources for learning.

Certainly one thing that's happening is that children grow up. As all parents are nostalgically aware, and every teacher to a lesser degree, time does pass by and those same girls and boys who once toddled their way around our homes and our classrooms have become women and men. The world begins to demand more of them, and they are forced to divide their cognitive resources in order to attend to these competing pressures rather than the answers to big questions. Those eager questioners that Chouinard and others observed have suddenly stopped asking so many questions.[55] As they mature, children become wise to this whole education game we like to play. They figure out what they need to do to succeed in school and become more strategic learners, "avoiding any challenges that will harm their academic performance and record, and often failing to develop deep understandings."[56] In fact, we put so much pressure on our children to succeed in school that some may actually stop caring about learning. William Deresiewicz, in *Excellent Sheep*, provides a scathing commentary on the counterproductive role of parents. He describes the all-too-common scenario of parents seeking the best for their children but pushing so hard that intellectual curiosity becomes a casualty of the education and status wars.[57] Furthermore, as they move through the school system, they are asked to take numerous standardized tests, the preparation for which positions education as something of utilitarian value. The question "Why?" steadily gets replaced by "What do I need to do to achieve X?" By the time these students enter postsecondary education, then, they have already had years to develop habits of mind that wall off curiosity.

As college instructors, it seems that the deck has been stacked against us when it comes to our students' curiosity. A network of systems has failed them, and other needs in their lives have taken over, but they arrive in our classrooms still, at some level, the learners who were driven by the biological need to know more and to investigate new possibilities. My position here and throughout the book is that the importance of basic mechanisms for human learning, like curiosity, does not change between the time someone is three years old and eighteen. It simply needs to be reinforced. As teachers, it is our job to help students reconnect with their curiosity and to use our courses as laboratories for discovery.

Don't Be Scary

Our first step in fostering our students' engagement with or rediscovery of their curiosity should probably be simply to make sure that we are not doing anything to inhibit their curiosity. As it happens, anxiety of all kinds has an extremely detrimental effect on the willingness of our students to explore new ideas and to ask questions. Let's take a look at some of the ways we might see this dynamic playing out in our classrooms. Hans-Georg Voss and Heidi Keller, in their book *Curiosity and Exploration*, provide a clear explanation of a model developed by M. Zuckerman that charts, among several things, the relationship between novelty and anxiety. As novelty increases, so do both curiosity (or sensation seeking in this model) and anxiety. At a certain point, the degree of novelty is such that curiosity wanes but anxiety continues to rise. When the anxiety is great enough, and the risk of pursuing the stimulus is perceived to be too high, people will withdraw rather than continue to press further.[58]

Novelty can take many forms in a college classroom: new ideas, new perspectives on old ideas, new kinds of assignments, and so on. Too much of any of these, particularly in a short period of time, can short-circuit curiosity, though, and lead to anxiety instead. This is why scaffolding of new material can be so important, especially for students who are new to a discipline. Presenting challenging ideas with which students have never worked before in stages rather than all at once can allow them to maximize their curiosity and lower the level of potential fear or anxiety. Even if the level of novelty is rather minimal, if the stakes for exploration are too high—in terms of grades, for example—anxiety can serve to diminish curiosity. As we will see in the section of this book devoted to emotions, students cannot learn if they are fearful or anxious.

Another way that anxiety can play a part in our classrooms, though, is through the responses of our students to our teaching style. In a series of widely cited experiments from 1978, Ruth A. Peters asked 152 college students in psychology and sociology courses at the university where she did her graduate work to rate themselves using inventories designed to measure "individual differences in curiosity and exploratory behavior" as well as "anxiety proneness in social-evaluative situations."[59] She then asked each student to rate their instructor on a scale to assess whether the teacher was threatening or non-threatening. In this case, the threat does not refer to an insinuation of violence but rather the level of intimidation students felt when interacting with the instructor. What Peters found is quite telling: "For students who perceived their instructors as nonthreatening, those with high trait curiosity initiated more than five times as many questions and declarative statements . . . than did low-C-trait-low-threat students. In contrast, when the student rated the instructor as threatening, the response rates for student-initiated verbal behaviors were low, regardless of level of trait curiosity."[60] In other words, even the most curious students will be inhibited if they feel intimidated by their instructors. These findings are important for (at least) three reasons. First, it is certainly true that students are not all the same when it comes to curiosity. Some report higher levels of natural curiosity than others, but this does not relieve us of the responsibility for drawing out and utilizing curiosity to enhance our students' learning. Secondly, it really does matter how we project ourselves in front of the classroom. If we stifle discourse, or are perceived as not caring about our students, or display a lack of empathy, or even if we scowl a bit too much,[61] we can shut down the processes by which our students learn almost before we can even begin. Finally, classroom environment is key here, but we should extend this to our assignments. The higher the stakes, the higher the potential anxiety. If we create more low-stakes assignments (or even, dare I say, ungraded assignments where students get feedback on their progress), we are creating an atmosphere that is friendly to curiosity. We cannot blame students for being uncurious if we have created courses that privilege high-stakes performance. I would very much like to see Peters's experiments replicated to see if the effects change in any way. I suspect they would not vary much.

GETTING STARTED

First impressions go a long way. You can break down some of the invisible barriers separating you from your students (while still maintaining professional distance) by talking to them about yourself on the opening day of the semester. Depending on your degree of comfort, this could mean telling them about your own academic journey, how you got into the field, what excites you about it, or what obstacles you faced along the way. You might even tell them a bit about who you are outside of the classroom—your hobbies, interests, and the like. It may sound a bit silly, but simply showing students that we too are human beings can help to mitigate any natural anxiety they feel about working with us. Even this small degree of openness can lay an important foundation for trust with your students. When they trust us, it is very difficult for them to feel intimidated by us.

Inquiry as a Design Principle

If intimidating teachers stifle curiosity, then it seems fair that we ask ourselves to be more thoughtful about our classroom presence. Once we move away from doing those things that can possibly inhibit curiosity, though, our attention can then turn to the ways in which we can cultivate a sense of wonder and discovery. Chouinard and others have shown us how intricately interwoven questions and curiosity can be, so it would make sense that inquiry should form the foundation of any pedagogical approach that wishes to place fostering curiosity at the center. And it needs to be present from the very start. Before we can turn to classroom practices, we need to think carefully about integrating inquiry into our course design. L. Dee Fink has argued that the course design phase is the most important for any implementation of what he terms "significant learning experiences" because everything we do in our courses derives from this process.[62] Building inquiry into the framework of our teaching is no different. We need to consider from the outset how inquiry can be present not just in our assignments and exams, but also how it drives our learning goals and our interactions with students.

Fortunately, there are already some very good models out there for us. Perhaps the most well known of these is derived from the work of Grant Wiggins and Jay McTighe, whose co-written book *Understanding by Design* is still a landmark in the field. Wiggins and McTighe argue for an approach to course design that is rooted in achieving understanding, a concept they define fairly broadly so as to allow for a range of pedagogical approaches. The key to their method is to begin the design process by thinking about our overarching learning goals for the course, with special attention toward those goals that will lead to deep understanding. To devise these goals, Wiggins and McTighe suggest that we need to develop the

"Essential Questions" that our courses will help students to answer.[63] They define essential questions as those that "push us to the heart of things—the essence. . . . Honest pursuit of such questions leads not only to deeper understandings, but also to more questions. But essential questions need not be so global. They can go to the heart of a particular topic, problem, or field of study. Thus we can say that each academic field can be *defined* by its essential questions."[64] Examples of essential questions for an introductory economics course, for example, might be "How do markets work?" and "How does the market reflect human behavior?" Every course we teach provides us with an opportunity to generate many similar kinds of questions. Likewise, if we structure our course from the outset so that every element is tied to one of our essential questions, then we have created a framework in which students will be using their curiosity throughout to pursue answers. Assignments provide pieces of the answers, as do activities, exams, papers, and all of the other elements that make up a course.

The model advocated by Wiggins and McTighe runs counter to the notion that course design should focus entirely on content we want our students to learn, which can be difficult to get used to, but it also has proven to pay great dividends in terms of student learning. Students learn the content, but they also figure out the significance of the material as well. Another design model that places inquiry at the forefront comes from a source much closer to home. I have the good fortune of working with a brilliant friend and colleague in Rice's Center for Teaching Excellence named Robin Paige. Robin's training as a social scientist influenced her development of a course design approach that focuses on what she calls a "metaquestion." Rather than developing a series of questions, as Wiggins and McTighe suggest, Robin argues that we should create one larger question that all of the work for the course seeks to answer.[65] The metaquestion leads to the generation of all the learning goals, assignments, even the text selection. The nature of the metaquestion will depend on the scope of the course. An introductory biology course may seek to help students to think scientifically about the living world, whereas an upper-level psychology course on cognition might ask students "What is learning?" Both design methodologies have similar ends in mind, though they take different roads to get there. In the end, providing our students with beautiful questions that govern their work in the course is one of our most important strategies for engaging their curiosity.

GETTING STARTED

Sometimes when we are in the weeds of designing a new course or revising one that we have taught previously, it can be difficult to take a bird's-eye view and think about essential questions or metaquestions. One suggestion I have is to set aside the syllabus for a moment and think about the key questions you want your students to explore over the course of the semester. Jot those down and then try to come up with a learning goal associated with each one. The rest follows from there. You might find that much of what you have been doing in the course, or planned to do in a new course, fits well with these questions. On the other hand, writing down the questions might also cause you to rethink your assignments or choose new activities. The key to gleaning the benefit of a question-driven course is to make this step an intentional part of the planning process.

Discussion-Based Pedagogies

The most familiar (and, to be honest, sometimes maligned) way to bring inquiry into the classroom is through class discussion. When class discussions are well executed, students have been found to learn more than when they are taught using what Jay Howard describes as "content-only instruction."[66] Indeed, Stephen D. Brookfield and Stephen Preskill have explained the many ways in which discussion is beneficial—everything from allowing our students to "explore a diversity of perspectives" to "affirm[ing] students as cocreators of knowledge."[67] The power of the method is well documented, but notice the qualifier I used two sentences ago. The devil of discussion is in the details. I don't think I'm going too far out on a limb when I predict that we have all taken part in some class discussions that have succeeded and some that have fallen flat. Sometimes students will argue and debate, while other times one can hear the crickets chirping. Because of the potential benefits for students, though, it is worth taking some time and effort to make our discussions as effective as possible.

Much of the success or failure of discussions begins with setting expectations. As Howard notes, "Because college classrooms are social settings where definitions of the situation are continually being negotiated, we can employ strategies that create new norms, including the expectation that all students will participate in discussion."[68] Such an expectation should be clearly outlined in the syllabus, and it could be accompanied by a description of the ways in which discussion will contribute to the learning for the course along with the value of inquiry for accomplishing your course goals. A mechanism for accountability, which usually takes the form of a participation grade, is useful as well. I think it is important to note, though, that grading a discussion is not always necessary, but some level of accountability and incentive usually is. Once students understand how discussion will fit into the course, it then becomes essential that we frequently reinforce its value early and often. The easiest way to do this is simply to offer ample opportunities for discussion early in the semester. James Lang argues that "several weeks of listening to lectures will condition students into a passivity that will be harder and harder to break as the semester continues."[69] Even if you intend to devote some time during your class meetings to lecturing, it is more important to build this up as the semester goes on rather than frontload it, so that students have time to become accustomed to the discussion format (and to become comfortable participating). As instructors, this also gives us a chance to model conscientious debate and productive disagreement.

In my own courses, and in the courses I have observed, one truism has emerged: discussions are most successful when instructors employ more open-ended questions than closed-ended ones. Although fact-based questions can sometimes serve to get the ball rolling at the beginning of class or at the outset of talking about a particular topic, nothing will shut down a discussion faster than too many questions to which there is only one answer (especially if that answer already resides in the teacher's head and students are then forced to play an exhilarating round of "Guess What I'm Thinking"). One way to shift from closed to open is to move deliberately from asking "who," "what," "where," or "when" questions, and shift instead to "why" questions—questions that really delve into the significance of the issues the class is addressing. Think back for a moment to Chouinard's work on children's questions. Very young children will always ask fact-finding questions before moving to conceptual questions, because it is the latter that truly engages their curiosity. So it is with our students. College students need to move quickly from the closed-ended questions that focus on collecting information to those that stimulate their curiosity. When we ask them to engage each other in working through significant issues, intriguing questions, and unresolved problems, on the other hand, their natural learning mechanisms are freed to explore and make connections. So it is vital to move from "Who is credited with developing the theory of special relativity?" and "What was the name of the town that George and Lenny travel to?" and "What is stereotype threat?" to "Why is the theory of special relativity so important for understanding our universe?" and "Why is Candy's dog significant for interpreting the last scene with George and Lenny?" and "Why is stereotype threat so detrimental to our mission as institutions of higher education?" if we hope to help our students to learn through discussion. An easy way to change fact-based questions to questions that will help to generate discussion is to ask ourselves "So what?" every time we come up with something we want to ask our students. If we have developed a closed-ended question, this instigation will provide the impetus to change our question into something that addresses significance rather than memorized material.

While I've established that open-ended questions are necessary for good discussions, my last piece of advice would be this: avoid questions that are *too* open. If you haven't just thrown the book on the ground in frustration over my semantic splicing, then please let me explain what I mean. Whereas the "why" questions above often provoke meaningful, sustained conversations, questions like "So what do you think about X or Y?" can often generate the kind of silence that makes up the stuff of our nightmares. These kinds of questions are too wide-ranging and leave little for students to really grab onto. Recall that curiosity can only be activated if we are invested in the answer. Questions that are too open allow students to fall back on easy opinions in which they do not have much at stake.

I acknowledge that it can be sometimes be challenging to develop discussion questions that hit all of the targets I have mentioned. In fact, it can be among the most difficult skills for teachers to develop, but it is so important for our students' learning.[70] As an illustration of this importance, when I asked Susan Engel how she put her findings about curiosity into practice in her own classroom, she talked about leading class discussion. She said, "By asking questions I don't have a set answer to, I am modeling genuine inquiry and sharing my own curiosity."[71] In the end, this might be one of discussion's greatest values.

GETTING STARTED

If you are already using discussion in the classroom, try taking some of the questions you intend to ask in an upcoming class session and see if there are any you could revise to draw more on students' curiosity. Alternatively, you could also take five minutes at the beginning of your next class and ask students to jot down one question they are curious about with respect to the topic at hand. If you are not yet using discussion as one of your teaching strategies, but you would like to do so, select some key concepts from one of your lectures and think about open-ended "why" questions you could pose about these areas of knowledge either to reinforce them or to amplify them by asking students to apply what they have learned. Test out a few of the questions and see how students respond.

Developing Questions

Another potential strategy for cultivating curiosity centers on what is perhaps the most important thing we can do as college instructors, which is to teach our students how to ask the right kinds of questions. Noted philosopher John Dewey has outlined the necessity for such instruction in this way:

> [The teacher] has to avoid all dogmatism in instruction, for such a course gradually but surely creates the impression that everything important is already settled and nothing remains to be found out. He has to know how to give information when curiosity has created an appetite that seeks to be fed, and how to abstain from giving information when, because of lack of a questioning attitude, it would be a burden and would dull the sharp edge of the inquiring spirit.[72]

These questioning attitudes and inquiring spirits are exactly what we need to nurture, but students often need guidance on how to move from these habits of mind to constructing valuable questions themselves. Indeed, Susan Harter explains that there "are many paths to framing a question, yet the path we choose needs to be thoughtful, insightful, innovative, and groundbreaking to move the field forward. . . . Merely taking an existing measure or comparing two measures, without a burning question, is unlikely to generate very meaningful findings."[73] Although it is unreasonable in most cases to ask students to "move the field forward," we need to help them learn how to formulate the kinds of questions that urge them toward deep understanding and engagement with the discipline.

Dan Rothstein and Luz Santana lay out an intriguing process for how we might effectively assist them with this. In their book *Make Just One Change*, they outline a strategy—which they have termed the Question Formulation Technique—for helping students to develop their skills with question asking that begins with choosing a focus for the question and then proceeds through stages of refining, revising, reflecting on, and prioritizing the questions.[74] This technique, they argue, is effective because it combines authentic practice (students formulate their own questions and choose the most viable from among those that are generated) with the metacognitive reflection that allows them to improve. Rothstein and Santana developed the Question Formulation Technique during their work in adult literacy programs and have since applied it to K–12 education, but there has not been much crossover into higher education. Given what we know about curiosity and the importance of question asking, their strategy or one like it could greatly empower our students.

Practically speaking, it is essential to consider what such questions might look like. As we know, the best questions lead not necessarily to answers but, as Wiggins and McTighe suggested, to larger questions. Getting to the point where they can do this, though, is sure to be a messy process for students. They will likely begin by looking to the well-run discussions we lead in class as examples of the kinds of questions they need to ask. This is a good place to start, but a question designed to instigate discussion can often be different from a powerful research question that leads students to new revelations. So, as instructors, we need to move beyond discussion in our classrooms and model for students this questioning process. After we engage in this modeling, though, it is time to let them work through the process on their own. A civil engineer, for example, might begin a class session by showing an image of a local bridge and then proceed by asking students "What do you notice? What do you wonder?" Although the questions might begin at the surface level, they quickly move into more complex terrain. The instructor's role in this activity is simply to guide the process, to push students to go deeper, and to connect questions as much as possible to material covered in class. Peter Newbury, Director of the Centre for Teaching and Learning at the

University of British Columbia's Okanagan campus, is the architect of the Notice/Wonder activity, and it can be applied to a wide variety of disciplines.[75] Similarly, a sociologist might do the same activity with a small dataset, while a historian could use a short primary source. There are many other strategies we might employ, but the key is this: until students understand the importance of questions and know how to engage in meaningful inquiry, their learning will be inhibited because their biggest tool—their curiosity—will be left unused.[76]

Exploring Constructivism

All of these pedagogical approaches fit neatly into a constructivist model of learning. Constructivism is a theory of learning that has often been seen as the conceptual underpinning for inquiry-based teaching.[77] Very simply put, constructivism posits that people cannot fully learn or understand unless they have been active participants in building concepts and knowledge for themselves. Curiosity is of fundamental importance to constructivist approaches. If, as Catherine Twomey Fosnot suggests, constructivism "construes learning as an interpretive, recursive, building process by active learners interacting with the physical and social world," then our natural curiosity drives this process by generating the motivation for these interactions in the first place.[78] Only if we are first curious about something will we bother to interpret or desire to build. Thus, constructivism provides for us a different way of thinking about the absolute necessity of curiosity for learning and in our educational systems.

Teaching using a constructivist framework is not necessarily intuitive. We are not taught how to do this in graduate school, and it requires close attention to course and assignment design. Implementing these approaches need not be altogether difficult, however, and can in many ways be transformative to our practice. Elaine Howes has a terrific take on constructivism from the perspective of teachers: "The very idea that my students' ideas would *shape* what they learned altered my vision of teaching from one in which my responsibility lay in accurately relaying intriguing ideas to one in which my role was to provide learning contexts within which students would create *their own* ideas, as individuals and as a social group. I cannot stress enough how much more fascinating, complex, and challenging this simple concept of students as knowledge-makers makes the work of teaching."[79] At its core, constructivism is about empowering students to take control of their own learning, and Howes demonstrates how meaningful and effective this can be for them and for us as teachers.

Although the theory of constructivism has been well known by K–12 educators for a long time (which is not the same thing as saying that it has been widely adopted), there seems to be less awareness of it among college educators and scant attention paid to it in the literature on college teaching, though this is starting to change. Among those who have explored constructivism in college, there has been some disagreement as to its effectiveness as a methodology. In particular, one group of researchers has argued that constructivist pedagogy is a "failure" because it requires so little guidance from teachers.[80] Such an argument misconstrues constructivist approaches, which can vary widely in terms of how much direct instruction is provided by instructors.[81] Indeed, the only thing constructivist strategies share is their emphasis on the agency of the students in our classrooms. Whether or not we agree with every single way constructivism is employed in the classroom, there can be no doubt from the research on curiosity as to why the theory has merit for student learning. The key here is to think carefully about strategy, so let's turn now to a few ways constructivist approaches have been used in several college courses.

Constructivism in the Classroom, Part 1: Donald Saari, University of California, Irvine[82]

I have already cited Ken Bain's *What the Best College Teachers Do* a few pages ago, and it is a book that has been very influential for me. When I first read it, I was finishing my graduate work at the University of Connecticut, and I remember being struck by Bain's description of a mathematician named Donald Saari, who explained his teaching philosophy as follows: "I want the students to feel like they have invented calculus and that only some accident of birth kept them from beating Newton to the punch. . . . I want my students to construct their own under-standing so they can tell a story about how to solve the problem."[83] This manner of teaching was bold enough to catch my attention even then. I wondered what it all might mean. Elsewhere in the book, we find out that one way Saari tries to accomplish his goal is by bringing in a roll of toilet paper and asking students to cal-culate the volume without providing them with any knowledge regarding the conventional methods by which mathematicians solve such problems.[84] Inventing calculus? Toilet paper? It was enough to make a graduate student's head spin. I soon moved on to more pressing concerns, but the description of Saari's teaching stuck with me. Since that initial reading, I have found myself returning to this book many times and have even used it as a required text in the graduate seminars on pedagogy that I teach at Rice. Each time, I have added more notes beside the passages illustrating Saari's pedagogy, all of which amount to the same question: "How the heck does he *do* this?" So I finally just decided to contact him and find out.

Saari, who is now a Distinguished Professor of Mathematics and Economics at the University of California, Irvine, opened our conversation by sharing with me that when he was an undergraduate he had a "triple major—varsity sports, student politics, and social life." This combination, he claims, was not exactly conducive to attending class, so he had to devise a way to teach himself the material. Eventually he began to develop stories to contextualize the subject matter and found that he was succeeding in his courses as a result. I'm not sure how much of his claim about poor attendance I should take on face value, but he does make clear that storytelling became the key to academic achievement for him. "You can't," he says, "tell a story about details, only about concepts." Storytelling became a way for him to build complex concepts, and it is primarily this strategy that he has brought into his courses. He works with his students to tell a story about a mathematical idea rather than beginning by talking about a formula, because he believes this latter approach stifles students' creativity. "Students and I explore the story," he explains, and—as the story unfolds—they build key concepts together.

At the heart of Saari's stories there is always a puzzle. One day he might walk in talking about gambling on a football game and as they work through the odds and discuss their rationale for the decisions they are making, they develop an understanding of hedging and arbitrage. It is not until students have arrived at the core concept themselves that Saari then gives them a formula they can use. I attentively listened to several other examples, but finally my desire to know was too much for me. "What about the toilet paper?" I blurted out. If he was taken aback, he was too much of a professional to say so. I, of course, provided him with the context for my query, and he happily revealed that he will sometimes bring a roll of toilet paper that is not a perfect cylinder to his introductory calculus class. He sits it down on the desk and tells his student that they need to help him figure out the volume of the bathroom product before the class ends or they will all be fired. At this point in the semester, students have not yet learned how to calculate the volume of objects that are not perfect cylinders, so he tells me that he is often met with silence for a few minutes. Finally, students start to ask questions and make suggestions. For each offering, Saari will push students to provide feedback, and they work together to assess whether or not a particular strategy is viable. Eventually, someone will venture the hypothesis that if they rip off one square of the toilet paper and calculate its volume (which they have learned how to do in a previous class), they could then do the same for all the squares and add them up at the end. This, ultimately, provides the conceptual basis for the formula they will use to find the volume. Sometimes, instead of toilet paper, Saari does a version of this activity with an apple. His rationale here is that students are using the same sorts of observations that Newton himself might have used when he developed calculus. By the end of our conversation, I left not only with new knowledge about the volume of toilet paper, but also with a reinforced sense of how effective constructivist teaching can be.

Constructivism in the Classroom, Part 2: John Hutchinson and Lesa Tran Lu, Rice University[85]

By 1985, John Hutchinson had taught the same two courses, Quantum Chemistry and Statistical Thermodynamics, for three years running. His students had been very successful, and he knew the material so well that he no longer needed any notes in order to lecture. But at that three-year mark, something happened. Hutchinson began to find the dynamic between lecturing and silent note-taking to be unfulfilling. As he prepared for his fourth year of teaching at Rice, he made the decision to try out some Socratic questioning in class. He was inspired to run this pedagogical experiment because his wife Paula was in law school and had been sharing her learning experiences with him. She convinced him to try it out, and he began to see a level of engagement in his classes that had been eluding him. To the degree that teaching awards are markers of success, it is fair to say that Hutchinson's experiment succeeded, because he won two teaching awards over the next several years.

But he did not stop there. In 1988, after continuing to expand the role of discussion in his courses, he brought his approach to General Chemistry—a course that he has taught ever since, even after assuming an administrative role as Dean of Undergraduates in 2010. General Chemistry courses enroll famously large numbers of students, so Hutchinson thought it would provide a nice proving ground for the technique's efficacy. The results were similar and the experience was transformational for him. Indeed, the student response to his use of the Socratic technique encouraged him to ask even more questions about pedagogy. What did he *really* want his students to learn and how could he get them to achieve those goals?

He tried out a number of approaches and, by 1992, had found an answer to this question: he wanted students to achieve a deeper understanding of chemical concepts by discovering, so to speak, the ideas for themselves. Arriving at this conclusion led Hutchinson to grow dissatisfied with textbooks and other teaching materials that were available to him because, as he says, "they gave away all of the answers." So he set about writing his own textbook that took as its touchstone foundational ideas in the discipline. The result was *Concept Development Studies in Chemistry*, an open-source textbook that prioritizes reasoning and understanding before application. The governing pedagogical framework for the book is this: "In each concept development study, a major chemical concept is developed and refined by analysis of experimental observations and careful reasoning. Each study begins with the definition of an initial Foundation of assumed knowledge, followed by a statement of questions which arise from the Foundation. Analysis of these questions is presented as a series of observations and logical deductions, followed by further questions. This detailed process is followed until the conceptual development of a model provides a reasonable answer to the stated questions."[86] In Hutchinson's view, students are too often asked to approach chemistry as if it were a set of formulae to memorize rather than a process leading to beautiful discovery. Only through nuanced understandings of key concepts could students get a sense of the nature of this discovery.

Hutchinson was aware that the prospect of constructing chemical concepts might seem daunting to a college freshman in an introductory science course, so he devised two strategies to make the approach more manageable for students. The first of these strategies was to draw upon history. In order to bring students into the discovery process, Hutchinson encourages them to forget everything they may have learned in high school chemistry courses. He then asks, "What if we didn't know anything?" It is a question, he says, that drives his entire pedagogical philosophy. When he poses this question, he does not actually intend for students to imagine a world where nothing is known. Instead, he wants them to consider only the data that would have been available to those who made particular discoveries. As one example, very early in the first semester of the General Chemistry sequence, students construct the atomic molecular theory for themselves simply by observing data about mass ratios of molecules made up of the same elements (nitrous oxides are the particular examples Hutchinson uses in his textbook).[87] He could, of course, just explain the atomic molecular theory to them, and many college instructors do so, but he has found that students understand the concept better when they build it for themselves. As we have seen elsewhere in this chapter, the research on curiosity and constructivism supports his claims.

The second strategy Hutchinson employs to make the concept development process more intuitive is to use interactive demonstrations conducted by the students themselves. To help students begin to understand Einstein's photon model of the photoelectric effect, for instance, students attempt to knock over a heavy textbook positioned on a table in a number of different ways. They try blowing on it and throwing foam balls at it. Only when they are given tennis balls, though, do they actually succeed in felling the mighty book. From this activity, they glean that one particle with sufficient mass can do what many particles of insufficient mass cannot. The demonstration may seem, at first blush, disconnected from the waves and particles that interested Einstein. But students are then given a simulation of data from the photoelectric effect, and they are able to connect the textbook demonstration to the action of photon packets in the photoelectric effect. Students use the same observations Einstein used, and—with help from this demonstration—they reach the same conclusions. Time and again, Hutchinson has witnessed how empowering moments like these are for his students.

In 2012, Hutchinson recruited Lesa Tran Lu to teach additional sections of General Chemistry using his constructivist methodology. Tran Lu has been instrumental in embedding even more active learning methods in the courses and in assessing the effectiveness of the pedagogy. She described for me another of the interactive demonstrations, this one used to help students understand dynamic equilibrium, which is—I learned—the state achieved when rates of forward and reverse chemical reactions are equal. [88] Students are given a box of Legos (with fifty pieces of one color and fifty pieces of another per box) and then form groups with each having a role as either a Shaker, an Assembler/Disassembler, or a Timer. They then take part in four different activities. For each group, the Shaker moves the box, the Assemblers/Disassemblers manipulate the blocks, and the Timer, well, he or she keeps track of time. In the first activity, the goal is to put together as many dimers (two linked blocks, one of each color) as possible within three minutes. The second activity focuses on disassembling as many of those dimers as possible in the same time frame. The students keep track of the data, and then they graph the results. They quickly see that the reverse process (disassembling) happens at a quicker rate, because separating a single dimer into individual entities is simpler than assembling two pieces into a dimer. It turns out that this quicker disassembling happens with chemical compounds too! For the third demonstration, twenty-five individual pieces of one color, twenty-five of the other, and twenty-five dimers are placed in the box, and Assemblers put blocks together while, at the same time, Disassemblers are taking the blocks apart. Students are asked to make predictions on how many individual pieces vs. dimers will be present at the end of the experiment if these processes are competing. The fourth and final demonstration asks students to do the same thing with respect to assembling and disassembling, but this time there are only individual pieces in the box. What students discover in the third and the fourth demonstration is that dynamic equilibrium—which is marked by an unchanging number of individual pieces and dimers—is reached. Regardless of how many each of the teams started with, the number of individual pieces slightly exceeds the number of dimers in both experiments, which is consistent with what students found and recorded after the first two activities.[89] Students leave these exercises with a more thorough grasp of a concept that can be rather tricky.

However, both Hutchinson and Tran Lu are quick to say that building these concepts through working with historical data and using interactive demonstrations is not enough. Students enjoy these elements of the course, but the learning in this constructivist model is dependent on assessing the ways in which students are then able to apply the concept. The homework and exam questions they develop, then, are designed so that students must analyze data and explain the reasoning leading to their conclusions. If it is important enough for students to learn, Hutchinson emphasizes, then you have to test it. I think this is a valuable lesson. Constructivist activities in and of themselves can only take us so far. We need evidence that students have gained conceptual understanding, and assessments are vital for collecting this information.

What about the Humanities?

Sharp readers such as yourselves, of course, will observe that both of these examples come from STEM fields. This should not be taken as an indication that constructivism is only possible in these disciplines, however. To illustrate this point, I can draw on an example from my own teaching career. I was an English professor at Columbus State University in Georgia from 2006–2011. As a part of my standard 4–4 teaching load, I was typically given at least two sections of World Literature 1 each semester. World Literature 1 was, and continues to be, a general education course for non-majors designed to introduce students to multicultural texts from the beginning of the written record to (roughly) 1600 C.E. I always thought it was important to have my students themselves tackle the kinds of questions scholars of ancient, medieval, and early modern literatures ask on a regular basis.

One of the most important of these scholarly questions has to do with source study and the transmission of stories. In order for my students to be successful, I wanted them to see that stories and literary archetypes develop over many, many years (sometimes over millennia) and may have their ultimate source in material that is now lost to us.

To enter into this discussion fruitfully, I asked students to read the flood story from the *Epic of Gilgamesh* alongside the narrative of the deluge in Genesis. Conservative estimates suggest that *Gilgamesh*'s flood story was finalized around 1200 B.C.E.,[90] though I have seen earlier dates put forward for pieces of the tale, while scholars believe that the oldest versions of Genesis were written between 922–722 B.C.E.[91] Famously, the stories share many similarities in tone, structure, and details, and it is easy to see shades of *Gilgamesh* in Genesis. The most likely reason for these similarities, though, is that the two are analogues stemming from an older Mesopotamian source that is no longer extant.

I wanted my students to be able to construct this knowledge for themselves, so—after a class discussion about the flood narratives and their respective dates—I asked them to develop possible models for the transmission of the stories. For the purposes of the exercise, I would withhold any information regarding what scholars believe to be the most likely answer. Through all five years of teaching this class, students would always come up with three potential models: 1) *Gilgamesh* is the source for Genesis; 2) Genesis is the source for *Gilgamesh*; and 3) there is an earlier, unknown source for both. I would draw the models on the board and then split students into smaller groups. At this point they would need to argue for which model they found to be most convincing and use evidence to support their claims. As we know, the third of the options is perhaps the most well-founded answer, and many of the groups would discover this for themselves as they tried to make sense of the differences between the texts and the likelihood of *Gilgamesh* being used wholesale as a direct source for Genesis. A smaller percentage would disagree, suggesting that the story of King Gilgamesh and even the physical tablets on which the text is inscribed could have found their way to ancient Palestine through migration, so that it is possible that *Gilgamesh* was the source for Genesis. The debates would often be spirited as both sides tried to marshal evidence in their favor.[92] I always loved this exercise, because in those moments students became burgeoning scholars of ancient literature, and I think it serves as evidence that constructivism can be fruitfully employed in a wide variety of disciplines.

Curiosity Makes Us Human

Creating inquiry-based, constructivist courses designed to cultivate curiosity takes time, and time is one of those resources that is, unfortunately, finite. The question then becomes one of costs and benefits. We need some indication that putting the time into developing pedagogies that target curiosity will have a significant enough impact on our students' learning that it will be worth the effort in the long run. Recent research seems to be pointing in this direction. A 2011 study, for example, has suggested that intellectual curiosity, as a trait, is a predictor of academic success in college.[93] In addition, Ken Bain's newer book, *What the Best College Students Do*, contains an entire chapter devoted to demonstrating how those students who utilize their curiosity are more successful in college and in their lives afterward.[94] If these studies and the many others covered in this chapter are accurate, then fostering curiosity in cases where it is apparent while finding ways to draw it out in those where it might seem less active will make learning more effective for our students.

But it is more than this, isn't it? Although the pedagogical value seems clear, there is a deeper importance to focusing our attention on curiosity as well. In 2015, I taught a course on the Pixar films, and one of the movies we studied during the course of the semester was *WALL-E*. The protagonist of the film, a robot named WALL-E, is quintessentially curious, collecting trinkets, videotapes, and other fragments of cultural artifacts that remain in the aftermath of an environmental apocalypse. While discussing this element of the film, I asked students why the film emphasizes this trait of WALL-E. One of them very astutely remarked, "Curiosity is what makes us human." This was a poignant observation, as well as an ironic one, since WALL-E is a robot. As the film reveals, though, he embodies more human traits than many of the actual people themselves. In the end, I think my student was absolutely right. Our heightened curiosity has shaped us as a species—our intelligence, our ability to learn, our understanding of the world. It is indeed hard to separate our humanness from our ever-present desire to know more.

I began this chapter with a fond memory of my daughter's appraisal of red cups, and I want to return to her for a moment. Lucy is now five and her curiosity has already found new targets in everything from pondering why crickets make noise to deep interrogations of the movie *Trolls*. Eventually, I hope she applies her sense of wonder to the great problems of our world. As college instructors, we have a major role in helping to guide this process—not just for Lucy, but for all those who bring with them their natural human curiosity into our classrooms.

KEY TAKEAWAYS

- Our long evolutionary history has primed our brains to seek out answers, particularly those that have eluded us. Curiosity is therefore intertwined with cognition and rests at the heart of the educational process.

- One of the most basic mechanisms for engaging curiosity is through asking questions. Questions are an essential driver for cognitive development in children, and they remain an important tool for learning throughout our lives.

- We can utilize the pedagogical power of questions through effective course design, inquiry-based assignments, discussion, and activities we develop to help students create their own questions.

- In order to build lasting knowledge, students have to play a major role in constructing it for themselves. Curiosity is a key component in these endeavors.

- Curiosity is certainly important at the course level, but departments might consider the role of curiosity in the curriculum as a whole. How can course sequences foster curiosity over time, and where are the critical points to teach inquiry-related skills so that students have the means to succeed in upper-level courses that privilege higher order thinking?

- P.S. Don't be scary! Anxiety of any kind reduces levels of student curiosity.

———

CHAPTER 2

Sociality

The need for *social belonging*—for seeing oneself as socially connected—is a basic human motivation.

> —Gregory M. Walton and Geoffrey Cohen, "A Question of Belonging: Race, Social Fit, and Achievement"

The true direction of the development of thinking is not from the individual to the social, but from the social to the individual.

> —Lev Vygotsky, *Thought and Language*

If we looked closely at the history of education in America, we would be hard-pressed to find many episodes that have made their way into popular consciousness. One exception, however, occurred in Riceville, Iowa, in 1968. On April 5 that year, Jane Elliott decided to try an experiment with her third grade class, which was made up entirely of white students. Martin Luther King Jr. had been assassinated the day before, and she needed a lesson with a significant degree of magnitude to help her students understand the kind of prejudice and racism that leads to such tragedies. She decided to split up the class into two groups: children with blue eyes and children with brown eyes. On the first day, those in the blue-eyed group were given all of the advantages (the best seats, etc.), which were then reinforced by Elliott, who told them they were superior to the group with brown eyes. In addition, "the brown-eyed children had to wear collars around their necks and their behavior and performance were criticized and ridiculed by Elliott."[1] Elliott switched the roles for the groups on the second day, but—in both instances—the privileged group quickly began to treat the disadvantaged group with disdain and meanness. Crucially, though, Elliott took time after the two class sessions to debrief the children, to ask them how they felt when they were being mistreated and to help them empathize with others who might be the victims of discrimination.

Although I'm not sure Elliott would have been able to get a protocol for her experiment passed through an institutional review board if she were to come up with the idea today, the documented results were powerful. She has been at turns praised and criticized for bringing the social world into the classroom, but we could argue that she was really showing that the social world is *always* a part of the classroom, that classrooms themselves are social spaces and essentially microcosms of the world outside their walls. All learning, then, happens in a social context because we are learning with and from one another. This is as true in college as it is in any other educational environment.

I began this book by discussing curiosity because it is what fuels our individual desire to discover, to inquire, and to figure out how things work. If we really want to know more about the interplay between teaching and learning, though, we have to delve into our nature as social beings. In fact, it is not a stretch to say that much of what makes us human stems directly from our sociality. It is such a vital element of who we are that we can actually feel physical pain when we experience social exclusion,[2] and prolonged isolation can lead to health problems as we grow older.[3] At a very fundamental level, we need others in order to live functioning lives. As an extension of this, our sociality drives our learning in many essential ways. Sure, we can learn things on our own, but we rarely learn them as deeply, because so much of our learning derives from our social nature and our visceral need to communicate with other people. Understanding the complexities of our students' sociality is therefore necessary if we are to design effective educational experiences.

Why We Need Other People

We are profoundly social creatures because of our evolutionary history, but human sociality surpasses in its complexity and its scope that found in many other species for whom community is fundamental.[4] After all, humans are primates, and Clive Gamble, John Gowlett, and Robin Dunbar have argued that "the great evolutionary invention of the primate family is sociality."[5] Elsewhere, Dunbar (one of the leading researchers on the evolution of sociality), along with Susanne Schultz, has explained that the distinguishing feature of the primate social world is the notion of "bondedness."[6] Thus, it is not just that we are social and that this characteristic is embedded in our development as a species, but also that our sociality is of a particular type. We establish groups through bonds that have both biological and practical bases. It turns out, then, that our drive to bond in pairs, when combined with males who devoted resources toward parenting, was an important innovation in human evolution because it led to strong family bonds, extended kin groups, and even larger social networks consisting of these more basic units.[7] Our bonds with other people are an integral part of being human, and they are the starting point for the way we experience the world.

Based on these group dynamics, the great biologist E. O. Wilson, among others, has even gone as far as to suggest that humans fall into a special category of sociality called "eusocial." In a eusocial species, a cohesive group is formed where "adult

members are divided into reproductive and (partially) nonrepro-
ductive castes and the latter care for the young."[8] Members of a
eusocial group live together at the same site and work as a cooperative unit.[9] Insects, especially certain types of ants, make up the
largest proportion of eusocial species, but there are some excep-
tions to this, like humans and naked mole rats (august company
indeed!).[10] The extent of our eusociality is debated, of course, but
the mere fact that human beings are even a part of this conversation puts us in the very small category of the most social species in
the world. This alone goes a long way toward explaining why our
interactions with others are so important to us.

Indeed, our sociality is fundamental to everything we do,
including learning. Our nature as social creatures gave rise to our
unique modes of communication as human beings, and thus
became the bedrock for the ways we share knowledge. In turn,
these interactions eventually led to more sophisticated kinds of
learning. *How* we came to learn from each other is a bit more complicated, though.

Imitation, Gestures, and Language

Our all-encompassing sociality can be seen as the starting point
for several developments that would greatly enhance our abilities
to teach and to learn: our capacity for imitation and our adeptness
at conveying important information through gesture and language.
Social species thrive only to the extent that they can communicate
with each other, so these human capabilities began as responses to
that need, but they would ultimately prove to be revolutionary.

Let's first take a look at our innate processes for imitation,
because this was the precursor to more advanced communication.
Marco Iacoboni of the University of California, Los Angeles, has
rightly noted that imitation "is an important aspect of human

behavior, facilitating learning and being associated with social cognition and transmission of culture."[11] It is no secret that we can watch someone do something and mimic the movement ourselves. Ask a toddler to copy your actions and you're in for approximately seven hours of delightful entertainment. Babies, too, start to imitate expressions very soon after they are born. The capacity to imitate is embedded in our makeup as human beings, and it has very long evolutionary roots.

I could have quoted lots of other scientists in the last paragraph about the importance of imitation, but I decided to cite Marco Iacoboni because he has been at the leading edge of research on the mechanism that may be responsible for our ability to imitate so thoroughly and productively—mirror neurons. As it happens, we share some of our propensity for imitation with our ape and monkey cousins, so the capability to do so must have developed very early on. Iacoboni and others have theorized that this may be because we have similar groups of neurons that play a major role in both the completion of an action ourselves and processing a similar action when we see others do it.[12] Here is my version of a widely used example regarding the function of mirror neurons: some of the neurons that fire when I reach for a bottle of water are the same as those that do so when I see my wife grasping a bottle. These are the mirror neurons. They respond to the activity of another as if it were a reflection of my own, and they are key components of imitation because they help me to replicate the motor activity. As Iacoboni goes on to explain, "mirroring mechanisms are also critically involved in the early stages of imitative learning."[13] Mirror neurons, and the imitation they facilitate, are neural products of our sociality, and they represent a critical stepping stone toward more advanced learning and communication.

Mirror neurons have sometimes been lauded as a kind of holy grail in terms of unlocking the secrets of the human mind, but not all scientists are on board with such a broad interpretation. In his book *The Myth of Mirror Neurons*, Gregory Hickok pushes back hard on the idea that mirror neurons are somehow the solution to every problem. In particular, Hickok argues that mirror neurons do not help us to understand the actions and the intentions of others; they are simply mechanisms for imitation.[14] This, I think, is a key for our study of sociality and learning. Imitation was an important outgrowth of our social nature, and the mirroring process that causes imitation is fascinating, but other crucial elements were needed before we jumped from mimicking others to comprehending them.

Here is where gesture and language come into play. Michael Arbib lays out a logical argument for how humans moved from imitation to the ability to communicate through more complex means by suggesting that the "extension of the mirror system from *recognizing* single actions to *being able to copy* compound actions was the key innovation in the brains of our hominid ancestors that was relevant to language."[15] This development, Arbib explains, provided the groundwork for our brains to be "language-ready."[16] Scientists, however, are absolutely divided on what happened next with respect to the actual development of language. Some, like Arbib himself, posit that informative gestures were the next logical progression from imitative abilities and then gesture led to vocalization and finally to language. Others—like Barbara J. King and Ian Tattersall—hypothesize that gestures and vocal language evolved together and that then, as now, the two elements comprise a "unified" system.[17] The work of David McNeill, a researcher on gestures, reinforces this integrated interpretation, since he finds strong evidence that "gestures and speech really *are* parts of one process [and] the best theoretical approach is to regard this process as a dialectic of gesture imagery and verbal/linguistic structure."[18]

One of the things I have learned from my research for this book is that it is difficult to make overly precise causal arguments about evolutionary matters. The messier, more skeptical hypotheses seem to garner more support, because it is really hard to know for certain if one phenomenon explicitly led to another. To say that language evolved from gesture, then, doesn't ring as true to me as a possible interplay between gesture and language where both evolved alongside each other as our systems for communication became more fully developed.

My discussion so far has focused on *how* human beings moved from imitation to gestures and language, but the bigger (and, for our purposes, more interesting) question is *why* did this happen? Any answer to this question comes back to our sociality and need to communicate, but Daniel Dor, Chris Knight, and Jerome Lewis also indicate that an "unusual evolutionary dynamic" would have been necessary to make this leap as well.[19] What are some possibilities for the extraordinary conditions that may have contributed to the rise of language? Robin Dunbar attributes the beginnings of language use to the grooming habits of primates. As grooming groups began to get too large, there needed to be a more effective way to communicate with other members of the expanding social sphere.[20] Thus, our modern chats about sports and movies are descendants of ancient grooming behaviors. This is an intriguing (and somewhat unsettling) theory, to say the least. On the opposite end of the spectrum, Dean Falk has proposed that language evolved from the interactions between mother and child—that is, the babbling of babies and the "motherese" used by women to respond to their infants.[21] Falk suggests that this connection has been unnoticed for so long because of the undue emphasis placed by researchers on men as "evolutionary movers."[22] She has a good point.

There are many other theories about the genesis of language as well, but all of them—in one way or another—have to do with learning. In many ways, learning is as basic as communicating with someone else in order to share information. This process, though, is so essential that it is implicated in many of the evolutionary advancements that make us human. We might even say that our social natures were heightened by our need to learn.

The Necessity of Play

An important way that humans learn through interactions with others is play. Play behaviors are common in all mammals, and scientists have frequently pointed to the developmental and psychological benefits of play in a wide variety of species.[23] The markers of play are extraordinarily similar, regardless of which group of mammals one studies: "Culled from many sources some of the claimed characteristics of play are: no obvious immediate function; pleasurable affect; sequentially variable; stimulation-seeking; quick and energetically expensive behaviour; exaggerated, incomplete, or awkward movement; most prevalent in juveniles; special 'play' signals; a breakdown in role relationships; mixing of behaviour patterns from several contexts; relative absence of threat or submission; and the relative absence of final consummatory acts."[24] I'm sure we can all think of playful moments with pets that resonate with this description, but humans have their own expressions of each of these behaviors, and the types of our play range widely. We might see these features pop up in a baseball game, in a group of children "playing school," in a rousing turn of hide-and-seek, in a tea party with stuffed animals, and in a classroom spelling bee. The list, of course, could go on forever. Regardless of the format, play is a deeply ingrained mechanism for learning about the world and about other people.

In fact, play is a necessary component for certain kinds of learning. For example, as Stuart Brown and Christopher Vaughan have explained:

The real question, then, is why and how play is useful. One major theory is that play is simply practice for skills needed in the future. The idea is that when animals play-fight, they are practicing to fight or hunt for later on. But it turns out that cats that are deprived of play-fighting can hunt just fine. What they can't do—what they never learn to do—is to socialize successfully. Cats and other social mammals such as rats will, if seriously missing out on play, have an inability to clearly delineate friend from foe, miscue on social signaling, and either act excessively aggressive or retreat and not engage in more normal social patterns.[25]

If our sociality is intrinsically connected to learning writ large, then it may also be true that, like these cats and rats, we need play to form an understanding of some of these social dynamics. We are at least as social as a species, if not more, than the others described here, which may mean that a lack of play inhibits social development. In turn, that would lead to poorer learning. Indeed, new research is beginning to demonstrate this very effect in children whose preschool experiences are more "directive" than play-based.[26] Play governs the lives of young children, and—through play—they learn much about their worlds. More than this, though, play allows children to fulfill their biological need for socialization in ways few other activities can. As with the case of the young cats and rats, this engagement is necessary for child development and the learning that accompanies it. Other benefits of play for children include emotional maturity and analytical skills, both of which enhance our ability to learn.[27] The lasting effects of a playful childhood linger and aid us as we become adults.

Play often gets a bad rap for falling outside the realm of intellectual pursuits, but the biological evidence is clear. Without play, our learning is hindered, and we are unable to function at our highest levels.

The Evolution of Teaching

We've just explored the basic, fundamental links between our sociality and our learning processes, but some have even suggested that there exists an evolutionary rationale for the more complex interactions involved in teaching itself. One group of scientists approaches this question by asking whether or not teaching behaviors are unique to human beings.[28] Many of these researchers use a definition of teaching that, more or less, has to do with one individual (the teacher) modifying its behavior in order for another (the student) to acquire "knowledge or skills more rapidly or efficiently than it would otherwise, or that it would not have learned at all. This definition differentiates teaching from other forms of social learning, in which naïve animals acquire information from other individuals engaging in their usual behaviour."[29] One of the difficulties of this approach, as I see it, is that it allows for the inclusion of animals who are learning through what we might call behaviorism—ants who figure out running routes by following a partner and touching the partner with antennae to indicate their presence. The closest example, described by Alex Thornton and Nichola Raihani, to what we might think of as teaching is meerkats who instruct their young how to hunt by bringing them kinds of prey that gradually require more advanced skill levels (moving from dead to live prey, for example).[30] These examples ultimately lead many of those who work in this field to conclude that teaching behaviors have evolved in a variety of species, but while these behaviors are fascinating, they are of a different order than the complex teaching and learning relationships of humans.

Gergely Csibra and György Gergely are also skeptical of claims regarding teaching in nonhuman animals. Instead, they have theorized that in humans (alone as a species), evolution has led to what they refer to as a "natural pedagogy."[31] Their formulation refers to a particular way of interacting that they call natural, because they believe it to be innate, and pedagogical, because it results in learning: "We have speculated that communication of generic knowledge was selected for during hominin evolution as a consequence of the emergence of recursive tool making practices, which confronted the observational learner with cognitively opaque contents to acquire. . . . A new type of communicative learning system based on ostensive-referential demonstrations of knowledge could by-pass this problem by having the expert user actively guide the novice by selectively manifesting the information to be acquired and generalized."[32] There is a lot packed into this description, but the most important element is their hypothesis that we devised a system of communication that depends upon "ostensive-referential demonstrations of knowledge." Another way to think about this is that our pedagogical inclinations evolved from a more elaborate form of show and tell. The key evolutionary move was the systematized behavior of one individual drawing the attention of another individual to a particular object and sharing information about it.

The most basic way that we engage another person in this kind of interaction, Csibra and Gergely argue, is through eye contact, and the fact that babies are particularly attuned to this manner of communication "well before they show evidence of learning from such interactions" is an indication to these researchers that "natural pedagogy is a basic cognitive adaptation."[33] Csibra and Gergely go even further and suggest that "infants are also prepared to learn generic kind-relevant information directly and from a specific source that is not available to other species: from benevolent communicators who manifest generic knowledge 'for' them that would be difficult (if not impossible) to acquire without such support."[34] For them, the entire foundation of the teaching-learning relationship is thus rooted in the evolution of our sociality. The way infants respond to adults is both evidence of this adaptation as well as an extension of every other kind of teaching that happens.

The original study on natural pedagogy published by Csibra and Gergely has been cited well over 800 times and has become an important linchpin for any discussion about the evolution of teaching. Some researchers are not as certain that the ways in which we learn from teacher figures compose an actual adaption, however. For example, Amy Skerry and her colleagues note the absolute "centrality of social learning for the acquisition of adaptive information and skills," but they do not think we can identify one specific mechanism to account for this learning.[35] Unlike Csibra and Gergely, they theorize that our brains have instead been readied by evolution to respond to pedagogical interactions and to develop a "theory of pedagogy" as we move from infancy to adulthood.[36] The question remains unsettled, but the level of interest in the subject highlights the significance of teaching as an augmentation of our sociality.

Storytelling

Related to the evolution of pedagogical behaviors is the development of stories and narrative. The earliest humans probably shared stories to relay vital information and to enhance social learning. Indeed, Louis Cozolino notes that: "Stories connect us to one another, help to shape our identities, and serve to keep our brains integrated and regulated. The human brain co-evolved with storytelling, narrative structure, and the tale of the heroic journey as told in cultures throughout the world. Stories are, in fact, so ubiquitous in human experience that we hardly notice their existence."[37] Any evolutionary forces that shaped our abilities to teach and learn were probably heightened by our nascent capacity for telling stories. With narratives, people were not only able to share information but to set that information in a context to make it easier for learning to take place. Primarily, it seems that our early ancestors were interested in social information, which would have aided our learning, and stories became a vehicle for conveying these details.[38] It goes without saying that stories are still a vital part of nearly every aspect of our lives—from local gossip to fine art to our classrooms.

In fact, Daniel Willingham has suggested that stories are particularly suited for the classroom because they "are treated differently in memory than other types of material."[39] Perhaps one reason for this effect is the evolutionary importance of narratives. Stories became a vital tool for communication, and so our brains began to process them differently. We can use this cognitive prioritizing to enhance learning, Willingham argues, by employing story structure effectively in our classes.[40] I go into more detail later in this chapter on the kinds of stories we might tell, but it is useful at the outset to know the degree to which narrative is valuable for learning new information.

A Caveat

I want to note at this point that our evolutionary history is only a springboard for understanding our sociality. It is not solely responsible for dictating the behavior of modern human beings. We are not robots who were programmed long ago and sent along our merry way. As Stephen Sanderson explains: "None of the tendencies identified above are rigid. Rather, they are behavioral *predispositions* that move along certain lines rather than others but that interact in various ways with the total physical and sociocultural environment. The behavioral predispositions tend to win out in the long run, but they can be diminished or even negated by certain environmental arrangements. At the same time, other environments can amplify these tendencies, pushing them to increasingly higher levels."[41] In other words, our sociality has been greatly influenced by evolution, but this nature can be mitigated by other factors in our lives. We see this when we teach.

Theories of Social Learning

Given how thoroughly science has demonstrated that our sociality is entwined with our learning processes, it is somewhat surprising that, as Jon Dron and Terry Anderson have noted, "many educators conceive of learning as an individual process, and assess it as such accordingly."[42] Okay, I suppose it's not that surprising. Educational systems tend to replicate themselves, and the history of education in America is dominated by a focus on individual achievement. Drawn by the promise of sociality for improving education, however, some important thinkers in the twentieth century provided us with different theoretical models in order to advance our understanding of teaching and learning. I am particularly interested in the work of Maria Montessori, Albert Bandura, and Lev Vygotsky because their frameworks for learning and sociality are still very influential. Though there are many researchers I could discuss in this section, I am drawn to these three because of the endurance of their ideas.

Maria Montessori could well be called the *grand dame* of early childhood education. Her famous method is guided by the philosophy that cohesive classroom communities are vital for learning.[43]

For Montessori, the education of young children must emerge from the group, not from instructing individuals. She saw this process as an extension of their development: "Children act in accordance with their natures, and not because of the teacher's exhortations. . . . This society created by cohesion, which children have revealed to us, is at the root of all social organizations. For this reason I maintain that we adults cannot teach children from three to six years of age. We can but observe them with intelligence and follow their development, at every hour of every day, in their endless exercises. What nature has given them develops with work."[44] Too much intervention by teachers in this society that the children construct can interfere with learning more than help it. Although Montessori admits that things change a bit as children get older, her emphasis on the group and the society of learning remains.

Albert Bandura is best known for his work on self-efficacy—which has taken higher education by storm of late and which I discuss in later chapters—but I am more interested at the moment in his concept of modeling. Modeling is the deceptively simple idea that we learn through observation of others (i.e., our "models"). First, Bandura suggests, we learn through verbal modeling—as with a child beginning to speak. Later, more complex behavioral modeling and intellectual kinds of modeling become important.[45] As he explains, "People cannot be much influenced by modeled opinions if they do not understand them. . . . In voicing opinions, models transmit ideas and preferences. But modeling does not itself guarantee that views which have been learned will be articulated."[46] A good teacher must move from modeling, then, to providing students with conceptual scaffolding they can use to build knowledge for themselves. Teaching is understood by Bandura to be a primarily social interaction in which we are serving as exemplars for the ways in which our students can engage with our disciplines. Given what we know about imitation from evolutionary biology, none of this should come as a shock, but Bandura's notion of modeling has been transformative for K–12 classrooms. I think it could have a similar impact on college teaching as well.

Finally, we come to Lev Vygotsky. I'm sure all of you have your own lists of your favorite educational theorists (right?), but Vygotsky is at the top of mine.[47] Prior to his untimely death from tuberculosis in 1934, Vygotsky produced incredibly innovative and influential work, much of which is still as relevant to education as it ever was. Furthermore, some of his research was conducted in response to Piaget's theories of child development. What I want to focus on, though, is Vygotsky's concept of the "zone of proximal development," which he outlined in his masterwork, the posthumously published *Mind in Society*.

For Vygotsky, the zone of proximal development is "the distance between the actual developmental level as determined by individual problem solving and the level of potential development as determined through problem solving under adult guidance or in collaboration with more capable peers."[48] In other words, for any given subject, an individual has a range—or a zone in Vygotsky's terminology—in which she or he is able to move from point A to point B, with point A being the current level of knowledge or skills and point B being the level of understanding that is possible for this person if given help from a teacher or fellow students. These zones fluctuate in size, so one person's zone of proximal development for, say, quantum mechanics may be bigger or smaller than another person's. Additionally, zones can vary even for the same individual. For example, one student's zone of proximal development for mathematical thinking may be broader than her or his zone for historical thinking.

I'll use myself as an example here as a way to help illustrate the point. My field of training is medieval studies. My zone of proximal development for studying works of medieval English literature, then, is broader than my zone for ancient philosophy, even though they are both fields in the humanities, and is certainly vaster than my zone for Keynesian economics. Going further, even within medieval studies itself, my zone for Continental literature will be smaller than that of English literature (because I do not have as much facility with Old High German as I do with Old and Middle English), and my zone for the paleography of medieval Arabic manuscripts will be smaller still. A good teacher or some of my brilliant friends can help me to learn more in these areas, but my achievement in one will proceed at a different pace than in another.

Although Vygotsky's original work dealt with young children, his theories on the zone of proximal development have certainly been applied to college level.[49] I believe he has come as close as any other scholar to truly capturing the power of human sociality in his formulation of these zones. Vygotsky understood that our ability to learn individually was quite limited. Eventually, we would need other people in order to reach our full potential as learners. The social element of education is not optional but necessary if students are to succeed.

One of the difficulties here, of course, is that these zones are not physical entities. We cannot see where they start and finish, so there is a great deal of trial and error involved as we try to work within them. In fact, part of our goal as teachers may be to help students become more aware of their own zones, their own strengths. Far from discouraging achievement, such metacognitive work can help students to build on areas of expertise. Vygotsky certainly never intended to suggest that learning had precise limitations; to the contrary, he hoped the zone of proximal development would allow teachers to understand students' vast potential in ways that would allow for more effective education.

Louis Cozolino has explained that the "curriculum and social environment of a classroom have a synergistic impact on learning. Supportive, encouraging, and caring relationships stimulate students' neural circuitry to learn, priming their brains for neuro-plastic processes."[50] Montessori, Bandura, and Vygotsky did not have the benefit of these modern neuroscientific findings to bolster their claims, but their theoretical models align nicely with this recent work. We can use the combination of these older frame-works along with newer science as we design and implement social pedagogies for our classrooms.

Social Pedagogies

The long road of this chapter has led to this point. The question that remains for us is this: how do we move from science and theory to practice? Some researchers have focused their attention on what they refer to as social pedagogies in an attempt to under-stand the degree to which our sociality influences the teaching strategies we use. One step in this direction has been an influential white paper for the Teagle Foundation written by Randy Bass and Heidi Elmendorf in 2011. Bass and Elmendorf rightly state that "the deepening role of social dimension in learning—which we take broadly to include all representation acts as constitutive of knowledge—is as yet very little understood," and then they suggest that social pedagogies are one way to bridge this gap.[51] They go on to define social pedagogies as "design approaches for teaching and learning that engage students with what we might call an 'authentic audience' (other than the teacher), where the *representation of knowledge* for an audience is absolutely central to the *construction of knowledge* in a course."[52] For Bass and Elmendorf, such pedagogies are social to the extent that they involve students in communicating with others beyond the walls of the classroom.

I would extend their framework a bit, however. They are focusing primarily on authentic assignments and discourse, which are both vital for learning and noble goals in and of themselves, but I want to look more closely at the ways in which students learn from each other and from the teacher.[53] My own characterization of social pedagogies, then, would include those strategies that maximize the characteristics of sociality I have outlined in this chapter and place our social natures as human beings front and center in the learning process. In what remains of this chapter, I want to delve into some of the most effective examples of these kinds of social pedagogies.

The Social Classroom

One element that is absolutely necessary for enacting social pedagogies is establishing what I am calling a social classroom. A social classroom, as I see it, has at least three important characteristics: a sense of belonging, a classroom management philosophy that privileges community building, and an instructor who effectively models intellectual approaches. There may be more, but I believe these are critical. Without first building a social classroom, it will be more challenging for any of the other teaching strategies I'll be discussing to take hold.

Belonging

One of the most interesting developments in educational research over the last decade or so is the degree to which it is either being performed by social psychologists or it is drawing on the work of important social psychologists. This represents a shift from more traditional work that centers on experiments designed to demonstrate how instruction and pedagogical choices influence student success. Instead, these new studies look beyond instruction to examine the social dynamics underpinning achievement. The interventions developed by these psychologists serve "as a catalyst . . . activat[ing] other forces in the environment that drive key outcomes. But those forces must be present."[54] In other words, social-psychological factors are necessary complements to cognition. Some of these interventions have improved student learning so much that they can almost seem like "magic," though—of course—they are not.[55] All of these efforts are as conditional as anything else in the educational research arena, but the results of the studies have been attracting the attention of scholars and institutions alike.

One subject that has emerged from this recent work as being crucial to students' educational experiences is their sense of social belonging. The lead researchers in this area have been Geoffrey Cohen and Gregory Walton at Stanford and David Yeager at the University of Texas. Walton and Cohen, for example, emphasize that "a sense of social connectedness predicts favorable outcomes. . . . In domains of achievement, we suggest people are sensitive to the quality of their social bonds."[56] There can be no doubt that college is a "domain of achievement," so it would follow that belonging becomes a salient factor in student success.[57] One study by Walton and Cohen dives deeply into this question. They set up an experiment to determine how a feeling of belonging, particularly among minority students, affects academic performance. In a pilot study prior to the experiment, they found that "minority students are more uncertain of their belonging than are majority students."[58] The two then developed an intervention in which they "provided minority students with an alternative hypothesis to use to interpret academic hardship. Black 1st-year college students were encouraged to attribute doubt about belonging in school to factors irrelevant to their social identity—in particular, to the struggles faced by students of all ethnicities during the transition to college."[59] Those students selected for the experimental condition were given survey data that demonstrated the extent to which more advanced students struggled with feelings of belonging early in their time at the university and how these feelings eventually faded. Both the treatment and the control groups were then asked to take notes on "each of the 7 days following the intervention" regarding "how much adversity they had experienced that day and their sense of fit in college."[60] The black students in the treatment condition outperformed all others when assessed on "self-perceived potential to succeed in college over time," even after seven days. In turn, those same students had an improved GPA over the next year.[61]

Walton and Cohen's work is just one example of a larger trend in the study of social belonging in education. Overall, as Yeager and Walton reveal, this body of evidence shows pretty conclusively that "if students feel more secure in their belonging in school, they may approach others in the academic environment more and with more positive attitudes, building better relationships, reinforcing their feelings of belonging, and laying the groundwork for later academic success."[62] Based on this research, colleges and universities should certainly be paying close attention to the degree to which students feel like they belong, particularly since this factor seems to affect decisions related to the much-ballyhooed retention, progression, and graduation rates. But if our institutions of higher learning are meant to educate human beings and not just numbers, then an emphasis on belonging is simply a signal of kindness and respect to those students with whom we work.

I would suggest, too, that an institution can put programs in place to enhance social belonging, but this is not enough. The classroom itself is the most immediate place where a student should feel like she or he belongs to a community of learners. The instructor, then, plays a major role in helping students to see that they belong in our courses, our disciplines, and our universities. One way to do this, following the work of Walton and Cohen, would be talking to students about how others have successfully overcome their struggles with the content of your course in the past. Another option, and one that is rather popular, is to have prior students talk to your current class about the same thing. Some faculty do this by hosting a panel early in the semester on which previous students talk about their challenges and triumphs, and then they take questions from the current students. Others ask students to write letters about their experiences in the course so that the next semester's class can learn how to navigate the academic terrain. As instructors, we can also be friendly and approachable, and we can maintain high standards for student work while being intentional about providing them with the tools to meet these standards. At the most basic level, though, we can enhance our students' sense of belonging by implementing a classroom management philosophy that prioritizes collaboration, cooperation, and community.

Classroom Management

We often think of classroom management as having to do with setting policies and monitoring behavioral issues in class, but I would like to encourage us to adopt a broader definition of classroom management. Specifically, our approach to managing our classrooms should include strategies for cultivating a climate that is conducive to learning and to productive social interactions. Two noted scholars of classroom management, Patricia Jennings and Mark Greenberg, suggest that one way we can do this as instructors is to promote "prosocial and cooperative behaviors through establishing warm and supportive relationships and communities, assertive limit-setting and guidance, and preventative strategies rather than controlling negative behaviors through coercive measures such as punishment."[63] Fostering relationships and communities is the key to this method, and students need to get to know each other and to trust their peers as part of this process. However, to make this happen in such a way that we avoid our class sessions devolving into a free-for-all of conversations about sports and the weekend, Jennings and Greenberg explain the importance of establishing clear ground rules in order to set boundaries. In other words, our policies can complement our efforts to build community by articulating which kinds of interactions are contributing to the goals of the course (group discussion about a problem set or a passage from a novel) and which are not (texting each other about party plans).

Establishing community through carefully constructed ground rules is even more important when teaching a course in which discussions about potentially sensitive subject matter take place. This frequently happens in humanities and social science courses. Without first creating clear guidelines about the parameters of the discussion, ways to productively respond to emotionally charged rhetoric, and the like, both the conversation and the community itself can suffer. It is not hard to think of hot button issues that might spark such a discussion. The trick is to make sure we have prepared our students to engage each other with respect and with the goal of learning in mind. Enlisting them in the process of developing these guidelines is an additional way to increase their investment in maintaining them during discussion. The classroom community is aided greatly by this kind of framework.

Unlike social belonging, which has been linked directly to enhanced academic performance, community building seems to be more aligned with improved motivation.[64] The two therefore work nicely together. They—and the social classroom in general—are helped along, however, by an instructor who understands the power of effective modeling.

Modeling

Albert Bandura's theories on modeling have been under-utilized in higher education. While Bandura was discussed in education courses I took in college, the emphasis was always on serving as behavioral exemplars and role models for younger children. This kind of modeling is not without its place in the college classroom, but the most obvious connection with Bandura's work and the teaching we do in higher education is our position as intellectual models for our students. If we want our classrooms to be enthusiastic communities and vibrant intellectual spaces, then we need to model these actions first and foremost. Some of the ways we can do this include:

- Exhibiting positive regard and empathy for all students in the class.
- Exploring multiple, diverse perspectives on scholarly issues and questions.
- Using logical argumentation to build our cases.
- Limiting our agonistic (competitive) approach to other scholars' work.
- Citing our sources orally and in visual presentations.
- Demonstrating methods for productive and collegial disagreement.

- Offering constructive, rather than destructive, criticism.
- Finding value in the contributions our students make in class.
- Listening.

This list is just a starting point, of course, but seeing ourselves as intellectual models and practicing these behaviors in our classrooms allow us to set an important foundation for students' social learning.

One aspect of modeling that Bandura rarely mentions, but recent research reveals is associated with learning, is gesturing. Through gestures, our physicality enhances our intellectual modeling. Susan Goldin-Meadow, one of the leading researchers on gesture and communication in the classroom, makes clear that "the gestures teachers produce have an impact on what learners take from their lessons and may therefore have an effect on learning."[65] As we have seen earlier, gesture played a major role in the evolution of our abilities to communicate, so it is not surprising that our gestures have an impact on our students' learning. The implicit power of gestures appears to cut across all disciplines, but there is a particular line of research demonstrating the importance of gestures for students who are learning foreign languages.[66] Regardless of what we teach, though, the moral of this story is that we need to be attuned even to how our movements are contributing to the efficacy of our teaching.

By cultivating a social classroom using these and other means, faculty pave the way for successful deployment of social pedagogies. The practice of teaching in ways that prime our sociality is complemented by the environment we create to support these strategies.

GETTING STARTED

Talk to your students about their own expectations for a classroom community. What standards for behavior do they themselves think are important? What helps them feel a sense of belonging? Think about drafting a short statement based on your discussion with them, including it on your syllabus, and revisiting it periodically a) to assess whether the standards have been useful and b) to consider additions or deletions based on the social dynamics that unfold over the course of the semester.

Discussion, Redux

It probably goes without saying that discussion is one of the most widely practiced and potentially beneficial social pedagogies, but I covered it in the last chapter and don't want to bore you already. Rather than rehash the same material, then, I want to include an anecdote of one of the most effective discussion facilitators I have ever seen.

In 2015, I had the good fortune to observe Dennis Huston, a now-retired professor of English and one of Rice's legendary teachers, in the classroom.[67] Dennis has won every teaching award our university offers, along with many national awards, too, including the highly regarded CASE/Carnegie US Professor of the Year Award. I happened to be observing a Shakespeare course, and Dennis was just beginning to discuss *King Lear*, one of the Bard's most heartbreaking plays. Dennis would masterfully intersperse discussion with an expert glossing of and commentary on the text. When a student would respond to a question, he focused intently, kindly, on each person who was speaking, often walking right up to where they were sitting in the room. He would listen and then push further. I must have heard him ask "Why?" dozens of times as he helped each student move beyond the surface to a more nuanced interpretation. For Dennis, each student, each speaker, is the most important person in the room while they contribute, and then he moves back to the group as a whole. They work as a team to put together a collective understanding of the text. To be sure, that interpretation may have existed before, many may have written about the same aspects of the play, but for these students, in this place, at that time, it was brand new—a thing that lived for each of them.

Going even further, they were only able to draw their conclusions by collaborating. Each person had a piece of the puzzle that she or he contributed to the group effort of developing a nuanced analysis of *Lear*. Dennis's interactions with the students, though, really serve to highlight the promise of discussion as a social pedagogy. Some discussions operate more like fact-finding missions with students participating in rapid succession and with very little connection between responses. Only when we engage students (as individuals and as a group) in ways similar to what I observed in Dennis's class that day can we actually say that our discussions are maximizing our sociality for learning.

Collaborative Learning vs. Group Projects

Collaborative learning, an umbrella term that covers many different kinds of social pedagogies involving small groups of students, has had a significant impact on higher education. This type of teaching has also been one of the most frequently researched pedagogical topics, which makes sense because of its ubiquity and the difficulty that comes along with efforts to teach in this way.[68] In fact, one of the questions I am often asked in my work as the director of a teaching center is not "Should I use collaborative learning?" but rather "How do I make sure I'm using collaborative learning well?" This is a valid concern. While collaborative learning holds great promise for our students, it can also have a detrimental effect if not structured properly.

There are so many different collaborative learning techniques that it is impossible to enumerate them all. The category includes everything from the well-known "think-pair-share" (otherwise known as "talk to the person beside you"), to interviews, to debates, to group testing, to team-based learning. Unfortunately, I don't have the space in this chapter to explore all of them in detail, but by outlining the contours of successful collaborative learning and the ways in which these strategies draw on our sociality, I hope to provide a template for you to choose those techniques that work best for you and your students.

At the heart of any collaborative learning strategy is a group of students collectively and cooperatively attempting to achieve mastery and understanding together. Assembling productive groups is therefore a key to successfully implementing these pedagogies. In an ideal world, and for maximum learning gains, groups would have five students in them, and they would be heterogeneous in makeup. We are not always in a position to construct groups with exactly five students, so groups of any size from 2–6 students can also be effective.[69] Heterogeneity within the groups is important regardless of the size, however, and we need to focus some attention on the composition process in order to ensure diversity in all of its forms. Sociality can drive our learning in group settings like this, but we place limitations on the possibilities for achievement if our students are only learning from people who share similar backgrounds and worldviews.

In their outstanding book *Collaborative Learning Techniques: A Handbook for College Faculty*, Elizabeth Barkley, K. Patricia Cross, and Claire Howell Major lay out five essential components that effective collaborative learning strategies share: positive interdependence, promotive interaction, individual and group accountability, development of teamwork skills, and group processing. Most of those elements are self-explanatory, but I'd like to pause for a moment to talk a bit about positive interdependence.[70] Positive interdependence suggests that the group's learning—not the grade, but the learning—hinges on the contributions of the individual students who compose the group. In other words, the solution to a problem or the interpretation of the text needs to emerge collectively in order for the process to be truly collaborative. If each student can complete the group's work on his or her own, then the task has not been designed with cooperation in mind.

The research on collaborative learning suggests that when these activities are designed well, students benefit significantly from them. One particular study on group learning in engineering courses, for example, found gains in many specific areas like problem-solving and higher-order thinking skills, as well as achievement on verbal, mathematical, and procedural tasks.[71] But there's a problem, and I'm going to wade into both anecdotal (because I don't have exact numbers) and controversial (because a lot of us do this) territory here. The trouble is that, too often, collaborative learning in classrooms across the country takes the form of a group project or a group presentation that lends itself to a "divide and conquer" mentality among students. Each completes her or his own part of the project, sometimes without even talking to other members of the group. We cannot entirely blame them for this. Some of the fault needs to be borne by the assignment design. Carol Colbeck, Susan Campbell, and Stefani Bjorklund explain further:

The conditions for group learning in higher education settings rarely meet the standards advocated by cooperative learning scholars. . . . As a result, many well-intentioned faculty assign group projects without providing students the information and guidance prescribed by cooperative learning advocates. A survey conducted with participants in group projects at a single university found that many students had negative reactions to group learning experiences. Students were particularly frustrated when they believed that the instructor had poor group skills or shirked responsibility for helping the groups.[72]

We can probably all think of group projects like this that we were asked to complete as students. I've even been guilty of assigning activities like this in the past, much to my students' dismay.

The quandary here is that students simply do not learn as much in this context. They learn teamwork,[73] certainly, but there is a real question here about whether a college course is the ideal venue for them to master this goal or whether we should be attending to other kinds of learning. I don't have an answer to that, but I do know that collaborative learning in its finest forms can achieve more than just this limited outcome. The methods that work best embrace the kind of structure that positions cooperation as a means to the end of generating collective knowledge through social interaction, not the end in and of itself.

Designing these kinds of projects for students can be challenging, however. We need to develop assignments that do not have pre-conceived conclusions if we are going to maximize collaboration for learning. An archival project or one that draws on fieldwork would be good options because students must rely on each other to gather evidence. Both of these examples, though, require students to go outside of the classroom. More traditional assignments that ask groups to develop their own research question or to tackle a previously unknown dataset can also achieve the goals on which we have our sights set. Each student needs the other group members in order to approach a solution, which is a fundamental attribute of all effective collaborative learning exercises.

GETTING STARTED

You may already be using group work in your classes, in which case one easy thing you might try is a quick assessment of how closely the activities match the attributes for successful collaboration I have outlined here. If these activities align well, then you're way ahead of me! On the other hand, you might find aspects of group work assignments to tweak and improve. For those who aren't yet using much in the way of collaborative learning but would like to do so, try selecting a short assignment that you would normally ask students to complete individually and transform it into a low-stakes group project using the guidelines. You may find that students really like it and that the new activity is meeting your learning goals as well as or better than the previous approach.

The Peer Instruction Revolution

In my humble opinion, one of the most important advances in collaborative learning (and therefore social pedagogies) has been the development of Peer Instruction, a strategy designed in the 1990s by Eric Mazur of Harvard University to gauge conceptual understanding. To clarify my terms up front, I am not talking about students teaching each other more generally. Yes, that can be effective, too (when used appropriately), but I want to focus on the specific technique Mazur created when he became aware of the fact that his students were giving him high teaching evaluations and getting good grades, but they did not understand the conceptual underpinnings of Newton's Laws of Motion. They could memorize the information and the formulas, and they could plug-and-chug the equations, but when they tried to answer questions that relied on deep learning of concepts, they were not very successful. Intrigued, and somewhat distressed, Mazur began integrating items from an instrument called the Force Concept Inventory into more of his class sessions to determine the extent of these misconceptions.[74] His idea for Peer Instruction was born.

A typical use of Peer Instruction looks something like this: an instructor gives students a problem to solve. Students first work individually for a few minutes to solve the problem. The instructor then reveals a selection of possible answers to the problem either on the board or on a screen, and students vote on the answer that best matches their own. Frequently, these votes are cast via a classroom response system, but colored note cards work just as well.[75] After observing the voting process, the instructor will put students in groups to work through the problem again and convince each other of the right answer. A new vote is then taken to see what answers the process has yielded, and a debriefing discussion about the solution follows.

Research on the effectiveness of Peer Instruction is very telling. Seven years' worth of data, beginning in 1990, show double the normalized gain on post-test scores in calculus-based physics classes using Peer Instruction over more traditional methods. In this case, the test in question was the Force Concept Inventory. By 1997, the increase in normalized gain was nearly four times that of traditionally taught courses.[76] The strength of these learning gains is not an anomaly either, as many other studies on Peer Instruction reveal consistently robust results. Furthermore, Michelle Smith, a biologist at the University of Maine, has shown convincingly that Peer Instruction not only improves scores on tests but even leads to better performance on follow-up conceptual questions in class. Students, that is, are more likely to answer a second, related conceptual question correctly during class after going through the Peer Instruction process for the previous question. Perhaps most striking, this improvement was observed "even when none of the students in a discussion group originally knows the correct answer" to the original question.[77]

At this point, you may be asking yourself the same thing I was when I first delved into this area of research: *why* does Peer Instruction work so well? It seems that even those who do research on Peer Instruction are still mulling over this question. Smith lays out several possibilities: "Previous explanations for the value of PI have maintained the 'transmissionist' view that during discussion, students who know the right answer are explaining the correct reasoning to their less knowledgeable peers, who consequently improve their performance on the revote. Our finding that even students in naïve groups improve their performance after discussion suggests a more constructivist explanation: that these students are arriving at their own conceptual understanding on their own, through the process of group discussion and debate."[78] As you can see, there are theories here, but no definitive answers. Mazur himself attributes the success of Peer Instruction to its being an active pedagogy rather than a passive one, but there are a lot of teaching techniques designed for active learning that do not have the same magnitude of effect.[79] I would suggest that we add sociality to this list of reasons. If our learning stems, in so many ways, from our interactions with other people, then those pedagogies that take the most advantage of this are going to have higher degrees of success. Peer Instruction draws on our sociality in ways that very few teaching strategies do, and this could help to explain its high success rates.

Peer Instruction was originally developed for STEM disciplines, but there are plenty of ways to use Mazur's model in the social sciences and humanities. We just need to change the emphasis a bit in order to make it work. Rather than collaborating in order to determine the correct response, students would try to persuade each other and defend their positions using evidence. Here is one example:

We might argue that L. Frank Baum's *The Wonderful Wizard of Oz* is

1.   A metaphor for growing up and leaving childhood behind.
2.   An exploration of individual differences and the ways in which society constructs those differences.
3.   A reflection on the journeys we all take in life and the need for intelligence, compassion, and courage on these journeys.
4.   A fun story for children that teaches them about overcoming obstacles.[80]

If we follow the general methodology for Peer Instruction, students would answer this individually, then talk with their peers, and then vote again. There is no right answer here; all are plausible. The point is to get them really thinking about how they would defend their position and what evidence they might use to construct an argument.

In short, Peer Instruction is exactly the kind of teaching strategy that can be substantiated by the research on how human beings learn. It uses social interaction as the actual means for learning rather than merely a single step in the process. In this way, it makes important use of our most deep-seated mechanisms for learning.

Stories, Play, and Games

Like monsters on medieval maps, storytelling and play tend to inhabit the margins when it comes to discussions of social pedagogies. Because of their evolutionary links to sociality and learning, however, it might pay some dividends to look a bit more closely at these areas. For example, we know from our earlier discussion that stories evolved as a means to communicate, to inform, to teach. Drawing on these roots, we can bring stories into our classroom in productive ways. I should note that I'm not talking about lectures here. They are a whole other ball of wax, and I will get to them later in the book. There have been many times when I have entered into a debate about lectures, and someone defends nonstop talking in the classroom by telling me that stories have always been used to teach people. That particular fact is true, but stories and lectures are very different genres. Stories are narratives with plots and beginnings and endings and even a character or two. Lectures, especially ineffective ones, are often litanies of facts and details. Some successful lecturers may include stories among the particulars, but lectures themselves are not inherently stories.

Now that I have that off my chest, let's turn to how we might incorporate stories into our teaching. I would suggest that any information we might wish to share with our students can be turned into a story. Rather than jumping into the theory of relativity, for example, what if students heard a story about Einstein's life and his intellectual journey prior to his development of $E = mc^2$. Housing data in a sociology course could be supplemented by the kinds of stories about evicted individuals that make up the subject of Matthew Desmond's award-winning book *Evicted*.[81] When I teach *Beowulf*, I begin with the story of J.R.R. Tolkien, his love for the poem, and his allusions to it in *The Lord of the Rings*. We might even tell stories about our disciplines. How did an idea change over time? What networks in the field led to these alterations? Since we already know that our brains respond positively to narratives, we should use this information to help our students learn through story. It is just easier to remember information when we have a structure into which we can put these details. Stories provide that for us and for our students.

As with storytelling, play can also be a useful component of our teaching.[82] Although it might at first seem anathema to the college classroom, K–12 instructors have long understood the importance of play in education. This awareness goes back at least as far as Friedrich Froebel, who originally developed the concept of kindergarten in the nineteenth century and built his entire pedagogical philosophy on the foundation of play.[83] Today, games and friendly competitions abound in the classrooms of younger children. We know play is of pedagogical value since it provides a biological impetus for learning. I suggest we break down the barriers and let play into the college classroom where it can do some good for our students. Thankfully, some faculty have already been doing so, but we still have a long way to go.

Play helps to cultivate creative thinking and provides students with an opportunity to explore multiple sides of an issue in ways other teaching strategies might not allow for.[84] This freedom of exploration is in part due to the low stakes of the play environment and the promotion of more informal social interactions. One of the most common ways that play makes its way into college curricula is through educational games. As Claire Howell Major, Michael Harris, and Todd Zakrajsek note regarding the value of such games:

> Academic games are a form of experiential learning, and as such, they have a particular potential benefit to higher education. That is, they provide the opportunity for learners to use

course content and skills in a contextualized environment. In this way, gaming provides an authentic learning experience for students. While playing games, students are engaged in the learning process; when games are designed well, students build strong connections to course content that aid later retrieval.

Educational games have the potential to help students reach important educational goals such as acquiring important foundational knowledge.[85]

Some of the benefits of play, then, are similar to those that students get from stories—such as engagement and boosting memory functions—while others are tied more to the active, experiential nature of play.

Puzzles, video games, trivia competitions, and scavenger hunts are just a few examples of academic games that work for student learning.[86] For a game to work in your course, it should be tied to your learning goals, but other than that, it need only be engaging and fun. Video games, in particular, have received a lot of press lately, and there has been a solid uptick in the number of educational video games since those days long ago when I was but a lad playing *Oregon Trail* in my elementary school. Just do a simple Google search for video or computer games that involve the study of bacteria, for example, and you'll see what I mean. Video games have become such powerful pedagogical tools because they require students to "learn a new literacy" in addition to the course material.[87] These games have truly become an educational force to be reckoned with in our colleges and universities.

Students are willing to invest their time in play and games because they are intrinsically motivated to do so by genuine interest, excitement, and fun. As a result, they are learning—sometimes without even realizing it. One important new pedagogy that combines all of these components is Reacting to the Past, a humanities-based teaching method using role-immersion games developed in the 1990s by Mark Carnes at Barnard College.[88]

GETTING STARTED

Every discipline has a treasure trove of stories connected to the major discoveries, landmark papers, and important theories that shape our knowledge of the field. See if you can find just one of these stories connected to a concept you will be teaching in your next class session. You may already know one or you may have to investigate a bit. Perhaps one is even connected to people you have known throughout your career. Use this story in combination with the other work you will be doing in the class and ask students to give you some feedback at the end of the meeting to determine whether your inclusion of a narrative was successful. I have a hunch you will receive a collective thumbs-up!

Reacting to the Past: Gretchen Kreahling McKay, McDaniel College

Early in the fall of 2014, I traveled to McDaniel College, a liberal arts institution in Maryland, in order to watch how Gretchen Kreahling McKay—a professor of art history—uses Reacting to the Past (RTTP) in her first-year seminar. McKay has long been a staunch advocate for RTTP and has even served on the national board for the Reacting Consortium, a group of colleges and universities that are active in the RTTP community. A few months prior I had read an essay by McKay about RTTP and contacted her about observing the pedagogy in action.[89] She enthusiastically agreed to let me sit in, and even participate, as her class played "The Threshold of Democracy: Athens in 403 B.C."[90] The game picks up in the period following Sparta's defeat of Athens after many years of war, and each student had been assigned a role to play as a member of the Athenian Assembly. Some were playing actual historical figures, like Thrasybulus the general, whereas others represented broad categories of people. Members of the Assembly are then divided into historically accurate factions like moderate democrats, oligarchs, and Socratics. The goal is to successfully navigate the complex political terrain and be declared the winner. To achieve this end, students read primary texts from Plato and Thucydides, write substantial essays grounded in thorough research, and give rhetorically sophisticated speeches on the floor of the Assembly in class each day.

McKay's students had already been playing the game for a few weeks before I arrived. In fact, they had just tried and executed Socrates in the previous class session. (The poor guy never could catch a break.) On the day of my first observation, Gretchen and I walked into a classroom that was already buzzing. Students were practicing speeches, working out strategy, and nefariously plotting against rival factions. If this was happening before class even started, I thought, then the session itself was going to be incredible. Reader, it was.

So much happened on that first day. There were wily arguments about ship voyages—where to go, how many ships to bring, who would comprise the crew—and a complex discussion about ostracism ending with a vote that led to the exile of a fellow named Krystos. I didn't always know what was going on, but the students sure did, and the class ended with a remarkable dialogue about social welfare that mirrored contemporary political debates on the subject. This level of engagement far exceeded anything I had seen in even the most active humanities classrooms, and it is this engagement that sets RTTP apart from other types of teaching. Students must not only have a good handle on the relevant content and information for the course, but they must be willing and able to work with each other in a way that goes beyond what most students are asked to do. They build their historical knowledge and critical thinking skills together in the context of this interactive game.

Before the second day of class, McKay asked me if I would be willing to play a small part in the game. She assigned me the role of a poor Athenian farmer, and I needed to give a speech that would convince the Assembly to pay people from rural areas to come participate in the democracy. My turn was to come up early in the next session. I devised something quickly, and the Assembly voted in my favor. Huzzah! As I gave the speech, I could immediately see the draw of RTTP. There is an energy that emerges from the real-time interactions that gives a kind of urgency to the work you are doing. If you haven't done enough preparation, then it shows, and you risk alienating your fellow farmers who may not get their chance to vote because you gave a poor speech. Thankfully, this did not happen, but it does illuminate the way sociality can motivate student success in RTTP.

The rest of the session went quickly with impassioned pleas to bring back the glory of old Athens, rolls of a dice that led to a character's death, and a unanimous vote to build a wall (I'm not kidding). Thus ended the Athens game for this group of students, and McKay announced that the following week would focus on a debriefing session comparing the outcome of the game with the actual historical events. This post-game discussion is a key feature of RTTP and helps to provide important context for students.

The Athens game is one of the oldest RTTP games and has been played at dozens of colleges and universities since its development.

Other games span historical time periods, and some of the newer RTTP offerings are moving into fields like biology and environmental science.[91] Interested faculty lead the game design process, and new games are often tested at an annual summer conference sponsored by the Reacting Consortium.

The evaluation of RTTP is in its early stages, but the first swath of research on this role-playing methodology seems to indicate gains in academic achievement, particularly with respect to student-reported increases in both their learning and their preparation for class, instructor-reported improvement in students' writing abilities, and larger assessments of student engagement.[92] There are also signs that students develop in psychological and social domains as well.[93] One thing that is absolutely consistent in every report on RTTP: students have fun while taking part in the games. That is not a result you see every day in educational research, and I think we should take this outcome seriously.

Strikingly, proponents of RTTP admit that "the specific cause of the obtained effects [of the method] is unclear."[94] Like Mazur hypothesizes regarding Peer Instruction, there is a kind of consensus that RTTP works in part because it is so active and engaging (and therefore, it is sometimes implied and sometimes stated outright, different from most other college classes). But this is not enough for me, especially because RTTP is so clearly unlike more standard teaching strategies. Mark Carnes himself considers RTTP to be a type of "subversive play" akin to football and fraternity life. For Carnes, the success of RTTP can be attributed to the enjoyment students take from learning in a context that breaks the rules, so to speak, of traditional higher education.[95] I, on the other hand, don't see anything especially subversive about RTTP, and categorizing it as such undersells its power. I would argue that RTTP helps students because it is exactly the kind of pure social play that research is demonstrating to have significant cognitive benefits. Indeed, as Stuart Brown and Christopher Vaughan have shown:

> During play, the brain is making sense of itself through simulation and testing. Play activity is actually helping sculpt the brain. In play, most of the time we are able to try out things without threatening our physical or emotional well-being. We are safe precisely because we are just playing.
>
> For humans, creating such simulations of life may be play's most valuable benefit. In play we can imagine and experience situations we have never encountered before and learn from them. We can create possibilities that have never existed but may in the future. We make new cognitive connections that find their way into our everyday lives. We can learn lessons and skills without being directly at risk.[96]

It sounds as if those writers are specifically describing RTTP, doesn't it? They are not, of course, but the passage does highlight what I think lies behind the effectiveness of RTTP. Play is deeply connected to our sociality, and through this connection, the neural systems for learning are engaged. RTTP taps right into these interactions and succeeds because it utilizes them so well.

The role-playing methodology of RTTP is not without its detractors, though. A frequent criticism is that the games take up too much time and do not leave enough time for the coverage of content. My response to that is probably predictable by this point: we really need to think carefully about the degree to which content needs to be our priority. Certainly, students have to leave our courses with a handle on important content, but—by the same token—there are serious issues with the methodology of trying to cram as much content as possible into the semester. Instead of going that route, let's think about choosing content carefully as a way to help our students develop a framework for thinking about the discipline. This is exactly what RTTP does through social interactions, and it's why I think the carefully designed role-playing games at the heart of this pedagogy can have a significant impact on the humanities (and beyond) now and in the future.

Being Together

I want to conclude this chapter by tackling a rather thorny issue: whether being together in the same physical space matters for learning. After reviewing so much of the literature on sociality and its effects on our teaching, our classrooms, and our students, I am going to go out on a precariously shaky limb and say that actually being in the same place matters a great deal for educational success as it allows for the full expression of our social nature as human beings. This is obviously a hot-button topic because of the prevalence of both social media and online education at colleges and universities today. Social media sites like Facebook, Twitter, Instagram, Snapchat, and others are being used more and more to augment face-to-face instruction,[97] while online courses and programs have proliferated exponentially since the dawn of the internet age in the 1990s. As an aside, when I use the term "online" here, I will be referring to courses that are taught almost exclusively—80 to 100 percent—at a distance without students and faculty interacting in a physical classroom space.[98] Certainly, we can experience some social connections through all of these technological means, but whether the technology allows us to tap into our sociality *enough* to maximize learning is a very different question.

Because social media is really an auxiliary tool for learning in most courses, I will focus on online education, where the platform itself is the vehicle for course delivery and instruction. It is impossible to work in higher education without having heard a great deal about, and forming an opinion on, online education. In 2014, 5.8 million students took at least one online course, which represents nearly 30 percent of college students in the United States.[99] With so many students pursuing online learning, there has understandably been a lot of interest in measuring the effectiveness of these courses, particularly as compared to the outcomes of face-to-face courses. To be sure, research looking at the differences between online and face-to-face courses is ongoing and much of it has been mixed, fraught with the difficulties of comparing these very different modalities. In her book *Minds Online*, Michelle Miller does an excellent job reviewing the broad swath of this research in a balanced way.[100] While it is certainly true that face-to-face teaching is not always as effective as it might be, I also think it is important to note that new evidence from large, recent studies has begun to indicate that online courses have not lived up to their promise for student learning.

For example, one 2017 study looked specifically at students enrolled in online or traditional face-to-face courses at the for-profit DeVry University. The researchers chose DeVry specifically because every "course is offered both online and in-person, and each student enrolls in either an online section or an in-person section. Online and in-person sections are identical in most ways."[101] After analyzing the performance of 230,000 students in over 750 courses, they found that "taking a course online reduces student grades by 0.44 points on the traditional four-point grading scale, approximately a 0.33 standard deviation decline relative to taking a course in-person."[102] They also found that students in online courses were more likely to leave the institution before graduating.[103] It is worth noting, though, that the mission of for-profit institutions and the inequities perpetuated by many of these institutions could play a role in leading to these outcomes as well.[104]

Similarly, research on California community colleges has revealed more bad news. An investigation of 3,011,232 enrollments in 57,270 courses that covered the span of time from 2008–2012 showed that students were performing more poorly in online courses than in face-to-face environments.[105] In particular, the "results suggest that students are 8.4 percentage points less likely to complete, and 14.5 percentage points less likely to pass, the online course that they enroll in compared to the courses they take through FtF instruction. They are 11.0 percentage points less likely to receive A or B grades in online course than in FtF courses."[106] Perhaps most telling was this conclusion: "the fact that online students perform less well on all three measures of course performance even when instructor-course factors are held constant suggests that course delivery mode per se is related to contemporaneous student performance."[107] Here, the online format is specifically found to be the key factor in lower student performance. Notably, neither of these studies distinguishes between synchronous online courses (where students and instructors interact at the same time) and asynchronous courses (where they do not).

There could, of course, be lots of reasons why studies like this are finding online courses to be detrimental to student performance. Poor institutional incentive structures for designing courses, limited professional development opportunities with respect to online teaching, and lack of agreement on the goals for online curricula are all likely culprits. Part of the problem may be connected to our sociality, though. Alfred Rovai has explained that the physical separation from other students and from the instructor that occurs in online contexts may cause the high rate of dropouts in these courses and affect the learning in other ways too.[108] The reason for this is that the separation creates a kind of psychological distance.[109] In turn, this distancing has a negative impact on what researchers refer to as "social presence." Very simply, social presence refers to the degree to which a student feels connected to fellow human beings within an interactive learning community. Chun-Wang Wei, Nian-Shing Chen, and Kinshuk have closely explored the issue of social presence and have found that "if learners perceive a high degree of social presence, they will engage in learning interactions, which would result in their enhanced learning performances in online courses."[110] Michelle Miller, too, has noted that the level of social presence felt in a course is "an important predictor of success."[111] There are ways to improve social presence in online courses, and many of the best instructors work hard to do so, but it does seem to be the case that students must have their fundamental sociality engaged in order to learn most effectively. Face-to-face courses have an easier time with this because everyone is in one place, but online courses do not have this luxury, and a lack of social presence brings with it a cost to student learning.

I recognize that online education has served some groups of students moderately well, especially nontraditional and working students. It has also benefited some instructors too.[112] But when we look at it as a whole, we really need to ask a) what are the institutional motivations for online learning, and b) is it helping more students than not? I wish I could say that many colleges and universities have developed online courses because they are thoroughly convinced that such environments are the vehicles for superior learning, but I am not sure that this is the case. No comprehensive review of all the online programs in the United States has ever been attempted, so we do not know for certain. However, many institutions are competing hard to increase their non-residential enrollment, while—at the same time—charging extra fees for students to take an online course, so we could take

Deep Throat's suggestion and follow the money if we really want to pursue this line of inquiry. Anecdotal data indicate that for every stellar online course prepared using principles of outstanding instructional design there is another one that is a compendium of PowerPoint slides and multiple-choice quizzes that require rote memorization. When you add to this the significant amount of time it takes an instructor to put together an online course, I do not see many points in favor of online programs.

I am skeptical by nature, but I did want to approach the research on online courses with an open mind. After writing this chapter, however, I now believe it is impossible to discount the educational value of being together in the same place and at the same moment, responding to each other's verbal and nonverbal cues, building knowledge not individually but as a community. As we continue to investigate the best possible learning environments for our students, we may discover that our sociality is even more important than we had realized.

KEY TAKEAWAYS

- Human beings comprise one of the most social species on the planet. Our evolution was closely tied to our sociality, and—specifically—many of our modes of communication and learning developed as a result of these social bonds.

- Because of these deeply ingrained connections, the most effective teaching techniques will be those that maximize student interaction and collaboration. I refer to these strategies as social pedagogies.

continues ➤

KEY TAKEAWAYS *continued*

- To cultivate an environment in which social pedagogies can thrive, it is important to first establish a social classroom. Social classrooms have at least three vital components: a sense of belonging, a focus on community building, and a teacher who models effective intellectual engagement.

- Research is beginning to reveal just how important social belonging is for learning, but individual instructors cannot do all of this work on their own. Institutions should consider developing collaborative programs between academic affairs and student life offices to help enhance levels of belonging for students.

- Collaborative activities only enhance learning when students need to build knowledge together. Traditional group assignments that can be completed by "dividing and conquering" fall short of this goal.

- Let's not forget about the usefulness of play for learning. If we can incorporate more opportunities for playfulness in the curriculum, our students will benefit.

- Social presence is an essential component of a successful learning environment. This kind of presence is easiest to achieve in face-to-face courses, but even then, instructors need to be intentional about building it.

CHAPTER 3

Emotion

In short, learning is dynamic, social, and context dependent because *emotions* are, and emotions form a critical piece of how, what, when, and why people think, remember, and learn.

—Mary Helen Immordino-Yang, *Emotions, Learning, and the Brain*

Through more than five decades of teaching and mothering, I have noticed that children (and adults, too) learn best when they are happy.

—Nel Noddings, *Happiness and Education*

Like many others who are from small towns, I have a somewhat complicated relationship with the place where I grew up, but I have always appreciated the education I received while a student in my little corner of Pennsylvania. Lots of teachers and classroom moments from those days stand out in my mind—including a terrifying experience in fourth grade where I was asked to recite the Gettysburg Address from memory while dressed as Abraham Lincoln (I'm still recovering from this)—but one educator truly made a difference in my life. Tom Scheivert was known to be a tough teacher with high standards, so when I began eleventh grade English with him, I really did not know what to expect. I soon figured out, though, that his class would not be like any other I had taken before. He taught me how to read closely, how to write with economy, how to approach literature from a number of different angles, how to think carefully and logically, how to build an effective argument, and how to appreciate the beauty and power of great art.

Importantly, he also did something else. I took a creative writing course with him during my senior year and worked for weeks and weeks on a short story. He dutifully read multiple drafts, giving me feedback on each one. When I turned it in, I was unsure of the grade I would get, but I felt good about the piece. A few days later, he gave the story back to me. Honestly, I forget what the grade was, because something else stood out to me. On the first page, in capital letters, he had written, "I am proud of you." He knew how hard I had worked on the story and was acknowledging my efforts, but—more than that—I felt at that moment like he cared about me as a student and a person. It drove me to learn as much as I possibly could from him and to trust him as we moved on to more difficult assignments. Later in the semester, I turned in a piece that I had rushed through, and I got back another comment: "Boo, Josh." In other contexts, this may not have had a particularly favorable pedagogical effect, but in this case it worked. I had not put forth my best effort, and he was helping me to see what was at stake when I took assignments too lightly. In the end, I learned so much from Tom because I was emotionally engaged in the intellectual work of his classes, which was in large part due to the fact that he simply showed he cared about me and my future.

Tom left teaching more than a decade ago to enjoy a hard-earned and well-deserved retirement. I spoke to him recently about this book and to let him know that he was one of the two teachers to whom I had dedicated it. To my surprise, he not only remembered me but also recalled specific things I had said and done when I was a student. All these years later, he was still the caring teacher who had seen potential in me when I couldn't see much of it for myself.

Thankfully, Tom is not an exception on this front. Teachers at all levels have long understood the pedagogical significance of emotions, and science has now caught up to these intuitions. We discovered in the last chapter that our sociality is responsible for the development and function of important features of the cognitive architecture connected to learning, but it is emotion that adds substance, nuance, and contours to our social interactions. Or, as Keith Oatley and Jennifer M. Jenkins put it, "Human emotions are the language of human social life."[1] This linkage between our nature as social creatures and the emotions that inscribe our interactions with meaning has considerable ramifications for student learning as well because emotion is similarly connected to crucial cognitive processes.

As we shall see, most of the time emotion and cognition cooperate quite nicely. Each needs the other, as dance partners do, in order to follow the choreography that leads to deep learning. Instructors can use this partnership to our advantage as we create assignments and activities that harness emotion for pedagogical gain, but we also need to know what to do when something goes awry and unregulated emotions begin to block out productive cognitive activity. What I think will become clear is that our emotions have great potential for enhancing learning but can sometimes undermine that process as well.

Getting Started

As someone trained in the methodologies of humanities research but who is, nevertheless, attempting to synthesize research from many other disciplines, I am continually trying to define the terms under investigation. I should have learned my lesson regarding classifications that seem too neat and tidy after wrangling with the various meanings of curiosity in the first chapter, but—alas—I did not. So it was that when I began exploring the ways in which emotion has been defined by various researchers and various fields, I found myself in exactly the same boat. I started to feel a bit like Dante wandering in his dark woods. Fortunately, I found Sarah Rose Cavanagh's book *The Spark of Learning*. Cavanagh, an expert on affective neuroscience (particularly as it applies to education) has pored over much of the research on emotion and consolidated the findings into three key elements that we might use as a kind of foundation for understanding these aspects of emotion: "feelings, physiology, and expression."[2] All three work in combination to form an emotive experience. For example, at times when we feel sad, our eyes will produce tears, and our facial expressions and body posture help to convey the unhappiness. Together, these components form an emotion.

The obvious follow-up question is what gets classified as an emotion. The answer turns out to be a resounding, "It depends." Happiness? Almost definitely. Shame? Sometimes. Anger? Usually, except when it's called "rage." The issue is complex and is rooted in arguments regarding the nature of our emotions. As Sarah Tarlow has explained, "The majority of writers on emotion recognize to some degree that emotions are both biological and cultural. The difference tends to be in what they see as more interesting and in need of exploration, and the potential problem is in continuing to think about emotion in polarized and binary terms despite acknowledging the limitations of doing so."[3] One way researchers have sought to establish some order amidst this vast array of possibilities has been to develop the concept of basic emotions. Basic emotions are thought to be the building blocks of more complex emotions and are thus, from an evolutionary perspective, much older than other affective responses. Table 1 represents different hypotheses as to what our basic emotions might be.

You will probably notice, along with Andrew Ortony and Terence Turner, that "there is little agreement about how many emotions are basic, which emotions are basic, and why they are basic."[4] Rather than continue to belabor the lack of consensus in these areas, I want to focus on the shared territory with respect to these attempts at classification and categorization. Clearly, our emotions are complex systems tied to our biology, psychology, and the cultures in which we live. Recognizing this is perhaps the first step in understanding the ways in which emotions influence learning. We will find no easy answers or strategies that work the same way every time. What is also evident, though, is that our emotions are deeply ingrained in our makeup as human beings and to develop any insights at all into their interplay with cognition and learning, we first need to understand their evolutionary story.

Where Did Our Emotions Come From?

Scientists have long been fascinated by the evolution of emotions. Darwin himself wrote a book on the subject, and from there things escalated rapidly.[5] Similar to what we saw with curiosity in the first chapter, human beings are not the lone possessors of emotion in the animal world. In fact, the emotional lives of many other species of animals are quite rich, and we are only beginning to understand their depth and nuance.[6] This developing research on animal emotions is of some importance to us as we think about our own emotions, because we are far closer to these fellow creatures than we often realize. At a base level, there is significant commonality in the way mammals' brains are laid out with respect to emotions:

Reference	Fundamental emotion	Basis for inclusion
Arnold (1960)	Anger, aversion, courage, dejection, desire, despair, fear, hate, hope, love, sadness	Relation to action tendencies
Ekman, Friesen, & Ellsworth (1982)	Anger, disgust, fear, joy, sadness, surprise	Universal facial expressions
Frijda (personal communication, September 8, 1986)	Desire, happiness, interest, surprise, wonder, sorrow	Forms of action readiness
Gray (1982)	Rage and terror, anxiety, joy	Hardwired
Izard (1971)	Anger, contempt, disgust, distress, fear, guilt, interest, joy, shame, surprise	Hardwired
James (1884)	Fear, grief, love, rage	Bodily involvement
McDougall (1926)	Anger, disgust, elation, fear, subjection, tender-emotion, wonder	Relation to instincts
Mowrer (1960)	Pain, pleasure	Unlearned emotional states
Oatley & Johnson-Laird (1987)	Anger, disgust, anxiety, happiness, sadness	Do not require prepositional content
Panksepp (1982)	Expectancy, fear, rage, panic	Hardwired
Plutchik (1980)	Acceptance, anger, anticipation, disgust, joy, fear, sadness, surprise	Relation to adaptive biological processes
Tomkins (1984)	Anger, interest, contempt, disgust, distress, fear, joy, shame, surprise	Density of neural firing
Watson (1930)	Fear, love, rage	Hardwired
Weiner & Graham (1984)	Happiness, sadness	Attribution independent

Note. Not all the theorists represented in this table are equally strong advocates of the idea of basic emotions. For some it is a crucial notion (e.g., Izard, 1977; Panksepp, 1982; Plutchik, 1980; Tomkins, 1984), whereas for others it is of peripheral interest only, and their discussions of basic emotions are hedged (e.g., Mowrer, 1960; Weiner & Graham, 1984).

Source. Ortony, Andrew, and Turner, Terence J. "What's Basic about Basic Emotions?" *Psychological Review* 97.3 (1990): 315–31. https://doi.org/10.1037/0033-295X.97.3.315. Published by the American Psychological Association. Reprinted with permission.

"As far as we know right now, primal emotional systems are made up of neuroanatomies and neurochemistries that are remarkably similar across all mammalian species. This suggests that these systems evolved a very long time ago and that at a *basic* emotional and motivational level, all mammals are more similar than they are different. Deep in the ancient affective recesses of our brains, we remain evolutionarily kin."[7] Underscoring these similarities across species is another way to emphasize the degree to which the neural structures for emotion in human beings are "evolutionarily conserved"—that is, extraordinarily old and, relatively speaking, only moderately altered over time.[8] Emotions, then, are inextricably a part of our actions, our behavior, our psychology, and our mechanisms for learning because they are connected to the development or the function of so many other networks in our brains.

As *Homo sapiens* continued to evolve, though, our emotional systems grew more complex as well. Some have argued that these changes led to advantages that increased our chances for survival,[9] but the scientific consensus seems to be that the evolution of our emotions was vital for enhancing our social connections. Oatley and Jenkins summarize the case for this interdependence between emotions and sociality rather succinctly: "Emotions arise largely with problems to be solved. So for recurring problems like escaping from predators, responding to strangers, meeting aggressive threats, caring for infants, falling in love, and so on, we are equipped with genetically based mechanisms that provide outline scripts for behavior that has been successful in the past, and has therefore been selected. Each kind of emotional pattern is triggered by distinctive cues. Each makes ready patterns of action appropriate to solving the problem that has arisen."[10] I particularly like the notion that emotions are tied to problem solving, and this is a

Table 1 (*opposite*). A Selection of Lists of "Basic" Emotions

theme that will reemerge later in the chapter. Problems, especially those that have to do with our interactions with other people, activate an emotional response that can help us to potentially find a resolution. Our emotions drive us to work together toward a common goal, to learn from one another, and to make important decisions about our safety or the well-being of others. Anyone who has ever been in an argument knows all too well that emotions can also make problems worse rather than better, but more often than not we are able to check our emotions even in these highly fraught situations.

Jonathan Turner, in fact, believes this kind of regulation is our most important evolutionary adaptation with respect to emotions. Other animals cannot control their responses in the same way. While problem solving is important, Turner thinks emotional regulation may have been responsible for augmenting the social bonds of our species to begin with.[11] Obviously, both parts of this social hypothesis (problem solving and emotional regulation) are compatible, and they need not compete with each other for primacy. They really represent two sides of the same coin, and their combined importance becomes especially clear when we look closely at the relationship between emotions and cognition.

Why Thinking and Feeling Need One Another

The debate regarding the relationship between cognition and emotion is a very old one. For a long time, the two were seen as being disconnected. Perhaps Descartes is to blame for that, but I suppose we will never know. By the latter half of the twentieth century, though, the nature of the conversation had shifted. Psychologists moved to a model where emotion and cognition were connected but—at the same time—one of these systems was the clear leader in managing our brain's response to stimuli. Arguments about *which* system was at the forefront began to dominate the discourse. One particularly lively iteration of this new turn occurred in the early 1980s between Robert Zajonc (who believed that emotion precedes cognition) and Richard Lazarus (who argued instead that cognition precedes emotion) amidst the pages of *American Psychologist*. As the volleys, featuring some rather pointed criticism, went back and forth between the two scientists, it was clear that there was a lot at stake in claiming one position or the other.[12]

Although the correspondence between Zajonc and Lazarus provides a bounty of rhetorical delights, the particular problem about which they were arguing was never solved. More recent research has begun to demonstrate that emotion and cognition depend on one another in extremely complex and crucial ways. Mary Helen Immordino-Yang, one of the foremost experts on emotion and learning, has explained that emotions act as a kind of "rudder" for cognition,[13] one that both guides the direction of our thinking and also alters our cognitive processes in ways that are sometimes productive and sometimes just the opposite. Luiz Pessoa takes a slightly different approach to detailing this relationship but arrives at the same end: "I will make a case for the notion, based on current knowledge of brain function and connectivity, that parceling the brain into cognitive and affective regions is inherently problematic, and ultimately untenable for at least three reasons: first, brain regions viewed as 'affective' are also involved in cognition; second, brain regions viewed as 'cognitive' are also involved in emotion; and critically, third, cognition and emotion are integrated in the brain. In the past two decades, several researchers have emphasized that emotion and cognition systems interact in important ways."[14] The emphasis on integration here seems to me to be the key. Our brains are not organized in such a way that emotional responses are isolated in one place and cognitive activity in another. Some areas are involved with both and other regions work interdependently. Cognition, therefore, can often serve to stimulate our emotional responses. Similarly, when our emotions are activated, they play an important role in allocating cognitive resources to the matter at hand.[15] This is particularly true, Immordino-Yang notes, with those "aspects of cognition that are recruited most heavily in education, including learning, attention, memory, decision making, motivation, and social functioning."[16] Thus, engagement with our emotions is vital for maximizing learning in all kinds of spheres, including the classroom.

If this news sounds too good to be true, or at least a bit too rosy, then rest assured: there is a downside to the connections between these systems as well. Recent research is beginning to show that "both positive and negative emotional stimuli interfere[ ] with performance," which runs counter to "previous suggestions that only negative, and in particular frightening, stimuli can interfere with online processing."[17] Initially, these findings gave me pause, and I wondered how all of the pieces of the emotion-cognition puzzle fit together, because there seem to be some areas of contradiction. It is true, of course, that if we are overcome by either positive or negative emotions, then we are probably not thinking too carefully. What seems to be essential, then, is the regulation of both types of emotions, and we will explore some strategies later in the chapter for targeting those positive emotions that enhance learning and minimizing negative emotions overall. As it happens, much of the groundwork for this sort of emotional regulation is established in childhood.

Children and Emotions

Developmentally speaking, the work of childhood is, in many ways, a process of harnessing the power of emotions in order to reap the rewards of cognitive gains. As much as anything else, "young children experience their emotions as being beyond direct, voluntary control—as something that involves their entire being and demands to be expressed."[18] I was reminded of this the first time I witnessed a toddler tantrum and the shrieking, stomping, fistful of fury that comes along with the outburst. Children who are experiencing such a response are clearly dealing with a swirling array of emotions that they are not able to rein in. Giggle fits work in much the same way, so we can't just blame negative emotions here. Not a lot of clear thinking happens when children are in the throes of an emotional storm. As children get older, their systems for emotional regulation mature, and they are able to develop strategies that allow for more control in this area. And then puberty hits, but that's an entirely different nightmare.

Interestingly, then, a developing child is very much a microcosm of the regulation process that we explored a bit earlier. Emotional regulation takes time, but the biological and psychological mechanisms that lead to regulation start quite early. Babies are dependent on their caregivers to modulate emotions for them. As Manfred Holodynski and Wolfgang Friedlmeier explain, infants rely extensively on this interpersonal system: "This emotional action regulation in infants is, nonetheless, still organized interpersonally, because emotions continue to be directed toward the other person. . . . Also with regard to reflective emotion regulation, infants still depend completely on an interpersonal regulation of emotions through their caregivers. They are still unable to control their emotions in line with higher motives and, for example, delay gratification. These tasks continue to be shouldered by caregivers."[19] Once children reach the age of three, however, they begin to move toward a more "intrapersonal" mode of regulation. Gradually, they require less and less assistance from their caregivers and are able to handle more on their own.[20] This, in turn, allows for a more complex interplay between the child's emotions and the cognitive processes that are developing at the same time.

Even as these regulatory mechanisms mature, emotions play an important role for children who are beginning to learn about the world. An interesting series of studies by Michael Lewis, Steven M. Alessandri, and Margaret Wolan Sullivan used a mechanism by which infants could pull a string to see a pleasing picture and hear a song. When they succeeded in doing so, they elicited largely positive emotions, but when they failed to pull the string or—more importantly—when they pulled the string and the experimenters did not present the picture/song combination, the infants cried. The researchers suggest that the "positive emotions expressed during learning (e.g., interest, surprise, joy) are likely to reflect active cognitive engagement with the contingency, 'mastery', and a sense of efficacy."[21] Thus, even in the youngest children, learning is connected to the kinds of emotions that enhance the desire to know more, whereas frustration occurs when efforts to learn are thwarted. Although the circumstances and contexts change as children grow older, these emotional responses to learning remain rather consistent.

The Role of Emotions in the Classroom

Despite this important research, we tend to think of a classroom as a space of purely intellectual work rather than a place for investigating the ways in which emotional engagement might enhance learning. This is especially true in college classrooms. I hope it is clear by now, though, that—as teachers—we ignore emotion at our own peril. Immordino-Yang starkly underscores the danger for us: "And students in the classroom struggle with very much the same problem: if they feel no connection to the knowledge they learn in school, the academic content will seem emotionally meaningless to them; even if they manage to regurgitate the factual information, it will lay barren and without any influence on their decisions and behavior."[22] That doesn't sound like a worthwhile pedagogical outcome to me. Although we need to be somewhat wary of making the connections too neat and tidy,[23] emotion does play an important role in our students' learning, particularly though not exclusively by enhancing our memory.[24] It behooves us then to think intentionally about productive means to help students make emotional connections with the material. One recent paper categorizes anxiety, enjoyment, and boredom as the "academic emotions" because of their impact on achievement, but I'm not sure we need to make such a sharp distinction. In fact, I would argue that almost all of our emotions are "academic" in the sense that they have an impact on student learning in one way or another.[25]

One strategy for drawing on this power of emotion for strengthening cognitive gains is to build opportunities into our courses for "encourag[ing] relevant emotional connection to the material being learned."[26] Easier said than done, right? When I present this idea to groups of colleagues, I am often asked discipline-specific questions about the viability of this approach. There seems to be a tacit agreement that it is one thing to suggest that we engage our students' emotions in the humanities, where the texts are often profound and poignant, or in the social sciences, where students are faced with very real instances of injustice and inequality, but it is quite another to generate emotional responses in other disciplines. I acknowledge the point, particularly because I have fond memories of those moments when, as a group, my students and I were moved by reading about Frankenstein's creature seeing his maker for the first time or watching the final scene of Margaret Edson's play *Wit*. That said, there is still more work to be done to maximize the effect of emotion on learning in the humanities and social sciences, and it is also possible to bring emotions to bear on STEM courses as well. A lesson on metastasis in cancer cells that is paired with interviews from survivors could engage students at a level that other methods might not. A discussion of pollination in plants could employ information about the endangerment of bees. An introductory computer science course might discuss Alan Turing's role in code breaking during World War II and the subsequent tragedy that befell him due to society's intolerant laws. There are possibilities in all disciplines; we just need to look for them.

So far, I have only been discussing emotion in terms of what instructors can do to design their courses to facilitate fruitful intersections of affective responses and learning. These are not the only ways that emotion is important for our classrooms, however. Sometimes, students respond emotionally to the work they do in our classrooms regardless of our intention. What makes a student happy or sad or amused or fearful in our courses can often have to do with past educational experiences, memories, events in their own lives, and many other factors over which we do not have any control. Sometimes, too, the emotional engagement they need in order to learn has nothing at all to do with the actual content and course materials.

GETTING STARTED

Toward the end of this section I listed a couple of topics that could, with just a bit of refining, resonate emotionally with students. Take a moment to think about the content that you cover in a particular course, and then try to identify two or three concepts that could be shifted in just this way. Where is the emotional angle in the material? How might it connect to students' lives and their emotional responses to the world? It's not possible to do this with everything we teach (nor is it desirable), but there may be subjects that would benefit from deeper levels of student investment. Helping our students engage the material in this way could be as simple as telling a story or providing them with a perspective they had not previously considered. We only need to find the places in our curriculum where such an approach will be both appropriate and fruitful.

The Extraordinary Power of Positive Emotions

There is a surprising (to me, at least) amount of literature demonstrating the benefits of utilizing positive emotions in order to catalyze student learning. Happiness, for example, lends its hand in some significant ways to students of all ages.[27] The associations between happiness and learning are not new, but researchers are beginning to make more substantive links that go beyond intuition.[28] Stephen Scoffham and Jonathan Barnes, for example, note that "within the full register of emotions experienced by humans, happiness is a positive force which enriches our sense of meaning, enhances our capabilities and enlarges the scope of our thinking."[29] Happy students seem to be more attuned to the work of the classroom and more expansive in the connections they make.

As an educational community, we do not necessarily need to have the same definition of happiness in order to see the benefits of the emotion on learning either.[30] We simply need to find ways to maximize this emotion for our students in order to enhance their learning. Some of this will lay outside of our sphere of influence, of course, but there is no reason that our courses and our teaching cannot generate happiness for students. If we can demonstrate for them the relevance of the material for their lives, their futures, their own sense of purpose, then we are likely to create a positive atmosphere in which students can experience a kind of joy in learning. Ideally, the college experience is not just about completing graduation requirements or amassing an impressive curriculum vitae, but instead about laying the foundation for a meaningful, happy life. Our courses can contribute to this by showing students how our disciplines lend themselves to achieving this goal as well. Taking the next step and designing assignments that allow students to make these discoveries on their own can be an even bigger boon, both for success in our courses and success in life. To some degree, simply displaying our own delight and enthusiasm for our subjects creates an atmosphere of happiness that cultivates learning. Enthusiasm is one of the most underestimated teaching tools at our disposal. Surely, we all gravitated to our work in higher education because we were enthusiastic at some level about our chosen fields. Modeling this for students helps them to see that coursework and happiness are not mutually exclusive and, thus, helps them to develop stronger academic skills.

Humor and amusement also help to enrich the learning process. First and foremost, laughter and humor have considerable physiological benefits, some of which are tied to cognition.[31] More specifically, though, humor focuses attention and drives students to reconcile disparate, and seemingly unconnected, ideas. Sarah Rose Cavanagh explains this further: "In the presence of humor, students detect and then have to resolve the incongruity between their original expectations and the humorous twist. This process of making one interpretation and then having to revise it results in a deeper level of mental processing than being exposed to the correct interpretation from the beginning; one is required to relate the information to more than one set of concepts and ideas, to reflect and elaborate on both the meaning of the initial interpretation and the revised interpretation."[32] We work harder than we realize sometimes when we are trying to understand a joke. This happens to me all the time, and it happens to students too when we use humor in the classroom.

Ronald Berk has spent years measuring the effect of humor on student learning. In one study of 316 students across several statistics courses and over two years, he collected considerable evidence from the students themselves to support the use of humor in class and in teaching materials (syllabi, exams, etc.) as a means to reduce anxiety, learn more effectively, and help them perform their best. They frequently rated all humorous strategies very or extremely effective in achieving these aims.[33] None of this is to say that we all suddenly need to transform into stand-up comedians. Indeed, jokes that repeatedly fall flat will probably not resonate with students and may even have the opposite effect of what we intend. That humor can augment learning is clear, but we need to find a style that meshes with our personalities in order for these benefits to be fully realized.

Without question, though, the research on positive emotions and learning reveals that the single most important strategy we can use to help our students to succeed in our courses is to care about them as learners and as human beings.[34] Researchers have called this approach pedagogical caring, and the effects are both greater emotional attachment in the educational context and higher academic achievement. Because I know very well that any time we blur the lines between teaching and personal relationships we risk alienating those faculty who (rightly) want to maintain clear professional boundaries between them and their students, I want to clearly define what we mean by pedagogical caring. In their poignantly titled article, "Please Don't Give Up on Me: When Faculty Fail to Care," Thomas Hawk and Paul Lyons offer a clear articulation of the scope of this method:

> Pedagogical caring and pedagogical respect would have us develop a repertoire of skills and dispositions that enhance the pedagogical relationship, a portfolio of pedagogical activities that offer guided participation and practice, and scaffolding approaches to help our students become more competent in the content and skills of the course, more self-directed in their learning, more cultivating of the value of relationships, and more capable in modeling an ethic of care to others. Faculty must extend recognition respect to all students as unique, developing human beings and appraisal respect for the development they make in the three arenas.[35]

In other words, we do not have to be best friends with our students to care for them in such a way that enhances their learning. Our teaching techniques, combined with our behaviors and attitudes, will facilitate the caring relationship.

I used the phrase "care for" in the last paragraph because the distinction between caring for someone or something and caring about that same person or thing is important. One of the first people to theorize about pedagogical caring, Richard Hult Jr., was careful to highlight this difference. Caring about something is a precondition of caring for it, but not all caring about leads to caring for. For example, I care about the Orioles winning the World Series (someday!), but I care for my daughter on a daily basis. Hult Jr. explains that the "caring agent, in addition to being attentive and concerned (that is, caring about), behaves with special skills to support or increase some condition of value in the cared for."[36] He then points specifically to the parent-child relationship, but extends his discussion of caring for a person to any relationship we greatly value.[37] This is where teachers play a role.

Nel Noddings, an educational philosopher who has done some of the most highly regarded work on caring and education, positions the "one-caring" (the teacher) in relation to the "cared-for" (the student).[38] Noddings frames the heart of the pedagogical relationship in this way: "When a teacher asks a question in class and a student responds, she receives not just the 'response' but the student. What he says matters, whether it is right or wrong, and she probes gently for clarification, interpretation, contribution. She is not seeking the answer but the involvement of the cared-for. . . . The student is infinitely more important than the subject matter."[39] That last sentence deserves a second read. A commitment to engaging emotions in our classrooms means embracing the notion that education is fundamentally about students, not bits of information. Noddings goes on to suggest that this pedagogical approach leads to "intrinsic interest or trust and admiration for the teacher," which—in turn—causes students to be more invested in their learning.[40]

Crucially, for our purposes as college instructors, Noddings explains that—even within this caring relationship—a teacher works with a student "directly but not equally."[41] I think this is a particularly important statement. It would be easy to reduce Noddings's approach to an *in loco parentis* kind of philosophy, and to suggest that it is dismissive of the content expertise of faculty in higher education, but I think it is so much more sophisticated than this. We care for students, not just for the sake of caring, but because it is necessary to fulfill our educational goals. Caring is a vital ingredient for learning.

One way to understand why caring pedagogies matter so much is to return to our old friend the zone of proximal development from the last chapter. Building on Noddings's work, Lisa Goldstein has suggested that the relationship between the one caring and the cared-for is an integral part of the work that happens in these zones. We know from Vygotsky that students need a knowledgeable peer or teacher to move beyond their zones, and Goldstein believes that trust, caring, and even love are necessary ingredients for making these intellectual advancements.[42] Further, Goldstein proposes that "in addition to being a region of intellectual development—a construction zone—the zone of proximal development is also a region of affective development—a relational zone."[43] The two zones are therefore dependent upon each other, just as we know emotion and cognition to be in a broader sense as well.

The tricky part here is figuring out how we bring all this to bear on our work as college teachers. What do caring pedagogies look like in our classrooms? Hawk and Lyons provide a useful road map here:

> For us as faculty, then, we should be continually aware that our students are unique individuals, leading to the realization that our relationships with them need to be contextual and concrete. An ethic of care asks for (a) our engrossment into their uniqueness, (b) a displacement or shifting of our motivation to what is constructively developmental for their well-being, without sacrificing our own, (c) a commitment to that relationship with the student as long as the formal and public role extends and even under conditions of difficulties for the student, and (d) a confirmation of the good and

positive in that student without sacrificing the recognition of that which needs further development.[44]

If we approach our teaching responsibilities with this as our guide, then it becomes easier to see how to employ specific methods in the classroom. Some techniques that have been put forward as examples of caring strategies include frequent feedback (particularly personal feedback that focuses on a student's own development, not just on the content or the argument),[45] high expectations, and even something as simple as showing students we care by coming to class prepared.[46] There are others too. Immediacy and being present for students when we are working with them also communicate that we care about them as individuals.[47] Knowing their names and developing course policies that treat students fairly can go a long way to establishing connections with them. Finally, the least that we can do is to take a few minutes to get to know who our students are as people. None of this is hard to do, but these sorts of relational strategies are vital for our students and their learning. I would even go as far as to say that this philosophy of teaching enhances the value of the work for us as well.

GETTING STARTED

Just a few sentences ago, I highlighted the importance of knowing students' names. Learning their names and using names during class together are two of the most basic ways we show students we care about them as learners. At some level, this task requires a bit of memorization for it to work as effectively as possible. However, if memorization stresses you out, or if you have a large class, make it

continues ➤

GETTING STARTED *continued*

easy on yourself. Provide students with card-stock table tents and ask them to bring these each day. This will allow you to use their names without necessarily having to remember them. Ideally, the table tents would help you to eventually remember the names, but—even if that never happens—you are at least showing students that you value them enough to use their names by any means possible.

A Classroom Where Everyone Matters: Kimberly Shaw, Columbus State University

For a concrete example of how to enact a pedagogy that places care at the center, we need look no further than the classroom of Kimberly Shaw, a physicist and professor of earth and space sciences at Columbus State University in Georgia. She was Georgia's professor of the year in 2015, and I recently had the opportunity to observe one of her courses for future science teachers.[48] In a single class session, I witnessed an array of strategies demonstrating the extent to which Shaw cares about her students as learners and people and how she makes them central to her pedagogy. To begin with, she opened the class by asking if anyone had heard from a particular student who had been out sick for more than a week. When nobody had, she said she would "give him a call" to make sure he was okay. It was clear that she was less concerned here about her attendance book and the participation grade of the student than she was about the student himself. Shaw values her students not because she evaluates them but because she prizes the classroom community forged by teachers and learners.

Later, when groups of students were working with a microscope, Shaw heard a young woman say, "I just can't do this." The student was clearly frustrated, and Shaw quickly came over and asked her, "What's with the negative self-talk?" Putting aside for a moment the fact that Shaw's action here is an important way to mitigate stereotype threat (which I will cover in the final chapter of the book), she also demonstrated positive regard for the student. Shaw's question opened up a conversation that ultimately led to the student realizing that she simply did not understand one of the directions. Her misstep had been nothing more dramatic than that. She went on to complete the activity quickly and correctly. This is an obvious instance where we can see that caring for students has nothing to do with lowering academic standards. Shaw did not give the student a free pass. They talked through the obstacle, and the student accomplished her goal as a result.

After the class ended and all the others had left, Shaw walked up to a student who had diligently and doggedly been participating throughout the session. She quietly told him that she was sorry to hear about his grandmother, who had recently passed away. "You've had a tough semester, I know," she said. The student did not say much. He nodded, thanked her, and left soon after, but the gratitude I saw on his face was quite telling. This is the kind of effect that a caring teacher can have. At that time, in that place, this student knew that someone was there for him, ready to listen. Although it may be conjecture or even projecting in some sense, I can't help but think that his active participation in the class had something to do with the fact that he knows he matters to Shaw, just as all of the other students do too. That day, I saw a whole host of innovative activities, scaffolded problems, and other evidence-based teaching from Shaw that clearly shows why she won such an important teaching award, but her commitment to her students (and vice versa) and the caring pedagogy I observed make this experience stand out for me more than almost any other I have had while writing this book.

The Effect of Unregulated Negative Emotions

I wish I could say that everything is always so powerfully positive in our colleges and universities, but I cannot. Negative emotions like confusion, fear, anger, and anxiety can often be found in our classrooms as well. By themselves and in small doses, negative emotions are not entirely problematic. A little bit of worry or some butterflies in the stomach might motivate a student to try her or his best. Difficulties begin to arise, however, when the prevalence of negative emotions prevails over a student's mechanisms for regulation.[49] As we have seen earlier in the chapter, this kind of regulation is crucial for maintaining the fluid and productive relationship between emotion and cognition. Once the balance tips too far toward the emotional register, learning is affected. This is especially true with negative emotions.[50]

It is now time to meet a character in the story of emotions and learning to whom we haven't yet been introduced but who plays a significant role in the plot: the brain's amygdala. Joseph LeDoux is a scientist at New York University who has spent a significant part of his career researching the amygdala, and he succinctly describes the structure as being "involved in both the acquisition and the expression of fear conditioning."[51] For this reason, the amygdala is has been widely studied,[52] and it can wreak havoc on our students' learning processes. Any instructor who wishes to design experimental assignments, try new techniques, or even introduce difficult and complex material for the first time needs to be aware of the ways in which the amygdala functions, and—perhaps more importantly—how the activity of this part of our students' brains might affect them.

The amygdala is made up of a group of nuclei found in both hemispheres of the brain. Although it is relatively small, the amygdala is an extremely important element of the brain's anatomy. Stimuli from any kind of environment (classrooms included) pass through the amygdala first, and it responds accordingly. From an evolutionary standpoint, the conditioned and unconditioned fear responses governed by the amygdala were essential for survival in even the earliest living beings. Indeed, our unconditioned fear response is simply the startle reflex that triggers the impulse to flee, fight, or freeze, which would have been vital for the continued existence of early hominids. Though this impulse may sometimes still be connected to survival, the startle reflex is mostly an evolutionary holdover. For example, when I was carrying groceries into my house the other day and was startled by my dog Gus, I did not have to flee, fight, or freeze. I merely had to pick up the groceries from off the floor.

Conditioned fear responses, on the other hand, are learned behaviors that emerge from the interactions between external stimuli and our memories. If we are in bed sleeping, for instance, and we hear a window break, our amygdala will take a leading role in connecting this stimulus with what our memories know about windows breaking in the middle of the night, and fear will result. It is important to note that the amygdala does not distinguish the reason for the window breaking; it simply responds to the stimulus. In this way, even conditioned fear responses have an evolutionary connection to survival.

Once the amygdala is engaged, the body's systems respond quickly. We can sometimes freeze up, our blood pressure and heart rate are affected, and adrenaline starts pumping.[53] Importantly for the subject of this chapter, the brain's cognitive processes are also inhibited.[54] It is easy to see why this would be the case. When faced with a situation where our distant ancestors needed to immediately flee, fight, or freeze, it would not have been advantageous for them to ponder the different choices, weighing each one out carefully through a consideration of the pros and cons. The reaction needed to be instinctual. This impediment to cognition, though, has serious consequences for our students. If a student's amygdala is responding to some kind of stimulus in the classroom (difficult reading material, a challenging assignment, a hostile classmate, etc.), he or she will not easily be able to think or engage in the work of the class.

Thankfully, the effects of the amygdala are not often long lasting, nor are most of us walking around fearfully on a constant basis.[55] This is because the body has a kind of checks and balances system put in place for the amygdala in the form of oxytocin. Like Batman to the amygdala's Joker, the neuropeptide oxytocin, once triggered, helps to modulate the fear response. In the popular press, oxytocin has sometimes been referred to as the "love hormone," but that is really an oversimplification. It is more typically described as deriving from and leading to "prosocial" behaviors,[56] including the nurturing responses of mothers toward infants, infant bonding with fathers, romantic behaviors, and close friendship.[57] But once it is "released during stress," it also plays an important role as a "modulator of anxiety and fear response" by reducing the activity of the amygdala.[58] As a result, oxytocin can cause or enhance feelings of trust and safety.[59]

The neurobiological workings of the amygdala and oxytocin are likely to cause a variety of responses in our students. I say *likely*, because we would need to design large-scale experiments employing an fMRI in order to prove these hypotheses more comprehensively. While my thoughts below are consistent with scientific research on the amygdala, I see what follows as the beginning of a conversation that I hope bears more fruit in the coming years. Also, it is important to recognize that our students' behaviors are most often due to a combination of very complex psychological and biological factors. To reduce any behavior to the mechanics of a single element of the brain's anatomy would be like staring at only a small piece of a very large, very nuanced painting and claiming, from that small bit of evidence, to have arrived at the definitive meaning of the work. By the same token, though, if we do not understand the role played by the amygdala in limiting cognitive processes, we risk losing a significant tool for understanding how to design the most effective courses and learning environments.

Having issued the necessary disclaimers, then, let's turn again to the possible impact of the amygdala on learning. There are some expressions of fear from our students that are likely to be connected to activity in the amygdala, of course, such as test or math anxiety, both of which are quite common. A comprehensive survey of test anxiety notes that the state "is directly related to fears of negative evaluation, dislike of tests, and less effective study skills. . . . HTA (High Test Anxiety) students hold themselves in lower esteem than do LTA students. They tend to feel unprotected and controlled by outside forces and are prone to negative qualities, such as other forms of anxiety. They experience more encoding difficulty when learning, more cognitive interference when tested."[60] This is consistent with what we know from the literature on the effects of the amygdala. Anyone who has ever experienced feelings like this when approaching an exam or an assignment, particularly under pressure, can acknowledge that this level of anxiety causes a whole-body response. Many of our students wrestle with similar issues, and cognitive activity is put on the back burner in situations like this.

Although test anxiety, and other circumstances where students are visibly anxious, are easier to detect, I would also suggest that the amygdala might be the culprit during some of those times when we would otherwise think that students were being standoffish, angry, dejected, or even disconnected. Those moments in our classes when students' expectations or assumptions have been challenged or when they are faced with new material for the first time are ripe for fearful responses. I want to be clear that I am not suggesting every instance of struggle in our classrooms can be attributed to the amygdala, but some of them might, so it helps us if we know what to do. One easy strategy we can use in allaying fear responses connects back to something I wrote about in the chapter on curiosity: don't be intimidating in class. Be approachable. So much research on the amygdala points to the simple finding that angry or frightened faces trigger the amygdala and happy faces modulate the response.[61]

I have been thinking about another possible strategy, however, that comes from an unexpected source. In their research on adopted children, Karyn Purvis, David Cross, and Wendy Sunshine have developed the idea of "felt safety," which they describe as "an atmosphere where children feel and experience safety for themselves."[62] The effect of felt safety, they argue, is that it "disarms the primitive brain and reduces fear."[63] This sounds like the amygdala to me, and indeed in other strands of this research Purvis and Cross target the amygdala specifically.[64] The concept of felt safety makes a great deal of sense for disarming the amygdala, then, especially because we know that its nemesis, oxytocin, can cause and increase feelings of trust and safety. Purvis, Cross, and Sunshine show that helping young adoptees to feel secure and safe reduces fearful responses dramatically.

I would like to consider what it might mean for us to import the notion of felt safety into our work as teachers. Perhaps this could be another tool for us when working with students who are experiencing unregulated fear or anxiety. What, though, would be the pedagogical equivalent of felt safety? One option might be to connect the material at hand back to students' prior knowledge.[65] One reason new or challenging content and assignments may cause anxiety is because they can look different from anything else a student has seen before. If we scaffold properly and show students how the work builds on previous things they have learned, it might help to induce a kind of felt safety. The feeling of confidence brought about by accessing information students have previously mastered provides a sort of safety net to help them work through the new material. Guided feedback on each part of an assignment can stem the tide of fear students may feel on large or complex activities as well. To be sure, students need to be challenged and to grapple with multifaceted problems, but there is a difference between the learning process and fear. One is necessary for cognitive gains and the other impedes them. That said, the amygdala need not be an obstacle for us as long as we have strategies we can use to help our students.

Although the amygdala and considerations of fear are important, they are not frequent topics at your average department meeting. Another matter tied to unregulated negative emotions, however, is everywhere in the press about higher education these days: the issue of trigger warnings. At its most basic, a trigger warning is a verbal or written statement given by an instructor prior to students encountering disturbing material of some kind—typically in a film or a text. The goal of a trigger warning is to "alert students who have had personal experience with the horrors you're about to cover (e.g., rape, childhood sexual abuse, suicide) that they may wish to activate their coping mechanisms so that they can regulate their emotions and avoid an affective drop in performance."[66] I would also add war and other kinds of violence to the list above, since trigger warnings are often framed in terms of their benefits for veterans. The actual word "trigger" is important for this discussion as well because of its associations with trauma and trauma therapy.[67] Trigger warnings, as a pedagogical concept, therefore have their genesis in the research on psychological trauma, and the movement to use trigger warnings in our courses is an attempt to avoid retraumatizing any of our students. This is an issue we must take seriously.

Catherine Denial is the Bright Professor of American History at Knox College and a strong advocate for trigger warnings. She recently wrote a blog post about her experience as a survivor of trauma and about what happens to her when she is triggered. I asked for her permission to quote extensively from the post, and she was gracious in granting it. Denial describes the totalizing feeling in detail:

> Sometimes I get overwhelmingly anxious. My body dumps adrenaline into my system and my heart races, my breathing becomes labored, and I often need the bathroom right away. I feel dizzy and overwhelmed. . . . Sometimes I dissociate. Things feel unreal and my body untethered, as if I can't feel myself walking on solid ground, or taking up space in a room. . . . Sometimes I get flashbacks. Flashbacks are, for me, the things that make me feel the most objectively out of my mind. I am at once in the present and in the moment of trauma. . . . Sometimes I am hyper-vigilant. . . . My brain scans constantly for danger, even in situations where I am objectively safe. My body is primed to fight or flee, so I am always on the edge of an adrenaline rush, my heart-rate elevated, my muscles tensed. Sometimes, because of all of this, I am very, very tired.[68]

Needless to say, any student who is feeling even a fraction of this cannot learn what we are teaching. More importantly, in these moments when life overtakes the walls of our classroom, the content knowledge of our discipline should be moved firmly to the background.

Trigger warnings have sparked passionate debate. Some find them to be important teaching tools, while others see them, at best, as unnecessary and, at worst, as a kind of censorship. One strand of this debate unfolded in the pages of *The New Republic* in 2015 because of an incident at Columbia University where students in a core course wanted a trigger warning during a class session on Ovid's *Metamorphoses*, which is a text well known for its intense descriptions of sexual violence. Several writers responded to the situation at Columbia, and the points they raise are in many ways illustrative of the various camps that exist in the arguments about trigger warnings. Jerry Coyne made his case first: "It's time for students to learn that Life is Triggering. Once they leave college, they'll be constantly exposed to views that challenge or offend them. . . . That's why one of college's most important functions is to learn how to hear and deal with challenging ideas. Cocooning oneself in a Big Safe Space for four years gets it exactly backwards. 'Safety' has been transformed by colleges from 'protection from physical harm' to 'protection from disturbing ideas.'"[69] For Coyne and many of his ilk, trigger warnings offer excuses for students either to deflect challenging conversations or to avoid doing work altogether.

Aaron Hanlon quickly followed with a rebuttal to Coyne: "Trigger warnings are nevertheless important because no matter how knowledgeable and comfortable professors are with the intellectually and emotionally challenging material we teach, our students are real people with real histories and concerns."[70] Hanlon underscores two notions that are important for this chapter. First, students are human beings. This is not a surprise, but it is worth repeating often whenever we are faced with making a teaching-related decision that may or may not disregard their essential humanness. Second, emotions can stand in the way of engaging with certain subjects, and we would do well to consider this. Hanlon then goes further to expose why the discourse surrounding trigger warnings is so fraught: "Still, unless we have a more robust discussion of what it really looks like to grapple with emotionally difficult or triggering material, arguing that trigger warnings are bunk and leaving it at that stops short of addressing the real issue of praxis: suppose trigger warnings are flawed, infantilizing, and impossible to deploy reliably, yet student concerns remain. What then? Ignore them, to the detriment of their education?"[71] There is no absolutely clear-cut answer to the question of how to work with students who are experiencing significant unregulated negative emotions or even potential retraumatization, but trigger warnings have filled the void, even if they are not a perfect solution.

I think the key to figuring out how to move forward is to make sure we are having productive conversations about students, emotions, and highly charged content. Arguments like Coyne's that portray students as trying to use trigger warnings to somehow game the system and circumvent the educational process are nothing more than straw men. How many students do we actually think are evading accountability in this way? Unless we see numbers here, I am tempted to suggest that such students either make up a minute segment of the population or they are figments of the writers' imaginations. Possibly devious or overly "fragile" students should be the least of our concerns in the trigger warning debate. Furthermore, those who take this position often seem to be more concerned about the current state of academic freedom in higher education than they are with student learning. Protecting academic freedom is certainly a noble cause, but I would strongly suggest that it is not the core issue when it comes to discussions of trigger warnings.

Another, more thoughtful argument I have heard against trigger warnings is that they are potentially problematic because faculty must subjectively pick and choose which content requires disclaimers and which does not. Unless we have data on the frequency of different kinds of traumatic incidents, it will always be difficult to reliably determine when a warning needs to be issued.[72] Our decisions to give trigger warnings, according to this argument, are therefore based on moral judgments that our students might not share and that could even be harmful for them. In essence, our choices signify our own perspectives on which traumas deserve warnings. This could unintentionally send damaging messages to students who have survived incidents of violence but who were not traumatized by them, and in a similar way communicate to students who have survived other kinds of traumatic events that their experience does not rise to the level of a trigger warning.[73]

Clearly, trigger warnings present a conundrum. They are "a partial and necessarily inadequate measure to enable some people to stay in the room so that 'difficult issues' can be discussed."[74] They solve parts of some problems but open up challenges in other areas. Faculty are not clinical psychologists (unless, of course, they have PhDs in clinical psychology), so we are not prepared to recognize trauma, and we have certainly not been trained to counsel students through a retraumatizing experience. Furthermore, there are students in our courses who will have intense negative responses to course materials but have not been traumatized. But we have to do something. We either err on the side of giving too much help or not enough. I know which side of that line I stand on, but perhaps, overall, it might help to reconsider the term "trigger warning" and work instead toward "content warning" or "content disclaimer," as some faculty have already done, because I think we need to preserve the value of such statements for survivors of trauma while making them more broadly applicable for helping students regulate negative emotions of all valences, even if they have never been traumatized. We can therefore aid survivors in participating fully in the educational experience while also providing access to difficult subjects for other students who a) may be flooded with negative, but not overwhelming, emotion or b) may not yet know that certain subjects will spark problematic reactions for them. It will never be enough to fully mitigate these responses, but it will at least be something.

GETTING STARTED

For both fear-related issues and trigger warnings, it helps to take a look at the content of our courses from a student's perspective. Just because a topic is fine with us, does not mean that it will be received in the same way by our students. This is particularly true with trigger warnings. Try to imagine different responses to course material, and if the subject necessitates it, consider giving a warning. You might also ask past students for their take on the content and whether or not they may have benefited from a warning. It is easy to put a catch-all warning at the top of your syllabus to address any potentially triggering material at the outset of the semester, but if you are on the fence about individual texts, topics, or films, then students can offer an additional viewpoint.

A Pedagogy of Empathy

I first heard the phrase "a pedagogy of empathy" from my friend Noreen Lape, who coined it for me when we were faculty together at the institution where I began my career. Noreen was widely known to be a kind and generous teacher, often inspiring her students both in the classroom and through her work directing the writing center. She is now doing great things at Dickinson College in Pennsylvania, where she has carried this idea with her. I would like to follow her lead and argue here for empathy as an essential element for effective teaching. All of the ideas I have explored in this chapter can be aided by an empathetic approach to our work with students. Trigger warnings or content disclaimers are the most obvious and visible (and politically charged) example, but the other strategies I have discussed will only work if we engage with our students empathetically. It is one thing to understand the connections between emotion and cognition, but it is quite another to take the extra step of considering how an individual student's emotions are enhancing or impeding her or his work in our course. Put more simply, we should follow the guidance of Sarah Rose Cavanagh, who suggests that "it is important for us, as educators, to appreciate the dizzying emotional complexity and competing priorities of our students' lives."[75] Such a move requires that we see and value our students as fellow travelers on this educational journey and that we actually care enough to help them reach their destination. It may not be easy, but it is a worthy goal—and one rooted in solid research—nonetheless.

KEY TAKEAWAYS

- Emotion evolved as an important part of our developing sociality. Our emotions give meaning to these social interactions, thereby strengthening the bonds that help to define our species.

continues ➤

KEY TAKEAWAYS *continued*

- The processes by which we regulate our emotions begin to develop when we are children. As we become adults, the framework put in place when we are younger becomes increasingly vital for successful learning to occur.

- Cognition and emotion work together in a delicate balance. When our emotions begin to supersede our abilities to regulate them, however, it significantly disrupts our cognitive systems. Simply put: overwhelming emotions have a negative effect on learning.

- Positive emotions such as happiness, joy, and humor are beneficial for student learning, but they are seldom part of our conversation about teaching in higher education.

- Perhaps one of the most significant things we can do as teachers is to care for our students as learners. Caring pedagogies do not require us to lower standards or to cross boundaries. They simply require that we be present for our students as fellow human beings and that we invest ourselves in helping them to succeed.

- Unregulated negative emotions impede learning in sometimes dramatic ways. The small part of the brain known as the amygdala may play a role in these kinds of emotional responses.

CHAPTER 4

Authenticity

We have cast our lot with learning, and learning will pull us through.
But this learning process must be reimbued with the texture and
feeling of human experiences shared and interpreted through
dialogue with one another.

—David A. Kolb, *Experiential Learning: Experience as the Source of
Learning and Development*

Old-fashioned pocket knives, for example, have a device for removing
stones from horses' hooves. People with this device may know its use
and be able to talk wisely about horses, hooves, and stones. But they
may never betray—or even recognize—that they would not begin
to know how to use this implement on a horse. Similarly, students
can often manipulate algorithms, routines, and definitions they
have acquired with apparent competence and yet not reveal, to their
teachers or themselves, that they would have no idea what to do if
they came upon the domain equivalent of a limping horse.

–John Seely Brown, Allan Collins, and Paul Duguid, "Situated
Cognition and the Culture of Learning"

When I walked into a class session of Donna Boyd's Introduction
to Forensic Anthropology course at Radford University, the first
thing I noticed was the real human skeleton that had been laid out
on a table at the front of the room. To be sure, the standard, plastic

teaching skeleton was there, too, but these were actual human bones. We later learned that the bones had once belonged to the victim of a murder, and they had been donated to Boyd by this young man's family after she had solved the crime. As a board-certified forensics specialist, Boyd is often called in by the state of Virginia on difficult cases where child abuse has led to death and the investigation is relying on osteology to determine explanations about the cause. For thirty years, Boyd has worked as a team with her husband Cliff Boyd, an archaeologist at Radford, to carefully exhume and examine the bodies of young victims and to provide both law enforcement and bereaved families with the answers they so desperately seek.

As if this weren't enough for one lifetime, it so happens that Donna Boyd is also a 2006 winner of the CASE/Carnegie US Professor of the Year award for her work at Radford teaching students to see, as she puts it, the stories our bones tell about us. These skeletal narratives, in fact, were important for framing the work we did in class on the day I attended. While Boyd was setting up her presentation, a student assistant walked around with a box of plastic bones, handing one to each student. Ever the egalitarian, though, this young man took requests. I heard shouts of "I want an ulna!" and "Give me a lumbar!" coming from different parts of the room. Diligently, the assistant did his part by gently tossing these bones to those who had asked. This was to be the first day that the class was formally studying osteology, and students were excited about bones even before the discussion had officially begun. Unfortunately, I missed out on acquiring a bone, because I was taking notes at an inopportune time, but the wonderful students around me were more than willing to talk to me about what they had been given.

Boyd utilized these plastic bones as soon as class began. "Everybody has a bone from Mr. Plastic Guy," she declared and then instructed the students to take a few minutes to figure out what the bone was and where it would be located in the body. Once they had a good idea of where the bone would be positioned, she encouraged them to feel for the bone on their own bodies—a practice called palpation that is commonly used by osteologists. Boyd then asked what I consider to be the epitome of the kind of meaningful questions I described in chapter 1 of this book: What could we learn about a person from this bone (meaning the particular bone that each student had chosen)? One student had selected a patella and talked about an ACL tear he had endured a few years back. Boyd asked him some questions about the surgery, which led to a discussion about the visible damage to the bone and about the presence of screws in the knee. In other words, Boyd noted, a forensic anthropologist would be able to tell that this injury had occurred simply as a result of the evidence from the bone itself. Boyd then asked other students about their bones. She asked one student, who had chosen an ulna, what breaks to this bone might reveal about the lifestyle of the person. For other bones, students hypothesized, arthritis would suggest age or injury. As a class, they were putting forward the sorts of questions that practitioners in the field use in order to make a compelling case.

Boyd then turned to the actual human bones she had brought with her. She told the class that they were going to walk through the clues offered by the bones and that they were going to solve the case for themselves. To get the ball rolling, she asked them what information they would need first in order to develop a hypothesis. She was silent for a few moments as she waited for them to start asking questions. Finally, one student suggested that they would need to know the sex of the individual. As a response, Boyd told the class about the size and shape of the pelvis, skull, and jaw. Then another student asked about the age. Boyd explained to the class that a clavicle, which was broken, had growth plates that had only recently fused. They asked about the height of the person, and she told them that, while any bones can be put into a regression formula to calculate the height, the femur is best. Eventually, as a class, they estimated that the person had been a male of average height in his early twenties. This was exactly what Boyd's original report had said as well.

At this point, students began to inquire about the injuries to the bones. Without getting too graphic here (is it too late?), I will just say that there were a variety of shattered bones throughout the torso. Theories regarding the cause of death were shared—car accident, beating, and so on—and Boyd asked students to defend their positions with the evidence from the skeleton. Like many expert teachers I have observed, she was helping them get to the point where they could make the last, and most important, leap to the correct answer. To do so, she asked one final question: what could possibly explain the fact that the broken bones are all in different locations? Students jumped on this question. It must be a gun shot, one of them said. Another echoed this and argued that the sites of the injuries could be explained by ricocheting bullets. They were right. The death had been caused by a shotgun, and Boyd had helped them solve the mystery on their own. When I left the classroom that day, students were still gathered there asking Boyd follow-up questions, clearly proud of themselves and intrigued by the day's discussion.

Later I interviewed Boyd about her teaching philosophy. Why, I asked, did she believe it was important to engage students in this way? "We learn things much better when they're real," she told me.[1] Boyd is absolutely right, and this realness, or authenticity, is the subject of the current chapter. I have chosen the term "authenticity" carefully, as I am aware that it has come under fire for being too vague or for its equation with poorly designed experiential learning activities.[2] If we look at the work of cognitive scientists, though, "authenticity" means something very specific. For those researchers who study this subject, a truly authentic learning experience must have "as much fidelity as possible to what students will encounter outside of school in terms of tools, complexity, cognitive functioning, and interactions with people. Therefore, creating an authentic learning context requires more than just presenting students with realistic problems or situations—it also means that students must address the problems or situations realistically as well."[3] The human brain is pretty adept at detecting the degree to which an activity, assignment, or exercise is authentic or artificial. The greater the authenticity, the deeper the learning. By contrast, artificiality leads to weaker, or more strategic, learning behaviors. Students quickly zone out (and their cognitive functions go on holiday) if they are not asked to apply their knowledge meaningfully in realistic conditions.

Cognitive Authenticity and Situated Cognition

What does it mean to be real? I don't mean to steer us too deeply into philosophical territory here, nor to sound as if I am quoting from *The Velveteen Rabbit*. Realism lies at the heart of any discussion of authenticity, though, so it is worth exploring what researchers mean when they broach this subject. A learning experience, for instance, can seem real even if it is only a simulation. Fighter pilots clock many hours in flight simulators before venturing into the open sky. On the one hand, learning in a simulator is a much less expensive proposition than testing out some new strategies in an actual F-16, but at the same time the knowledge gained is equally salient. The reason for this is that the learning is embedded in a domain-specific context. It does not matter whether the learner, in our example, is in a simulator or a jet. The brain registers the situation as being realistic (and therefore useful) and, thus, learns more than if the scenario had been contrived without attention to this authenticity. Researchers refer to this quality as cognitive realism or cognitive authenticity, and it is a central element of human learning. Indeed, some have even argued that the cognitive authenticity of the learning experience is even more important than absolute fidelity to the actual environment in which the knowledge would be applied.[4] It does no good to be in a real kitchen, for example, if one does not yet know how to cook. One could, however, learn to chop onions quite well in a classroom, as long as the right knives are provided.

Why might cognitive authenticity be so important? Let's think for a moment about the ways in which babies learn. For infants, every instance of learning is an authentic one. We do not create artificial assignments for babies. There are no lectures on how to eat. They grab an actual spoon, fling some food around, and experiment until they get it in their mouths. The same is true with every other aspect of a baby's world. Deep learning demands authenticity, and it is no different with college students. Adult brains are still cast in the same mold. Like babies, we continue to learn the most from realistic problems and authentic scenarios.

Creating courses, assignments, and activities that prioritize cognitive authenticity means allowing students to do significant work within the domain of a particular discipline in a way that goes beyond brief forays into applied problem solving. This kind of learning requires what some have called situated cognition. Cognition is situated insofar as it is heavily dependent on context and environment, which means that instructors should strive to more deeply encase learning experiences within authentic disciplinary contexts. In other words, a student in a sociology course learns more successfully when she is given assignments that mirror the kind of work professional sociologists do. As John Seely Brown, Allan Collins, and Paul Duguid are careful to note, however:

This is not to suggest that all students of math or history must be expected to become professional mathematicians or historians, but to claim that in order to learn these subjects (and not just to learn about them) students need much more than abstract concepts and self-contained examples. They need to be exposed to the use of a domain's conceptual tools in authentic activity—to teachers acting as practitioners and using these tools in wrestling with problems of the world. Such activity can tease out the way a mathematician or historian looks at the world and solves emergent problems. The process may appear informal, but it is nonetheless full-blooded, authentic activity that can be deeply informative—in a way that textbook examples and declarative explanations are not.[5]

Although it is not our job to use our classrooms to produce mini versions of ourselves, we can achieve great results by treating students as burgeoning scholars rather than novice thinkers. Certainly, we will encounter a few students over the course of our careers who will go on to graduate school and the academy, but the main function of our teaching is to help all the students who walk through our doors to learn. Far from keeping the secrets of our disciplines locked behind a door, this learning requires us to give our students access to the problems, the frameworks, the data, the methodologies, and the domain-specific knowledge of our fields in order enhance their understanding of the material.

The trouble is that courses do not always focus on authenticity. Assignments often center on mastery of content rather than an immersion in the discipline. Ironically, as researchers on cognitive authenticity and situated cognition tell us, students may learn all the content we teach them and still not know how to utilize this information beyond the walls of our classrooms. A biology student might memorize all of the bugs he is told to remember and yet not be able to identify any of them out in the field. In large part, this is due to the fact that the activity itself is an artificial learning exercise. The student knows that he will not have to identify any real bugs in this scenario, so he just goes through the motions to get a satisfactory grade on the exam. Authentic assignments, by contrast, are connected to the broader context in such a way that they are impossible to complete without being able to identify the bugs, so to speak.

Even more problematic, from the perspective of privileging authenticity, are the teaching techniques that have been traditionally employed in the classroom: "we consistently rely on decontextualized instructional strategies. In our desire to cover as much material as possible, we focus our instructional activities on abstract basic skills, concepts, and technical definitions. We believe that decontextualized skills have broad applicability and are unaffected by the activities or environments in which they are acquired and used. However, when we do this, students do not learn when to apply those skills or within what kinds of contexts they work."[6]

What we do in front of the classroom can sometimes be disconnected from both the real work of our disciplines and also the world beyond our classroom doors. To the degree that we want to build authenticity as an important element of our courses, we need to choose strategies that allow students to engage in work that feels genuine and real, which in many cases means that we will provide them with opportunities to replicate the activities of scholars in the field. Leading a discussion, for example, can be an authentic strategy, as long as students are grappling with questions that are central to the discipline. In the pages that follow, I will outline some other ways to make our learning environments more authentic, and I will also question the viability of one popular teaching strategy that is particularly inauthentic: prolonged lecturing.

Authenticity and Immersion

One key element of cognitive realism or cognitive authenticity is the degree to which the learning experience is immersive.[7] An assignment, activity, or course that focuses on immersion is one that feels "compellingly" real to students because the components of the experience are genuine, not contrived.[8] A great example of this kind of authenticity can be found in the classrooms of our colleagues in modern languages. It has become more and more common over the last few decades for language instructors to favor immersion pedagogies. Immersion-based language instruction has long been hailed as coming closest to the ways in which young children naturally acquire language. In many immersion classrooms, students receive very little direct instruction about a language; instead, they are taught in the second language and must construct meaning through experience, context, etc. This method is very different from older models of language teaching in which students focused on memorizing vocabulary and working through grammatical structures.

Evidence for the success of immersion teaching has been piling up. A recent study has shown that adults are not only able to achieve high levels of proficiency in a second language (something about which scholars had been skeptical for a long time) but also attain "native-like syntactic processing in the brain" when taught using "immersion or immersion-like experience" as opposed to explicit instruction on grammar and syntax.[9] This is an important finding that underscores the efficacy of authentic learning activities. In many ways, immersion learning exemplifies my larger argument in this book as well. Our learning mechanisms do not fundamentally change as we grow older. They simply mature.

Learning from Experience

Immersion, of course, must be connected to a specific experience, and researchers have—for decades now—been deeply interested in studying the kinds of experiences that will generate the most authentic learning. One of the leaders in this area of inquiry is David A. Kolb. His work on experiential learning has been highly influential in shaping pedagogical approaches that focus on students making meaning from their experiences. Kolb argues that "knowledge is continuously derived from and tested out in the experiences of the learner."[10] We cannot truly know anything, according to Kolb, unless we directly experience it first. This view connects to the idea of authenticity perfectly because the genuine experience is the driver of learning. For Kolb, however, having the experience is only the first step. He designed a now famous cycle for experiential learning that moves from concrete experience to reflective observation, abstract conceptualization, and active experimentation.[11] The experience itself is the locus of authenticity and the launch pad for learning, which can only happen after reflecting on the experience, building a conceptual framework from the reflection, and then applying this new knowledge to other scenarios, problems, or questions.

The work of Kolb and other researchers has led to the development of models for experiential education, which is an umbrella term covering a wide variety of pedagogical methods and instructional programs that formalize experiential learning.[12] As a part of his recent book on experiential education, Jay Roberts reviewed much of the research on the topic and found no fewer than twenty-six types of strategies that have at some point been associated with the general category of experiential education—including active learning, adult learning, adventure education, career and technical education, environmental education, service-learning, and vocational education, among others.[13] What this list makes clear to me is that the net we cast when we talk about experiential education is perhaps too wide. It's like eating at a chain restaurant where the menu is ten pages long. You can pick something, but it's hard to tell whether or not it will be any good, because there are just too many options. The abundance of pedagogical choices here can cause us to lose sight of authenticity. Instead, we need to direct our attention to those methods that help students learn effectively by reflecting on and applying the knowledge gained from their experiences.

Service-learning is one such approach. Faculty who utilize service-learning in their courses and assignments typically ask students to volunteer in the local community, to ruminate on this experience, and to design a project demonstrating what they have learned. The type of service ranges from spending a few hours working with an organization to larger-scale undertakings that involve developing a proposal for sustainable change and pitching it to a community board. Janet Eyler, an expert on this methodology, explains that service-learning "is specifically designed to counter the isolation of learning from experience and the artificial division of subject matter into disconnected disciplines that lead to what cognitive scientists call the 'inert knowledge' problem, or the tendency to acquire knowledge which cannot be accessed and applied in new situations."[14] Authenticity, then, is at the very heart of this method. Studies are beginning to show that service-learning has a positive effect on academic outcomes for students as long as the corresponding assignments, particularly the reflection exercises, are well structured. Service-learning, then, provides us with an outstanding example of authentic experiential education that improves student learning.[15] The general benefits of learning from experience are amplified, however, when students are doing domain-specific work in a particular discipline.

GETTING STARTED

Experiential education is incredibly valuable, but it can sometimes be hard to know where to begin. Start by looking at your learning goals. What kinds of experiences might augment the learning in your courses? Is it several trips to a museum? Working closely with a community partner? Once you identify an experience you might want to pursue, there will probably be offices on your campus that can help you set things up, provide you with community contacts, and offer guidance on structuring the experiential component. There's no need to go it alone!

Authenticity and Experience within Our Disciplines

When students are directly involved in the work of our disciplines, they are taking part in, arguably, the most authentic learning experiences we can provide for them. This kind of engagement frequently takes the form of undergraduate research, which has seen dramatic gains in popularity, and in programming budgets, over the last few decades. Undergraduate research is a broad umbrella under which many kinds of activities and assignments rest. A student who works for years in a biology lab under the guidance of a PI or a graduate student is certainly participating in undergraduate research, but so is a student who is co-writing a paper on econometrics or on representations of disability in medieval literature. We often think of undergraduate research, however, as being something that happens outside the classroom, but this need not be the case. In fact, many universities have had great success encouraging faculty to develop assignments for their courses that allow students to engage in this same kind of authentic activity for some or all of the semester. We can transform our classrooms into laboratories where students explore, discover, test, and then do it all over again. This is as true of STEM courses as it is of those in the humanities and social sciences. The key is simply to develop assignments that allow them to dive into the work of the discipline. I often hear claims that students don't know enough of the content to be able to engage in this kind of research, but I don't think this is either accurate or fair. Students sometimes only need a little bit of information or a critical framework in order to begin the process of authentic research.

Studies on the efficacy of undergraduate research for enhancing student learning have been almost uniformly positive, which—I have to say—is quite a feat. A 2007 paper in *Science* identified an increase in conceptual understanding as one of the most important benefits of undergraduate research.[16] In another study of seventy-six rising seniors (which incorporated 367 interviews), significant gains were reported in the application of students' knowledge from the classroom to the research activity, in critical thinking and analysis skills, and in "understanding of conceptual connections between sciences."[17] Although there has not been as much work yet on the values of undergraduate research in the humanities and social sciences, signs are pointing in directions that indicate similar results.[18] Based on what we know about cognitive authenticity, this intuitively makes sense. Give students work that is deeply rooted in disciplinary contexts and that replicates the activities of scholars in the field, and they will learn the material more than if we simply ask them to build knowledge in environments that are void of contextual frameworks or artificial in design.

Embedding research opportunities in our courses is not the only way to prioritize authenticity, however. It is not entirely necessary to devote large portions of our semester to this kind of intensive work in order to engage our students in authentic learning tasks. As Donna Boyd demonstrated, even activities that last no longer than the span of one class session can be powerful and effective in their own right. At their best, this is what lab and recitation sessions can offer students in STEM courses, although the continued prevalence of "cookbook" labs can be problematic in this regard. Spending some time collecting samples and specimens out in the field for a biology class would also be a good example.

Once again, these activities are not limited to STEM classrooms, though. Cameron Hunt McNabb, an associate professor of English at Southeastern University in Florida, makes authenticity a central element of her literature courses. In fact, when I interviewed her in the fall of 2016, she used the phrase "authentic pedagogy" before I even had a chance to ask any questions.[19] She wants her students to engage in the "same discourse that scholars do." For McNabb, the product "of authenticity is agency," and she wants her students to feel they can take ownership of their learning. Her approach is perhaps best seen in the performance activity she has designed for students in her Introduction to Shakespeare course. In order to underscore for her students that each play was (and is) a "live text, not a fixed text," McNabb crafted a three-part assignment for her students. First, she brings in actors to workshop a scene for a week, and then she puts her students into groups. Each group must choose a scene to perform from one of the plays they have studied. They make all the interpretive choices and are responsible for props, costumes, and other related materials. Additionally, students annotate a prompt book for the scene with notes about directing choices, shifts to the setting or the language, questions they want to answer, and problems they need to solve. Finally, after performing their scenes, they must turn in both the annotated prompt book and a co-written analysis of the prompt book that explains the choices they made when preparing their scenes.

Performance-based pedagogies are not new, of course, and are frequently used by faculty when teaching drama (like my own experience in Chris Fee's Medieval Drama course described in the introduction). McNabb, though, takes the authenticity even further by artfully showing her students that the performance is, in many ways, the play itself. In a wonderful turn of phrase, McNabb suggested that this work allows her courses to have a kind of "afterlife" with students. They carry with them what they have learned from their performances and from the other creative assignments McNabb has constructed for them as they move on. This strikes me as not only the goal of learning in general, but the particular role of authenticity for learning as well. Working within a discipline-specific context makes the knowledge gained in our courses ultimately more potent and accessible for our students.

GETTING STARTED

If you are interested in developing authentic assignments for students that mirror the work of scholars in your discipline, one easy first step in this direction is to bring some of your own research into the classroom. Talk to students about what you are working on, what questions are driving you, what obstacles you have encountered, and in what direction you hope to proceed. Give them a chance to respond and ask questions. Some fantastic assignments can emerge from this process that are connected to your work in some way, which will benefit both the students, with respect to their learning, and also your own research agenda. For those in STEM disciplines, a discussion like this may also lead you to find new student collaborators for your lab.

The Inauthenticity of the Lecture

Just as there are a wide range of authentic activities that work well for student learning, there are also some that do not effectively produce learning because they are less authentic. The answer I'm delicately moving toward here is one that will win me just as many enemies as it will friends, but I feel that I must enter the fray. The simple truth is this: despite its predominance in classrooms across the country, prolonged lecturing is one of our most inauthentic teaching strategies. Yes, I said it, but now let me explain myself before you either applaud or start heckling me. I want to emphasize that I am concentrating my attention on *prolonged* lecturing. I am not tossing the baby out with the bathwater here. I do believe that short lectures still have their place and can be useful for providing students with key information or context, among other things.[20] In fact, Donald Bligh has shown that lectures are as good as anything else if our only goal is to "transmit information."[21] Rather than targeting all types of lectures, then, I would like to focus on something closer to the notion of what some have called "continuous exposition"—that is, lecturing for long periods of time with very few breaks (if any) for student engagement.[22] Those situations where instructors are talking for the bulk of the class period, and therefore limiting their interactions with students, are the least authentic of all classroom environments. Such environments are artificial insofar as they do not resemble in any way the natural circumstances under which human beings have learned for much of our history, and our brains are easily able to detect and ignore these kinds of contrived scenarios (unless we force ourselves to pay attention for the sake of a grade). Could you imagine our ancestors holding lectures about hunting and gathering? Me neither. How about a colloquy for infants on the intricacies of speaking? Nope.

So why, as Donald Bligh has suggested, is "lecturing still the most common method" of teaching in college classrooms?[23] Some history is in order. The original purpose of lecturing was patently clear. About a millennium ago, students in the first medieval universities did not have access to books. Gutenberg and his printing press were still centuries away, so scribes were responsible for producing texts. This meant that the teaching (if we may call it that) in these scenarios involved declaiming the work verbatim so that students could copy the correct words. The monks, priests, or other clerics who were instructing would often offer some commentary or glossing as well, but the emphasis was on careful recopying. One could argue that as books became more widely available, lecturing became much less necessary. The inertia brought about by tradition is difficult to overcome, however, and the technique has continued to reign supreme. The inauthenticity of lecturing has also remained constant. Students rarely do more than listen and sometimes take notes in courses where prolonged lecturing takes place. They are in many ways separated from the intellectual activity because the learning environment lacks the contextual richness of the strategies I outlined earlier, and they are not asked to do the work of the discipline in any meaningful way.

It is largely because of this lack of authenticity, I would suggest, that so much research has found lectures to be ineffective means for engendering student learning. Indeed, there is a very long history of this research. Here, for example, is a gem from an article published in 1916:

It should be obvious that the lecture in these days of easy and cheap book printing has no necessary place in the teaching of economics. It consumes valuable class-room time—time when minds should be actively engaged—in the thought-deadening business of receiving and recording another's thoughts, which might better first be read from a printed page and discussed later in the class-room. The supreme business of our course is to get as much effective thinking done in the year as possible. Right economy of time demands the retirement of the lecture. Consideration of its effect on the student's business of thinking actively enforces the demand.[24]

We have certainly been debating this issue for quite some time, haven't we? One of the most important papers demonstrating the negative impact of lecturing on student learning was just published in 2014, however. In June of that year, Scott Freeman, Sarah Eddy, Miles McDonough, Michelle Smith, Nnadozie Okoroafor, Hannah Jordt, and Mary Pat Wenderoth put out the "largest and most comprehensive meta-analysis of the undergraduate STEM education literature to date" in *Proceedings of the National Academy of Sciences*.[25] Freeman and his colleagues analyzed 225 different studies, many of which compared the efficacy of active learning strategies to that of "traditional" lecturing (i.e., prolonged lecturing or continuous exposition—take your pick), and their work yielded some rather dramatic findings: "The data reported here indicate that active learning increases examination performance by just under half a SD [standard deviation] and that lecturing increases failure rates by 55%. The heterogeneity analyses indicate that (i) these increases in achievement hold across all of the STEM disciplines and occur in all class sizes, course types, and course levels; and (ii) active learning is particularly beneficial in small classes and at increasing performance on concept inventories."[26] There has yet to be a more definitive word on the subject, and there is certainly no equally convincing rebuttal that lectures are, in fact, the better way to go.

In seeking answers to the question of why prolonged lecturing is so ineffective, some researchers have argued that the issue is connected to our attention span, with 10–15 minutes often cited as the average attention span for traditional-age college students.[27] I should note that there is a bit of disagreement in the research with respect to the precise length of time for which students can pay attention,[28] but I feel confident in saying that the attention span of human beings has its limitations (we've all been to academic conferences, right?), and that college students probably begin to reach some of these limitations between 10–20 minutes. But let's think less about using a stopwatch for a moment and consider the pedagogical ramifications of this information. Once the threshold of a student's attention span is crossed, he or she is able to focus less, retain fewer pieces of information, and encode less of this knowledge in long-term memory.[29] Learning takes a back seat as the mind begins to wander during the lecture.

As I mentioned earlier, though, I'm convinced that the problem is more rooted in the lecture's inauthenticity. In fact, I think the issues with students' attention spans are a symptom of this lack of authenticity. Remember that the human brain is ruthlessly pragmatic. It's not all that interested in anything it deems unnecessary or unimportant. Evolution has shaped the brain to make quick decisions as to what it needs to focus on. Authenticity is often a key indicator of relevance, and our cognitive processes are most engaged when both of these elements are at play. The inauthentic learning environment created by prolonged lecturing leads to a reprioritization and reallocation of cognitive resources, which in turn affects student's attention spans. In other words, the attention span becomes an issue primarily because the authenticity is missing. Students are not paying attention, because—from the perspective of their cognitive systems—there is no real reason to focus on the material other than getting a good grade. Brains, however, care very little about grades.

It should be said, too, that prolonged lecturing eliminates much of the necessary social engagement I discussed in chapter 2. When combined with inauthenticity, the absence of important social dynamics can make learning all but impossible. Yes, there will always be self-motivated or self-directed students in our class-rooms who have the potential to augment lectures by their own means and to learn in spite of us, but those students make up only a small percentage of the actual students we will teach over the course of our careers. It stands to reason, then, that prolonged lec-turing should rest at the bottom of our list in terms of the pedagogical options from which we might choose.

GETTING STARTED

Consider setting aside ten minutes during one of your upcoming class sessions to test out an active learning strategy you have read about in this book. Choose one that matches well with your philoso-phy of teaching, and be transparent with your students that you are trying something new. Most activities will require a little planning, but it need not feel cumbersome to be effective. After you implement the activity, ask students for some feedback so that you can gauge whether or not you could use such strategies more widely.

Authenticity and Closing the Achievement Gap

Perhaps unsurprisingly, two of the methods I have covered in this chapter—designing undergraduate research opportunities and eliminating prolonged lectures—have been shown to reduce the achievement gap for both women and underrepresented minorities, particularly in STEM disciplines.[30] These students simply do better in courses that implement approaches of this kind. This makes a lot of sense to me, since both of these pedagogical actions prioritize engagement, and the more engaging a particular strategy is, the more likely it will benefit these populations of students.[31] But I also think this research underscores the ultimate importance of authenticity. It is not a coincidence that these more authentic learning environments increase the success rates for groups of students whose academic performance has traditionally been affected by factors like socioeconomic inequities, the extent of their previous preparation in the subject area, the lack of inclusive pedagogies, and more. Authenticity is a basic requirement for deep learning, and it stands to reason that students who have experienced largely inauthentic environments will benefit just as much or more from exposure to these contexts than peers who have previously encountered them.

In general, we can think of authenticity as an element that will help all students to one degree or another. It must be built intentionally into our course activities, though, for it to be meaningful and for it to have the cognitive benefits that researchers have outlined. An assignment is not authentic simply because it exists; it must be embedded within disciplinary contexts or situated within a real domain in order for our brains to establish that it is a valid, and not an artificial, learning exercise. There are demonstrable gains that can be made when we utilize authenticity in this way. But let's be honest. It is also just a lot more fun for teachers to help students do work that applies to their disciplines and their lives in ways that are meaningful.

KEY TAKEAWAYS

- The brain is most attuned to information and stimuli necessary to its survival. It therefore prioritizes relevance and authenticity when learning. In other words, the brain doesn't mess around. If it registers a situation as being artificial or unimportant, it will allocate cognitive resources elsewhere.

- A learning environment or assignment with a high degree of cognitive authenticity adheres as closely as possible to the work performed by scholars in a particular discipline.

- Undergraduate research projects are among the most authentic learning activities that we can assign our students. These need not be cumbersome, semester-long endeavors, either. Some of the best projects can be completed in weeks or even days.

- Providing students with opportunities to learn through experiences in the field, in the community, and the like is an important way to build authenticity into our courses.

- Prolonged lecturing is an inauthentic pedagogy that can undermine student learning because of its effects on attention spans and its emphasis on passively receiving information.

CHAPTER 5

Failure

Far from being a sign of intellectual inferiority, the capacity to err is crucial to human cognition. Far from being a moral flaw, it is inextricable from some of our most humane and honorable qualities: empathy, optimism, imagination, conviction, and courage. And far from being a mark of indifference or intolerance, wrongness is a vital part of how we learn and change. Thanks to error, we can revise our understanding of ourselves and amend our ideas about the world.

—Kathryn Schulz, *Being Wrong: Adventures in the Margin of Error*

Failure is probably the most important factor in all of my work. Writing *is* failure. Over and over and over again.

—Ta-Nehisi Coates, qtd. in Angela Duckworth, *Grit: The Power of Passion and Perseverance*

According to author Mario Livio's version of the story, James Watson and Francis Crick stumbled pretty dramatically on their way to discovering the double helix of DNA. Watson had attended a lecture by a fellow scientist named Rosalind Franklin in 1951, and some of the knowledge he gained from Franklin's presentation was instrumental in the first model of DNA that he and Crick put forward. The two later presented their model to a team that included Franklin, and she ripped them to shreds. Unfortunately for the famous scientific duo, they had made a sizable error regarding the "reported water content" of DNA, which was caused in part by "Watson's misunderstanding of a crystallographic term that Franklin had used in her seminar a week earlier."[1] It seems that crystallography was one of Crick's specialties, and Watson's miscue led Crick to make some faulty assumptions. Following the presentation, their research on DNA was formally suspended, and they were only explicitly allowed to continue in 1953, after Linus Pauling published a model of DNA that turned out to be inaccurate.[2] Of course, they had been unofficially pondering the nature of the problem all along, and they learned much from the failure of their initial model that eventually led to the discovery that garnered them the Nobel Prize in 1962.[3]

Not all of us will go on to make world-changing breakthroughs like Watson and Crick, but I think it would be difficult to find a scholar who would deny the importance of failure in the academic research process. In fact, failures (both small and large) tend to make up quite a bit of the terrain on the road to discovery. Stuart Firestein explains that this is the natural way of things: "Failure is the expected outcome according to the Second Law of Thermodynamics. There are many more ways to fail than to succeed. Success, by definition, should be very limited. Failure is the default. Success requires an unusual, but possible, confluence of events in which entropy is temporarily reversed."[4] As academics, we are trained to learn from our failures, to use each as an opportunity to refine our hypotheses and to advance our understanding, until we reach a point where the collective gains we have made from these failures come to be labeled "success."

The same is true of our work in the classroom. We (ideally) try out a new teaching strategy or a new assignment, determine whether it has helped our students learn, and then we continue to refine these approaches to achieve better results. Why is it, then, that our educational systems stigmatize failure so profoundly for students themselves? We ask students to take high-stakes exams where the consequences for error are serious. We often design courses that privilege correct answers rather than exploration and discovery. We rarely give our students feedback on assignments for which we are not providing a grade. All of this is understandable, given the history of educational systems and the limits on our time, but these strategies do very little to decrease the negative view of errors and mistakes.

The tone is set early too. The prioritization of grades and correctness begins when children are very young. Errors are viewed as something students must target and eliminate. But this doesn't have to be the case. In her powerful book *The Gift of Failure*, Jessica Lahey describes a way to flip this script in elementary and secondary schools: "Failure is too often characterized as a negative: an F in math or a suspension from school. However, all sorts of disappointments, rejections, corrections, and criticisms are small failures, all opportunities in disguise, valuable gifts misidentified as tragedy."[5]

Lahey is right, and I think we can pick up on her cue in higher education. There is a great deal of research coming out now that is showing us how valuable failures can be for our students' learning. Much of it leads to one, solid conclusion: if we design courses that provide students with opportunities to fail when the stakes are low and then give them the support and guidance to gain understanding from these instances, we are creating environments where students can learn more effectively. Thinking of our courses in this way, though, requires something of a paradigm shift. Of all the subjects I cover between the many pages you have now graciously made your way through, this one has been the hardest to wrap my mind around. As a student, I was certainly never rewarded for my failures, and no one mentioned the value of failure to me when I was training as a teaching assistant in graduate school. I may even be guilty of creating some assignments and exams in the past that have prioritized correct answers rather than giving students the space to make meaning from their errors.

Yet here we are. The research is clear, and the classroom interventions developed from this research show demonstrable gains for students. So how, then, do we begin to build failure into our teaching? First, I want to clarify exactly what I mean by failure. For the purposes of this chapter, we should envision student failure as a spectrum that begins with small errors like inaccurate calculations and extends to significant conceptual misunderstandings that impede a student's ability to build knowledge. To some degree, these cognitive failures will also relate to poor performance or low grades, but we need not view failure exclusively in these terms. Some miscues begin long before we give any assignment and, likewise, some continue long after students have left our classrooms.

For our first step in building pedagogies of failure, we probably need to understand a bit about why, as a species, we are so prone to error in the first place.

Error Machines

In many ways, the brains of human beings are designed to detect and to learn from failure. There are clear evolutionary advantages to gaining insights from failure, of course, but we are also, in a lot of respects, error-making and error-correcting machines. On a daily basis we are wrong about an embarrassing number of things: our computer passwords, the formula for quadratic equations, whether a situation is as it seems, where to invest our money, whether the television show Big Brother is trashy or an interesting sociological experiment. Though I concede that we do get things right from time to time, much of our perpetual wrongness is apparently connected to our mechanisms for trying to understand the world around us. Because the brain would quickly become overtaxed if we deeply analyzed every single thing that we observe, it relies instead on quick assessments of probability. Kathryn Schulz, author of *Being Wrong*, describes our predicament nicely. "Human beings," she writes, "don't care about what is logically valid and theoretically possible. We care about what is *probable*. We determine what is probable based on our prior experience of the world, which is where evidence comes in: we choose the most likely answer to any given question based on the kinds of things we have (and haven't) experienced in comparable situations before."[6] As you might expect, this innate process can lead to some problems.

Let's take the example of the computer password, for instance. The latest Taylor Swift album has just been released, and you are desperate to log on to your favorite website to purchase it. You try the password you use for everything, and it does not work. You try a second time: nothing. You know it has to work, because this is the same password you use time and time again. You conclude that the website must be having issues, because clearly your password is correct. Unfortunately, both of these assumptions are wrong. The website, as it happens, is just fine. You've made an error about your password because you've been depending on your brain's estimation of probability. Yes, you do use this password a lot, and your brain knows this, so it quickly calculates that the only reasonable answer to the conundrum you are facing is your standard password. In doing so, this automatic response has obscured the memory of the time that the website you are trying to access had a security breach and forced you to change your password. After pondering the situation for a minute or two, you finally remember what happened and try out what you think you may have used for the new password. Success! It turns out that a bit of analysis and engagement with long-term memory were needed to override the brain's initial assessment.

This example and Schulz's illuminating description of our dilemma are ultimately illustrations of the work of Daniel Kahneman and his longtime research partner Amos Tversky. Although Tversky died before their work was complete, Kahneman became a Nobel Laureate in Economics in 2002 for their combined efforts to understand the ways in which people make decisions. They studied the flawed heuristics we use to make judgments and the biases that result from our reliance on these heuristics. In his book *Thinking, Fast and Slow*, Kahneman explains how he and Tversky "documented systematic errors in the thinking of normal people, and [they] traced these errors to the design of the machinery of cognition rather than to the corruption of thought by emotion."[7] The machinery to which Kahneman is referring here is the interplay between what he calls System 1 and System 2. System 1 generates "automatic" responses to stimuli using the heuristics Kahneman and Tversky laid out, and, thus, it often leads to biases. System 2, on the other hand, is designed to analyze the responses of System 1 in order to draw more reasoned conclusions.[8] The trouble, as Kahneman sees it, is that System 2 is often otherwise occupied by some other issue related to cognition, so our decisions frequently stem from the unchecked responses of System 1.[9] This gets us into trouble and is responsible for any number of errors we make on a daily basis. While System 2 is taking a long lunch break, System 1 will often make inferences without sufficient evidence,[10] or intuit causation when none exists. As Kahneman notes, "We are evidently ready from birth to have *impressions* of causality, which do not depend on reasoning about patterns of causation. They are products of System 1."[11] He argues that we need the critical elements of doubt and questioning supplied by System 2 in order to avoid such pitfalls.

Another way these two systems can lead us into error is through the construction of stories. Sometimes System 1 will generate a quickly gathered (and incorrect) conclusion that System 2 will accept without analysis because it is attending to other affairs. System 2 will then construct a narrative in an attempt to explain the supposed veracity of System 1's response, and the error will become deeply ingrained.[12] The primary issue here is not the misunderstood concept, conclusion, or fact, but the story that creates an "illusion" of correctness. Kahneman sees these illusions as being at the heart of so many faulty decisions and judgments: "The sense-making machinery of System 1 makes us see the world as more tidy, simple, predictable, and coherent than it really is. The illusion that one has understood the past feeds the further illusion that one can predict and control the future. These illusions are comforting."[13] Indeed, such illusions affect our daily lives and our interactions with the world. They are also prevalent in our classrooms.

Kahneman's complex theories about human error are revealing, but we also commit very simple errors as well. We may misremember a series of facts, probably because the information was not successfully moved from our working memory to long-term storage, or we simply transpose information when writing it down. These kinds of mistakes happen all the time to us and to our students. The good news about our overall propensity for making mistakes, however, is that our brains have evolved to register and to process cognitive errors. In particular, there is general agreement among neuroscientists regarding the existence of two processing signals that originate in the anterior cingulate cortex of the brain: the error-related negativity (ERN) signal and the error positivity (Pe) signal. The ERN has to do with "conflict between the correct and the erroneous response," whereas the Pe "reflect[s] awareness of and attention allocation to errors."[14] More precisely, the Pe can be responsible for "(1) conscious error recognition, (2) affective error processing or (3) performance adjustments after an error."[15] Recent research has also suggested that the two signals are "at least partially dissociable," meaning that the activity of one may not necessarily be related to the other.[16] It is also important to note that some of the activity described here can occur unconsciously, without our knowing that anything at all has happened.[17]

So what does all of this mean? The ERN monitors stimuli as they whiz by. Its job is really to detect whether an answer we've given does or does not match up with the correct response. The ERN doesn't go much further than this, though. It is simply recording the presence of an error.[18] The Pe, on the other hand, is where the magic happens. Through the activity of the Pe, and its role in allocating cognitive resources, we not only recognize our errors but can change our behavior, responses, and strategies as a result of having committed the error. In terms of our capabilities for using failure as a learning tool, then, the Pe ranks among the most important of our neural mechanisms. The work of Jan R. Wiersema, Jacob J. van der Meere, and Herbert Roeyers on early cognitive development reinforces this claim. In a study of the ERN and Pe processes in groups of children, adolescents, and adults, they concluded that the Pe "and the ability to adjust response strategies seem to mature at an earlier stage than early automatic error detection processes (ERN)."[19] The Pe is vital for learning about the world, and it develops earlier, perhaps even because of its importance. Human beings need this functionality. We need to make sense of our errors, and the Pe helps us to do this.

Speaking of children, psychologists have been interested in how kids make mistakes at least as far back as the work of Piaget, who perhaps deserves an award for most frequent cameo appearances in this book. He believed that babies younger than twelve months old had no clear sense of object permanence because they would look for a toy at a place where it had previously been hidden even though they were explicitly shown the location to which it had been moved. He found that this happened over and over again. The babies he studied (mostly his own children) repeatedly searched the area in which they first found the toy rather than the new hiding spot that had been revealed to them. This fundamental miscue became known as the A-not-B error.[20] Although researchers still argue about the cause of this error, it occurs with remarkable consistency in children.[21] Importantly, children's cognitive capabilities quickly mature to the point where the error is not an issue, but its prevalence does suggest how failure is deeply ingrained within our developmental systems. I would also suggest that the scholarly disagreement about this phenomenon in babies reveals that, in general, there is no easy answer when it comes to the question of causes. A failure in our thinking process is not caused by a single misfiring, but by a complex system of factors both psychological and biological.

The A-not-B error is one type of what is known as an "expectancy failure." That is, a baby expects something to happen, and it does not. Quite a lot of research has sought to understand these kinds of failures, and we have gained important knowledge about the strategies infants use to make sense out of what they perceive to be logical inconsistencies.[22] I wrote about one such study in the first chapter of this book. On the whole, it seems to me that the body of this research reveals an important idea for the study of education. When the expectancies about the structure of a baby's world are violated, the learning begins. This is a failure of sorts, but it is just as assuredly our earliest instance of learning from failure.

This process continues unabated during the early years of our lives. Kathryn Schulz notes that "being wrong . . . appears to be a key means by which kids learn, and one associated as much as anything with absorption, excitement, novelty, and fun."[23] But then something happens. Both at home and at school, children begin to see the consequences of failing. Far from being a source of joyful experimentation, mistakes now result in correction or discipline. Children are certainly still learning from their failures, and much of this learning benefits them as they progress through the educational system, but their orientation to that failure changes. They figure out how to navigate around and past failure rather than through it. Because of this, they begin to close off an important pathway to their success. As college teachers, we have the opportunity to effect change here, to reinvigorate failure as an educational tool. Let's dig deeper into how we might do this.

Why College Students Fail

Like the young children I just discussed, college students too can fail for many different reasons. Trying to isolate one particular cause, however, is fruitless because there is almost always a network of interrelated factors operating to generate the particular errors and mistakes we see in our classrooms. As a framework for understanding this complexity, I am going to use that staple of Psych 101 courses everywhere: Maslow's hierarchy of needs. In 1943, Abraham Maslow published a now-classic article called "A Theory of Human Motivation." Although he was proposing a schema meant to account for the entirety of our motivations, his work has often been applied to education. Essentially, Maslow argued that our needs as human beings could be divided into two categories: basic needs and higher needs. He suggested that our higher needs could not be met if we had not satisfied our most basic needs, hence the notion of a hierarchy. Still further, one sub-category of need could not be fulfilled if a more fundamental need had not yet been met, even if both needs fell under Maslow's larger category of basic needs.[24]

If you do a Google search for Maslow's hierarchy of needs, you will likely find many instances of a pyramid-like illustration of his theory. The pyramid is the most popular representation of Maslow's hierarchy, though he himself did not use this image in the original paper. It does, however, remain a useful tool for explaining the ordering of needs. At the bottom of this metaphorical pyramid are the two classifications of basic needs that are most essential for human beings—physiological needs and safety needs. Needs that would fall into these groups include hunger, thirst, sleep, shelter, and psychological safety from fear. Maslow speaks of cognitive needs, what he describes as "the desires to know and to understand," only later in the paper, and he signals that these kinds of needs are subservient to those that are more basic.[25] While it may at first seem out of place to mention such elemental concepts in a book about college teaching, the important work of Sara Goldrick-Rab and the team at the Wisconsin HOPE Lab has demonstrated that hunger and housing insecurity are issues facing a significant number of college students.[26] I hope it's obvious that if students are wondering where their next meal is coming from or whether they will have a place to stay for the night, then they will be either unable to learn or, at the very least, to maximize their learning strategies.

We might also look at the importance of sleep. I don't know about you, but students at my university pride themselves on getting as little sleep as possible. This may be a badge of honor in the residential halls, but it has serious consequences for cognition. Tired brains cannot learn effectively, because sleep is such a basic need. And this is only scratching the surface.[27] There are a variety of other factors contributing to academic success that align with the basic level of Maslow's hierarchy, and our awareness of these issues helps us to understand why our students might not be achieving at the level we think is possible for them.

Consider for a moment the fear of failure, which plagues college students everywhere. Unfortunately, we've gotten ourselves into a fairly dire predicament here. Jessica Lahey describes the situation starkly: "We have taught our kids to fear failure, and in doing so, we have blocked the surest and clearest path to their success. That's certainly not what we meant to do, and we did it for all the best and well-intentioned reasons, but it's what we have wrought."[28] There is evidence to suggest that this fear begins very early in the lives of our children, and they carry it with them into our classrooms when they enter college.[29] As Lahey explains, it does not matter whether parents and teachers intend to instill this fear (although I hope it is unintentional, of course). Instead, the fear is generated by the many different cues children are given. The effect on learning can be dramatic, especially once these children become college students:

> A fear of failure can poison learning by creating aversions to the kinds of experimentation and risk taking that characterize striving, or by diminishing performance under pressure, as in a test setting. In the latter instance, students who have a high fear of making errors when taking tests may actually do worse on the test because of their anxiety. Why? It seems that a significant portion of their working memory capacity is expended to monitor their performance (How am I doing? Am I making mistakes?), leaving less working memory capacity available to solve the problems posed by the test.[30]

Although this response is certainly tied to the cognitive processes of memory, learning is primarily jeopardized for students who fear failure because their psychological safety remains an unresolved need. Students may fail simply because of their perceptions of failure, and the subsequent fear that occurs, irrespective of whether they have actually failed very much during their years in education. Unfortunately, because of the heavy consequences for failure at many institutions—via their grades in courses, their progress through curricula, GPA systems, graduation requirements, and more—these fears are not altogether unjustified. At a minimum, we should empathize with students who are trying to succeed in a system that prizes success over development. Indeed, empathy is one of the dominant themes of this chapter.

Beyond Maslow's hierarchy, there are other potential causes of our students' failures that affect cognition but are not fully cognitive in nature. Chief among these is stress in all of its heart-palpitating varieties. Regardless of its source, stress may be one of the most powerful deterrents to learning for our students. Stress can wreak some pretty serious havoc on "a particular set of cognitive skills located in the prefrontal cortex known as executive functions."[31] As the name "executive functions" indicates, these processes serve as a kind of command center and are nothing to trifle with. The biochemical reactions induced by stress, not least of which is the release of adrenaline, gear up our bodies for a physical response. To do so, cognition is suppressed so that we don't think too analytically about whether we should run from the threat under which our brains now imagine us to be. These are not ideal conditions for solving equations or sussing out the nuances of the Treaty of Paris.

Under extreme stress, students might even choke when performing intellectual tasks in which they have demonstrated repeated success. I want to say up front that I actually dislike the violent physicality of this analogy, because I think it serves only to further stigmatize failure, but choking is a well-documented phenomenon. Sian Beilock has built a career studying instances of choking, as a matter of fact. Throughout her work, Beilock has examined a variety of different contexts (such as athletics, business, and academics) where "sub-optimal performance" happens specifically "in response to a highly stressful situation."[32] Perhaps surprisingly, Beilock demonstrates that students with a higher degree of functioning in their working memories are more prone to choke on tasks they have aced in the past. Similar to what happens with other kinds of stress responses, it seems that choking is the result of a severe taxing of the working memory and a subsequent depletion of the brain's glucose supply.[33] Beilock describes the problem in the following way:

> The ability to perform difficult tasks declines over time— much in the same way that a muscle tires after exercise. In fact, glucose (which is a primary source of energy for the body's cells, including brain cells) becomes depleted when you continuously exert effort on a difficult thinking and reasoning task. If you don't take time to recoup your resources, your performance on whatever you do next can suffer.
>
> Glucose depletion may be especially problematic for those people highest in cognitive horsepower. Higher-working-memory individuals often tap a more extensive network of brain regions for performance than low-powered folks, so their brain cells need a lot of energy. This is because high-powered people tend to use the most cognitively demanding strategies to solve a problem.[34]

When stress enters a scene where both glucose levels and working memory are exhausted, particularly if those memories generally operate at a high level, then choking can occur. Thus, the very skill that we think would help our students the most—the ability to use multiple tactics when considering a problem—can ironically lead some to fail when they are performing in situations that elevate their stress levels.[35] We have all seen students with great track records do poorly on an exam. The potential role played by stress in this failure should make us think twice about immediately attributing this performance to a lack of studying (or worse).

Stress can come from a variety of sources. It can stem from the actions or expectations of an instructor or it can be self-imposed or it can be some combination of these. Less frequently, stress can also come from social interactions in the classroom. Just a few chapters ago, I was touting the importance of sociality for learning, but—like everything else—there is more than one side to the story. Social pressures can sometimes serve to stifle our learning. In *Being Wrong*, Kathryn Schulz recounts the famous experiments of Solomon Asch, who was interested in seeing to what degree "social conformity" had an effect on the ability of subjects to give correct answers.[36] In these experiments from the 1950s, Asch would place a participant in a room with other people, all of whom (unlike the participant) were privy to the purpose of the study. An experimenter would show the group a series of flashcards. On one flashcard there would be a vertical line, and then the other would have a series of three lines with different lengths. Each member of the group was asked to choose which line from the series was the same length as the single line. After a few rounds, the group members who were part of the experiment began to intentionally give obviously incorrect answers. Faced with this scenario, the participants who were not in the know concurred with the incorrect answers nearly 37 percent of the time on average. Various attempts to replicate versions of the Asch experiments have been conducted in the time since the original studies were completed, but a series of recent tests using an fMRI machine produced data suggesting that we may not even realize that we are aligning with the incorrect answer.[37] In other words, social forces can be so strong that they actually change the way we perceive information. It is not hard to see how this might come into play in our classrooms, particularly if we place a premium on collaborative learning or discussion-based pedagogies. Since we know how beneficial such strategies can be for our students, we must pay keen attention to how social dynamics are playing out in our courses.

At the nexus of fear, stress, and social pressure is the issue of stereotype threat. Stereotype threat has been in the higher education news quite a bit lately, and for good reason too, as it is pervasive and threatens the achievement of many groups of students, including under-represented minorities and women. Claude Steele and Joshua Aronson were the first to conduct research on stereotype threat, and Steele's popular book *Whistling Vivaldi* both tells the story of how he became interested in the topic and also summarizes his and Aronson's most important findings. Steele's early research on the subject involved stereotypes regarding women and mathematics. He wanted to determine whether social stigmas affected academic performance, so he co-designed an experiment where talented women and men would take a standardized math test. In one condition, the participants were told that that the test would reveal differences between genders, while in the other condition, participants were instructed that the *particular* test they were taking would not reveal anything about gender differences. Steele's discussion of his findings is fascinating: "And the results were dramatic. They gave us a clear answer. Among participants who were told the test did show gender differences, where the women could feel the threat of stigma confirmation, women did worse than equally skilled men, just as in the earlier experiment. But among participants who were told the test *did not* show gender differences, where the women were free of confirming anything about being a woman, *women performed at the same high level as equally skilled men. Their underperformance was gone.*"[38] These results led to an entire research program. Steele and Aronson studied students from various minority groups and eventually revealed that these populations were similarly affected by stereotypes, particularly when the students were strong academically and when the stereotype connected directly to a personal identity that was of value to the student. Taken as a whole, their research ultimately showed that "these effects might play a significant role in the underperformance in school and on standardized tests of major groups in our society."[39]

There are now hundreds of studies on stereotype threat and its pernicious effects on academic performance and on learning.[40] This work has reshaped discourse about student achievement and has allowed us to craft more successful student retention programs. Good teaching means being aware of the degree to which we are priming stereotypes in our classrooms and establishing environments that may cultivate stereotype threat. In the latter part of this chapter, I will provide some suggestions for strategies we might use to mitigate the damage stereotype threat can cause, but for now it is simply worth noting that—of all the contributors to student failure I have outlined thus far—stereotype threat might be the most deeply ingrained.

You'll notice that I haven't said a word about those causes of cognitive failures that are connected to the actual material we are teaching in our classrooms. We're about to get to those, but I want to emphasize that I have spent so much time on these other issues because, with the possible exception of stereotype threat, we talk about them so seldom as educators. Too often it can be easy to slip into the trap of seeing our classrooms as separate from the world, an intellectual oasis from the life beyond its walls. Nothing could be further from the truth. Students do not drop their worries, stressors, and needs at the door when they come to learn from us. Having a sense, then, of the psychological and social dimensions that affect learning can be a powerful tool for teachers.

GETTING STARTED

Empathizing with student concerns and issues can certainly be accomplished through the caring approach to pedagogy I discussed in the chapter on emotions, but one immediate (and practical) thing we can do to help students who are experiencing extreme stress and other kinds of difficulties is connected to the information we provide in our syllabi. Make clear to students the resources available at the university for support when it is needed. Some statements to this effect are likely mandatory for all syllabi at our universities, such as a description of disability-related services, but we can do more than this. Information about accessing tutoring services and the writing center can help students for whom getting additional academic support could relieve some of the stress and anxiety. On the other hand, making sure students also know where to find counseling services and the student health center can be equally beneficial. Finally, Sara Goldrick-Rab has even advocated for including a "basic needs security" statement on our syllabi for those students who are experiencing food or housing insecurity to find the support they need.[41]

Failure in the Classroom

Once we get down to the business of teaching and learning, we see a host of other problems involving cognition that can arise from the work our students are doing in our classes. Perhaps the most common of these relates to the knowledge structures and cognitive frameworks—what Ken Bain has called "mental models"—that students bring with them to our courses.[42] The degree to which students already have a foundation in place for understanding the concepts we teach will vary widely, and this variance will be reflected in their mental models regarding a particular subject. Teaching can feel like smooth sailing when a student's mental model is correct and complete, but this is not always the case. Instead, students have often developed mental models over the course of their education that are inadequate or inaccurate, which can hamper their ability to build the kind of new knowledge we discussed in the section on constructivism in the first chapter of this book. Although it can be relatively easy to identify when a student is struggling due to an issue with prior knowledge, it can be very difficult to change the problematic mental models.

Part of this difficulty is due to the neurobiology of cognition. In our brains, knowledge and information are not arranged into abstract models, though Bain's use of mental models is a helpful explanatory tool. Instead, as James Zull points out, "every fact we know, every idea we understand, and every action we take has the form of a network of neurons."[43] Millions of neurons are involved here, and each network is forged by the firing of synapses. The stronger the synaptic response, the more deeply ingrained the knowledge, and once a neuronal network has formed, it cannot simply be erased. Zull describes the pedagogical challenge of this structuring of neurons: "Whatever neuronal networks are in the student brain, a teacher cannot remove them. They are a physical fact. As we will see later, it may be possible to reduce the use of particular networks, or to use other networks in their place, and some networks may die out or weaken with disuse. But no teacher, with a wave of the hand, a red pen, or even with a cogent and crystal-clear explanation, can remove an existing neuronal network from a student's brain."[44] This biological reality of learning is true regardless of whether the neuronal network represents accurate or inaccurate knowledge. We can only build on existing networks; we cannot change the fact that such networks exist in the first place.

I actually find this scientific explanation to be liberating as a teacher. All of us have had those moments when we just could not figure out why a student, or a group of students, or even a whole class did not seem to understand a particular concept. It can be confusing, and some can even be tempted to just give up and move on to the next topic. Recognizing the neuronal basis of learning, however, gives us an important tool for helping these students. If we know that simple corrections cannot change these networks, then we need to try another approach that might aid in weakening those synaptic responses. To achieve this, we first need to recognize the areas in which students have the most misconceptions. Many faculty in STEM fields use concept inventories for this,[45] but a simple, homemade pre-test given at the beginning of the semester can work well too. Next, and most importantly, we need to create scenarios where "learners must . . . face a situation in which their mental model will not work (that is, will not help them explain or do something)"[46] so that we can potentially interrupt the reinforcement of those faulty networks. If students repeatedly run up against the failure of their inaccurate cognitive models, we heighten the possibility for those neuronal networks to get weaker and weaker.

Here is a fictional example (that may or may not be based on a true story) of how such a process might play out. Let's imagine there is a boy sitting in a second-grade classroom where the teacher is dutifully offering a social studies lesson. We'll call this boy "Josh." And let's say the teacher happens to be talking about presidents of the United States on this particular day. In an effort to make things relevant, the teacher explains that a fair number of former presidents are on our coins and currency. Maybe she even holds up one of her own dollars to explain. While all this is going on, let's pretend that our friend Josh isn't paying very close attention. I'm sure he's thinking about something studious rather than, say, baseball or video games. Through his distraction, he imagines he hears the teacher say that the *only* figures adorning US money are former presidents. This is a fairly simple mistake and one that could be easily corrected but is not at that particular moment. A few months later, Josh learns that the image of Alexander Hamilton is on the ten-dollar bill. For several years afterward, Josh believes that Alexander Hamilton was a president of the United States, and it takes an enterprising history teacher to help him figure out his mistake. She shows Josh a list of presidents. Hamilton is not on the list, and the synaptic connections holding Josh's network together are weakened. Perhaps even when he is older, Josh still has to stop and think for a moment about whether Hamilton was a president. This lasts until he has a particularly effective history class in which he reads some of the Federalist papers and learns all about Hamilton's role as the first Secretary of the Treasury. As a result, the early neuronal network falls into disuse, and a new one is constructed using remnants of the old one.

One can imagine similar scenarios in other disciplines. Have students developed misconceptions about one of Newton's laws of motion? Do a demonstration that illustrates the law, and then have them do the same demonstration again in groups. Are they bringing to your course a mental model that positions disability solely as a biological reality rather than a social construction? Ask them to walk around campus taking a census of accessible buildings. Are they operating under the assumption that "negative reinforcement" refers to punishment? Start playing a song by Britney Spears and tell students that you will not stop until someone gives you the correct answer. The examples here are legion, and the point is a serious one. If students do not confront these incomplete or inaccurate knowledge networks, significant errors can result.

The situation gets even more complex when cognitive models and networks are tied to personal beliefs and deeply held convictions.[47] Bain notes that students can even undergo a kind of "emotional trauma" when these sorts of models are altered.[48] In our example above, Josh did not have anything personal at stake in knowing whether Alexander Hamilton was president. He just needed to move from being incorrect to being correct. If Josh, however, had spent much of his early life idolizing Thomas Jefferson and later encountered the cognitive dissonance of Jefferson's roles both as a slaveholder and as a writer of the Declaration of Independence, then learning could be a more difficult prospect than merely facing the failure of a model. In this case, part of his sense of self is implicated in the shift. This is not just a case of developing more accurate knowledge. The same can be true for any students who are tasked with learning material that runs counter to their personal belief system. As teachers, we sometimes see this struggle playing out in courses that deal with religion, politics, social norms, or even evolutionary biology. It will not be an issue with every student, but it is likely an issue with some. They certainly *can* construct new models and establish neuronal connections that build more accurate knowledge. They most likely even want to do this. But it will be a difficult process for them, both emotionally and cognitively, and the struggle can inhibit the ability to learn.

Another element that can have an impact on whether our students learn effectively involves the capacity of the brain to manage its cognitive load. Once an individual's cognitive load crosses the threshold from challenging to overtaxing, learning is affected. Two types of load have been identified in the literature: intrinsic cognitive load and extraneous cognitive load. Intrinsic cognitive load is "determined by the interaction between the nature of the materials being learned and the expertise of the learner."[49] Intrinsic load can often be an issue with learners who have less expertise in a particular area. When students are new to a subject area, they need to balance multiple ideas, theories, facts, figures, and any number of other concepts in order to make headway in the discipline. The trouble is that they are processing each of these pieces as independent entities, which can overtax the ability of their brains to make sense of the whole picture. As students become more expert in an area, they build complex networks, such that all of these elements are engaged simultaneously. This diminishes the cognitive load and allows them to move on quickly to more challenging material.[50] As an example, think about what it is like for a student in an introductory biology class to be learning about photosynthesis for the first time. That student is juggling a variety of components: learning the parts of the plant, trying to understand the role of chlorophyll, and attempting to memorize a chemical equation. If we ask this student a fairly conceptual question about the importance of the glucose produced in the reaction, it is conceivable that he or she might struggle with this answer due to the high demand of the intrinsic cognitive load. Certainly not every student will make an error here, but the conditions are ripe for failure to occur.

Issues of intrinsic cognitive load can be most difficult for teachers to balance in courses like those frequently found in general education curricula, where we may be working with a diverse array of students that includes everyone from majors in our department to those with very little preparation in our discipline. In situations like this, it can be challenging to design the course so that we can minimize the problematic effects of intrinsic cognitive load, yet at the same time making the course challenging enough for those with more experience.

Extraneous cognitive load, on the other hand, refers to that which is "not necessary for learning . . . and that can be altered by instructional interventions."[51] This kind of cognitive load is often the culprit when students are using technology for non-pedagogical ends during class time. Even if they are searching Google for information relevant to the work of the course, they are still burdening cognitive resources that could be devoted to the intellectual work of the class. Lest this sound too much like a kids-these-days style of rant, I remember times when I was distracted as a student too, even though I did not have the same technological devices at my disposal. The key to a successful intervention, then, is to minimize distractions as much as possible without affecting the quality of student learning. By all means, use technology in the classroom, and allow your students to use it too, but create sound accountability structures in your syllabus to tackle distracting uses of technology. Other kinds of extraneous cognitive load can be harder to address but are just as prevalent. If you are teaching about behaviorism in your psychology course, and a student is trying to remember the details regarding what his high school teacher once told him about a famous psychology experiment where a researcher conditioned a young boy to fear furry or fuzzy objects (John Watson and the "Little Albert" fiasco), then that student's learning may be affected. Even though the attempted recall is tangentially relevant, given the topic of the class session, the student's learning suffers because his working memory is now crowded with superfluous information. Providing time during class for students to ask these kinds of questions (and being open to answering these types of questions as well) can help to alleviate the problems that can be caused by extraneous cognitive load.

Even if we are successful with helping students to learn in our own courses (and I am confident that we can be), there is—sadly—no guarantee that this learning will transfer to other domains. Transfer is a thorny issue that many educational researchers have tried to tackle. In fact, anecdotally speaking, this might be the kind of student failure that is most frustrating for faculty. I'm sure you've heard complaints that sound something like this: "I know that they learned such-and-such a concept in such-and-such a course! Why can't they do it in mine?!" The consternation is duly noted, but it is also worth saying that students are not intentionally trying to thwart our pedagogical plans. The reasons why students sometimes fail to apply what they have learned in the context of one course to that of another are varied. In *How Learning Works*, Susan Ambrose and her colleagues suggest that transfer of this kind can be impeded either when students "associate that knowledge too closely with the context in which they originally learned it and thus not think to apply it—or know how to apply it—outside that context" or when they "do not have a robust understanding of underlying principles and deep structure—in other words, if they understand what to do but not why."[52] One or both of these conditions could cause students to falter when asked to utilize knowledge created in other contexts. The first condition, in particular, is supported by research on what psychologists refer to as task switching.[53] Thus, if students only associate a problem-solving or an interpretive strategy with information they learned in a specific course, they will have difficulty importing it to the new context. What seems like an easy leap to make turns out to be quite challenging simply because of the way our brains organize information.

Taken individually, any one of the cognitive, psychological, or social factors I have discussed in the last two sections could lead students to fail in some aspect of our courses. Only rarely do any of these elements occur in isolation, though, so there is no shortage of challenges that we and our students face. Rather than allow failure to serve as a blockade against learning, however, we instead need to use it to our advantage.

GETTING STARTED

I briefly mentioned pre-tests at the beginning of this section, and they are an easily implemented tool that can help with all of the cognitive issues I have just described. The goal of a pre-test is for you, as the instructor, to gauge the level of conceptual understanding that students are bringing with them into your course. A brief pre-test, then, will certainly help you to assess prior knowledge, but it will also allow you to manage cognitive load and locate points for transfer. Pre-tests can be short and to-the-point, or they can be a bit more involved. To design a useful pre-test, I recommend sitting down when you are developing your syllabus and thinking about the 10–20 concepts that students simply *must* know from the outset if they are going to succeed in your course. You can then build multiple-choice or short-answer questions from these concepts. If you are teaching a course that occupies a specific spot in a sequence for your department's curriculum, you could also talk to the instructor of the course that feeds into yours and make this discussion the basis of your pre-test.

Learning from Failure

This is the part where I give you the good news. Failure can be one of our biggest allies in learning if we utilize it appropriately. As we've seen, our brains are designed to find and to construct knowledge from errors. "When we make mistakes," explains Jo Boaler, a renowned scholar in the field of mathematics education, "our brains spark and grow. Mistakes are not only opportunities for learning, as students consider the mistakes, but also times when our brains grow, even if we don't know we have made a mistake."[54] All we need to do as teachers is to tap into this capability. A successful deployment of failure-based pedagogies, then, depends on two related strategies: 1) preparing students to learn from failure, and 2) designing opportunities where students can fail and then subsequently build conceptual understanding as a result of this process.

The first of these strategies, to prepare students psychologically and emotionally to handle and process failure, is essential but may seem at first to fall outside of the job description for most faculty. In his study of successful college students, Ken Bain has found that "strong measures of self-efficacy" are a crucial element to overcoming failure, but it can be challenging to see how we can cultivate this in our classrooms.[55] Thankfully, there have been some researchers who have found intersections between this kind of preparation and the work we do as educators. Carol Dweck is one such person. If you have been anywhere near higher education over the last few years, I would bet that you've heard of Dweck and her work on mindsets. Dweck contends that human beings essentially fall into two camps with respect to our beliefs about our own intelligence. Some people have a "fixed mindset," in which they "believ[e] that [their] qualities are carved in stone."[56] Those with a fixed mindset consider their intelligence to be static and see limitations on their ability to build new knowledge or skills. A "growth mindset," on the other hand, is different and is "based on the belief that your basic qualities are things you can cultivate through your efforts. Although people may differ in every which way—in their initial talents and aptitudes, interests, or temperaments—everyone can change and grow through application and experience."[57] Dweck's findings suggest that growth mindsets can be developed over time and are key to achieving success in many different spheres of life.

There is now a wealth of data from follow-up studies by Dweck and others to demonstrate that cultivating growth mindsets for students leads to substantial improvements in their academic performance, whereas fixed mindsets have detrimental effects on students' achievement. Furthermore, recent studies in the field of cognitive neuroscience have begun to confirm that growth mindsets do indeed lead to better gains in academic endeavors.[58] The question for us to consider, then, has to do not so much the value of a growth mindset but the ways in which we move students toward developing this kind of mindset. Some faculty are beginning to use surveys and other instruments developed by those who have been studying mindsets.[59] Some are designing their own interventions. More simply, just talking to our students about failures (either our own or the failures of well-known scholars) can go a long way toward helping them to see that perceived obstacles are not ends unto themselves, but instead are important points along the journey toward growth.[60]

Another frequently cited, though perhaps more controversial, approach to preparing students to persist through failure originates with Angela Duckworth, a psychologist who won a MacArthur Genius Grant in 2013. Duckworth has pioneered the study of what she has termed "grit," a concept that underscores the importance of effort and the ability to continue to work hard in the presence of obstacles. This capacity for perseverance is grit. According to Duckworth's studies, when all other things are equal, grit is the deciding factor in predicting who will succeed and who will falter.[61] Talent is simply not enough to account for success. As she succinctly notes, "what matters is grit."[62] Duckworth's findings, and her data to support them, have recently been met with some degree of skepticism, pointedly so in a new study by Marcus Credé, Michael C. Tynan, and Peter D. Harms. They especially see problems with her claims for grit's "predictive power."[63]

To be perfectly honest, I don't really have a horse in this race. Some of the evidence in the Credé, Tynan, and Harms article does suggest that Duckworth may have overstated her case, but she has defended her research in other forums.[64] The reason I am less interested in this question is because the emphasis on whether grit can predict achievement actually distracts us from what I think is most valuable about Duckworth's work with respect to education. If we look past the hype, there is something at the core of the concept that is valuable for instructors at any level, and it stems from Duckworth's time as a math teacher in middle and high school, which is when her interest in studying grit began. As she reflects on her experiences in those classrooms, she recalls the following:

> Gradually, I began to ask myself hard questions. When I taught a lesson and the concept failed to gel, could it be that the struggling student needed to struggle just a bit longer? Could it be that I needed to find a different way to explain what I was trying to get across? Before jumping to the conclusion that talent was destiny, should I be considering the importance of effort? And, as a teacher, wasn't it my responsibility to figure out how to sustain effort—both the students' and my own—just a bit longer?[65]

That last sentence really gets to the heart of grit's potential for education. If we can teach our students the strategies necessary for working "just a bit longer," we can help them to reimagine failure. From this perspective, we can show them that what they thought was failure might just have been a moment where they stopped too soon. A variety of basic metacognitive strategies can be used in teaching them how to delay this stopping point or to start up again, thus allowing them to break through the stigma associated with getting a wrong answer. I like this aspect of grit, and I think it is valuable to pursue.

Still other researchers believe that grit does not go far enough. Anindya Kundu advocates instead for teaching agency to students. "Like grit," Kundu suggests, "agency requires action but considers one's ability to act and create change, without glossing over structural inequalities. Agency is not an individual trait. Schools, groups, and communities can organize to grow agency for collective interests."[66] Kundu's criticism regarding inequity is crucial and applies not just to grit but to mindsets as well. So much of the research seems to gloss over the socioeconomic status of communities that would affect a student's ability to enact grit or foster a growth mindset. It may be much easier for a student from a privileged background even to think about grit, for example, let alone try to put it into practice. Only once we peel back the surface and acknowledge the structures that influence our students' perceptions of failure and impede their progress can we hope to make any gains.

This brings us back again to stereotype threat. Our work to cultivate growth mindsets, grit, and agency can be substantially undermined if we do not take proactive steps to minimize the risk posed by the presence of stereotype threat in our classrooms. My Rice colleague Robin Paige, whom you may remember from my discussion of her work on metaquestions and course design, has curated a series of very helpful strategies for reducing stereotype threat. These include:

- Teaching students about stereotype threat
- Providing students with a sense of belonging and external attributions for anxiety
- Providing opportunities for self-affirmation and priming

positive aspects of the self that are not related to performance in the classroom
- Providing positive role models and examples of individuals who have performed successfully in your field or discipline
- De-emphasizing threatened social identities
- Promoting diversity and diverse perspectives
- Creating an inclusive environment in the classroom[67]

By helping students to achieve a metacognitive awareness of the negative consequences of stereotypes on their academic performance and by prioritizing a classroom climate that privileges diversity and affirmation, we can create an environment that fosters their sense of psychological safety. As we have seen in other chapters of this book as well, this kind of security is necessary for learning in general and for working through failure in particular. However, fundamental to all the methods I have outlined—growth mindsets, grit, agency, and minimizing stereotype threat—is the notion that students must ultimately develop the tools that allow them to push through failure on their own. An effective teacher can help set students on this path, and the approaches I have been outlining over the last few pages can empower them to take the steps necessary to construct this crucial habit of mind.

Once students are mentally prepared to productively process their failures, we can then create opportunities in our courses that utilize moments of failure to enhance learning. This is the second of the two strategies that are essential for fruitfully incorporating pedagogies of failure into our teaching practices. As we begin to take a close look at some of these techniques, it is wise to consider the important admonition from Jessica Lahey: "Of course, there's a fine line between struggles that promote learning and struggles that doom learning and intrinsic motivation. First-year Latin students can't translate *The Aeneid* and asking them to do so would not result in learning but frustration and anger."[68] She is absolutely right. We cannot give students a task that lies so far outside their cognitive experience that they have no entry point for tackling it. Instead, we are interested in those moments of failure that are actually conducive to further learning. In order for this to happen, the challenge we give students must be accessible to them either through prior knowledge or scaffolded coaching, and it must also be generative in building new networks that serve to enhance students' conceptual understanding.

One of the early leaders in researching these kinds of teaching methods has been Robert Bjork. In a 1992 paper, Bjork and his co-author Richard Schmidt discuss the value of introducing "difficulties" into the learning process.[69] Bjork would later build on this concept and coin the term "desirable difficulties" to describe a series of techniques designed to help students learn new information more effectively. Much of his subsequent research agenda has been devoted to exploring desirable difficulties in more detail. Such difficulties, according to Bjork and Elizabeth Bjork (another of his frequent co-authors), "are desirable because they trigger encoding and retrieval processes that support learning, comprehension, and remembering. If, however, the learner does not have the background knowledge or skills to respond to them successfully, they become undesirable difficulties."[70] A typical desirable difficulty will be challenging enough to enact predictable moments of error or outright failure, but because Bjork's theories rely on frequent practice, students develop confidence that they will be able to surmount those instances when they encounter roadblocks.

Bjork frequently cites several strategies that make use of desirable difficulties for learning, which include working with students to space out their practice intervals, asking them to come up with their own answers rather than providing answers for them (the "generation effect"), and incorporating a technique known as interleaving. By way of explanation, Bjork and Bjork themselves provide what I think is a particularly illustrative example of interleaving: "When participants were asked to learn the styles of each of 12 artists based on a sample of 6 paintings by each artist, interleaving a given artist's paintings among the paintings by other artists—versus presenting that artist's paintings one after another (blocking)—enhanced participants' later ability to identify the artist responsible for each of a series of new paintings."[71] Although this approach was tough for students at first, they learned more than those who practiced blocking. Like many practices that employ desirable difficulties, you will find that students experience minor episodes of failure (and some degree of frustration) with interleaving, but the research clearly shows that the learning gains far outweigh the short-term setbacks.[72] In order to help students push through the initial failures, it is a good idea to keep the interleaving sessions as brief as possible at first until they can build up a tolerance for error, so to speak. Once students become accustomed to the complexity of the tasks, though, interleaving and other desirable difficulties can lead to significant cognitive gains.

Another strategy with great promise for improving our students' learning has been developed by Manu Kapur. Kapur's work is some of the most exciting I have encountered in the time I have been doing research for this book, and it centers on what he calls "productive failure." As opposed to the techniques that utilize desirable difficulties, where the emphasis is on encoding information with which students need to be (and should be) familiar, applications of productive failure focus on providing students with problems that lie outside of their immediate capabilities. At first this seems counterintuitive, since I took great pains to say earlier that giving students problems they cannot solve would stifle learning rather than augment it, but productive failure relies in important ways on the activation of prior knowledge. Kapur summarizes his approach this way: "Productive failure engages students in solving problems requiring concepts they have yet to learn, followed by consolidation and instruction on the targeted concept. By failure, I simply mean that students will typically not be able to generate or discover the correct solution(s) by themselves. However, to the extent that students are able to use their prior knowledge to generate suboptimal or even incorrect solutions to the problem, the process can be productive in preparing them to learn better from the subsequent instruction that follows."[73] Both stages of the process—the problem-solving attempt and the instruction afterward—are important for the success of this pedagogy, but the reliance on prior knowledge is equally as vital. If we do not provide students with a pathway into the problem, they will not make enough headway to justify the failure that is built into the method. As teachers then help students to compare their solutions and their procedures for tackling the problem to the correct answers, the students are able to target exactly where they themselves need to build more conceptual understanding. Because these areas of need will vary widely, productive failure allows us to tailor instruction almost to the level of each individual. Kapur's studies have begun to demonstrate the sizable gains students can make in this kind of environment.[74]

With productive failure, everything depends on the design of the task we give to students. An ideal implementation, therefore, would be to develop a problem that draws in part on a concept with which students are already conversant, but also hinges on one or more concepts that they have not yet encountered. The problem must also "admit multiple solutions, strategies, and representations, that is, afford sufficient problem and solution spaces for exploration" so that students can have a variety of entry points in attempting their solutions.[75] For example, let's imagine a basic, introductory physics course where students are already comfortable solving problems about force using everyone's favorite, well-known formula Force = Mass x Acceleration. As a next step, we want these students to have a solid understanding of pressure. The formula for pressure depends on first calculating force (Pressure = Force / Area), but we are not going to tell them that yet. Instead, we give them ten minutes at the beginning of class to solve a problem asking them how much pressure is being exerted by a pen weighing X grams when it is laying on its side (thus covering an area of Y mm) versus when it is balanced on its point (thus covering Z mm). Of course, because you would be more knowledgeable than me, you would fill in these variables with real numbers so that students could actually engage with the problem. As they work on it, they will most likely recognize that force is somehow an important element, but they may hit a roadblock in determining how force connects to pressure. Importantly for this methodology, we need to make sure they come up with an answer so that they can compare it and their solution process to the correct answer. As they identify where they went awry, the potential is there for them to develop an understanding of pressure that is deeper than if we simply gave them the formula at the outset.[76]

Productive failure is easiest to envision in those disciplines where problem solving is most common. What is less clear to me is how to import Kapur's method into humanities and social science courses, but I would like to offer some possibilities here. In some courses, students could analyze interviews, data sets, or studies that build on, but go beyond, concepts they have already explored. Having discussed the connections between demographic characteristics and smoking, for example, you could present students with data that shows relationships between demographic information and alcohol abuse. The context will be different, but students can use the tools they have already developed to interpret possible connections. The ensuing instruction would then reveal the strengths and weaknesses in students' logic. I could also imagine a similar approach with psychology experiments or formulas in economics. For courses in the humanities, I think primary sources are the key to introducing productive failure methods. In the humanities we often lecture briefly or lead discussions on philosophical ideas, historical background, models for literary interpretation, and much more. If we follow one of these sessions by providing students with a related primary source (but withhold any contextual information), and we ask them to make sense of what is going on in the source, then we might be able to constructively use Kapur's work for our own ends as well. Regardless of discipline, though, I think productive failure techniques have great potential for our pedagogical endeavors.

I would like to close this section on pedagogies of failure by mentioning one other method that intrigues me, although I offer the caveat that there is currently less data available by which we might judge its efficacy. This teaching practice, which I think could be easily imported into a variety of disciplines, involves students verbally identifying and explaining mistakes they find in a sample problem. The work I have found on this technique comes out of physics education research, but I think it is easy to see the transferability here to activities that move beyond problem solving. In many ways, it may be ideal for courses in which writing plays a key part, but we can probably push it even further, particularly with more advanced students, by providing them with sections from published studies or constructing intentionally flawed hypotheses for them to assess. One important feature of this strategy is that students need to actually verbalize their analysis, which allows them to learn from each other. Fundamentally, through this

206

process of recognizing and explicating errors, "students are them-selves able to examine whether a mistake is a conceptual misunderstanding" or just a logistical issue.[77] In turn, this can help them to refine aspects of their own comprehension.

There are, of course, many other approaches we could discuss here. Some teachers have even begun to periodically highlight their "favorite errors" from students and to explore these mistakes (with student approval) during class.[78] Personally, I'm not sure I would go this far, because it seems to me that the social dynamics would be difficult here, but it does speak to the range of methods people are now trying in an effort to aid their students as they attempt to learn from failure.

GETTING STARTED

If you are interested in implementing pedagogies of failure into your courses, an easy first step would be to try out a modified form of Kapur's productive failure method. Carve out some time to present students with a problem or question that you know they can only partially answer. Give them a few minutes to sketch out some possible approaches for a solution and then, as a group, discuss the difficulties they encountered. Where are the gaps in their knowledge? Where do they need a firmer grounding in the underlying concepts? Then you can use this discussion as a jumping off point for the work of the class session. This strategy allows you the benefit of introducing failure as a learning tool in a low-pressure environment.

What is the Error Climate of Your Course?

Effectively employing these various strategies that promote student learning through failure hinges in many ways on the error climate of the course.[79] Gabriele Steuer and Markus Dresel define a "favourable error climate" as "the perception, evaluation and utilization of errors as integral elements of the learning process within the social context of the classroom"[80] and have determined the following elements as being fundamental to a course's error climate:

1. Error tolerance by the teacher
2. Irrelevance of errors for assessment
3. Teacher support following errors
4. Absence of negative teacher reactions
5. Absence of negative classmate reactions
6. Taking the error risk
7. Analysis of errors
8. Functionality of errors for learning[81]

Ultimately, they found "significant positive associations" with respect to the "interrelation between error climate and achievement."[82] They conclude by saying that "not only emotional climate aspects, but in particular the cognitive aspects of the error climate in the classroom seem to be important for learning from errors."[83]

Although Steuer and Dresel are primarily focused on the perception of students in German secondary schools, I believe their findings are applicable to higher education as well.[84] As instructors in colleges and universities, we should strive to create what I would call an *error-positive* climate in our courses. In an error-positive climate, faculty believe that errors and mistakes provide valuable opportunities for growth and learning, and they design courses and assignments that reflect this belief.[85] There is plenty we can do to adjust error climate and move toward one that is more positive—including trying out some of the suggestions in this chapter—but we need to assess the climate before any changes we institute have the potential to make a significant impact. If we try to implement a pedagogy of failure, but we have not yet addressed one or more of the factors affecting the error climate of our course, then we are likely to meet with limited results. Failure can only be a mechanism for learning if it is valued as such by both the teacher and the students.

Patricia Taylor, an assistant professor of English at Briar Cliff University, has thought a lot about the power of failure and about developing an error-positive climate in her courses—so much so, in fact, that she now addresses the issue in her syllabus. She incorporates the following language into the requirements for all of her courses:

One of the greatest hindrances to a student's active learning can be fear of failure: fear of looking silly or stupid in front of a classmate or faculty member, or fear of not getting a good grade on a project. Students have sometimes been taught that they need to be perfect, or as close to perfect as possible, to be rewarded. This is especially true for many . . . students who have been taught, explicitly or implicitly, that their identity and intellectual worth is tied up in test scores and GPAs.

However, as a professor, I think that there are things more important than perfection: curiosity, risk taking, persistence, integrity, and self-awareness. College courses ideally are places where students learn the value of experimentation with ideas, techniques, and even failure itself. I want you, in the words of Edward Burger, to make for yourselves "a mind enlivened by curiosity and the intellectual audacity to take risks and create new ideas, a mind that sees a world of unlimited possibilities."

For this reason, a portion of your final grade (5%) will be based not on how much you fail, but how you handle failure. Have you been willing to challenge yourself to take risks that might result in failure? Have you been aware of when you have failed, and refused to give up in the face of failure? Have you found ways to use your failure to create something new and interesting? Have you grown from your failures? I hope this grade category will give you the freedom to try new things, and even to fail at them, and to come back having learned something from the experience. To earn these points, at the end of the semester you will write a reflection (300–500 words) that describes your risk taking, your experience of failure in the course, and what you learned from both.[86]

This is clearly a very thoughtful approach, and it achieves several ends. First, it makes evident to students that failure is vital for learning to take place. Additionally, though, Patricia destigmatizes failure for her students by making it an actual learning objective and by fusing it with curiosity, courage, and other intellectual values. From the outset of her courses, students know that they are not to view errors as obstacles but as steps toward the goal of understanding.

A Laboratory for Failure: Ann Saterbak, Matthew Wettergreen, and ENGI 120 at Rice University

By now, you're probably thinking, "This sounds good, but what would a course that truly valued failure look like?" I'd be thinking that, too, if I were in your shoes. The truth is that there are many problem- or project-based courses at universities around the world that could serve as models, but the one with which I am most familiar can be found at my home university. Every semester, Ann Saterbak and Matthew Wettergreen teach ENGI 120: Introduction to Engineering Design to a room packed with eager Rice freshmen. Only first-year students are permitted to take this course, and it fills up quickly despite that fact that it is an elective. At the beginning of the semester, students listen to pitches from members of the local community describing real-world problems to solve. Students are then put together into teams of four or five based on their project preferences. Their goal is to design a viable solution (or at least a prototype) by the end of the semester, which is when they make a formal presentation to the project's sponsors. When the students begin, they know that a range of possible solutions for the problem exists, but they do not yet have a sense of which direction they will take, nor do they have a clear idea as to what the design process will look like. At a global level, then, failure is always possible, while success may be elusive. Students are not intimidated by these conditions, however. In fact, they thrive in the environment the instructors have created for them.

During the design phase itself, failure is both expected and encouraged. According to the instructors, if the students are not open to trying out a host of different ideas and learning from multiple failures, then they will find it hard to develop a workable solution. Dead-ends are part of the process of discovery and invention. Ann and Matthew encourage students to make the most of their errors and then use them to push their ideas further. I have been fortunate enough to observe the work of this course on several occasions,[87] and I can tell you that there is a kind of excitement that I have only rarely witnessed among students as they work on their projects. Countless hours are spent outside of class time as well, because students are eager to put their best models forward at the end of the semester. Since its inception in 2011, the course has produced dozens of successful projects, including—among many others—a feeding apparatus for giraffes at the Houston Zoo, medical equipment for hospitals in Africa, and a wheelchair for a patient with arthrogryposis. Although the ostensible goal of ENGI 120 is to develop future engineers who are creative and who understand the hard work it takes to design solutions, Ann Saterbak and Matthew Wettergreen are also teaching students how to draw important lessons from their failures.

A Final Word about Grades

Thus far, I have been avoiding the elephant in the room, but it is time to address the most powerful obstacle to implementing pedagogies of failure in our courses. This unruly elephant trying its best to knock down everything I have set up in this chapter is grades. Grades seem like a good idea, and on the surface they appear to have the potential to be useful, but by the end they subvert all the work you have been trying to do. In an ideal world, grading "includes tailoring the test or assignment to the learning goals of the course, establishing criteria and standards, helping students acquire the skills and knowledge they need, assessing student learning over time, shaping student motivation, and feeding back results so students can learn from their mistakes, communicating about students' learning to the students and to other audiences, and using results to plan future teaching methods. When we talk about grading, we have student learning most in mind."[88] Although I would encourage us to work hard to make grades reflect more of these noble goals, the trouble is that they so rarely do. No matter how much we try, grades consistently communicate to students that they fall short of an ideal, regardless of the degree to which they may have improved over the course of a semester, a year, or an academic career. Grades stigmatize failure in ways that are sometimes unrecoverable. They increase the kind of competition among students that distracts from the goals we are trying to achieve in our classrooms. They become prizes for students to win rather than signs that point to actual learning. In the end, grades are the quintessential extrinsic motivator, whereas educational pursuits need to be primarily intrinsic if they are to be transformational.

My work on this book has led me to a singular conclusion regarding grades: while they can serve as markers of competence, they are antithetical to the natural processes by which human beings learn. Early hominins were not graded as they learned how to fashion tools. We do not give babies grades while they explore. If anything joins together the vast history of human learning, in fact, it is feedback, not grades. Although a case could be made for viewing grades as a kind of feedback, students do not build conceptual knowledge simply because we attach to their work an indicator of how closely they align with constructed norms. Instead, they only learn deeply when we give them suggestions for how to improve, when we ask them questions that allow them to spot their errors, when a conversation leads to a new way of seeing the world.

At the same time, we cannot singlehandedly change the educational system as it now stands. I wish we could, but—sadly—we cannot. If we truly want to build courses that position pedagogies of failure at the center, then we will need to work from inside a structure that places a high value on grades. One way to do this is to rethink the grading model for our courses. Designing courses with a limited number of assignments or exams, each of which is worth a significant percentage of the final grade, only reinforces the detrimental elements of grades. Instead, we can think about creating more frequent assignments that count for less in the overall scheme of the course. As we lower the stakes like this, we provide more freedom for our students to risk failing in order to learn. No student is going to take such risks on a midterm exam worth 40 percent of the final grade, because the potential consequences are too dire. We need to distribute this weight in order for our students to have room to learn. In fact, I am a strong advocate of implementing a variety of low- or no-stakes assignments for which we primarily give feedback. By doing so, we can emphasize to them that the value of our courses comes not from what grade they earn but from the knowledge they build, the understanding they achieve, and the interactions between teacher and student that allow for such gains.

Another way to overthrow the despotic reign of grades in our universities is to shift our grading philosophy entirely. More and more faculty have moved to contract-grading, specifications-grading, or portfolio-based systems in their courses as a way to get around the more damaging effects caused by the extrinsic motivation of grades. Although each of these grading methods have slightly different features, all of them (especially specifications grading) emphasize that students should be "graded pass/fail on individual assignments and tests or on bundles or modules of assignments and tests."[89] These models allow students to focus more on the process of learning instead of the outcome of every assignment. Ultimately, we still need to give final grades for the course, but at least we will have changed the nature of the game a bit with respect to our desired outcomes. Above all, one thing remains certain. If we are to teach our students to learn from their failures, we must pay attention to the role played by grades in our courses.

GETTING STARTED

To help our students shift their focus from grades to learning, we need to separate evaluation from feedback. One step in this direction would be to choose one of the courses you are teaching and develop a small assignment, or select one piece of a larger assignment, for which you will give feedback but no grade. Brief essays and short problem sets are always good options for this kind of activity. The purpose here is simply to give students some help and support without the stigma of evaluation. If it works in the context of this one assignment, think about ways you could make this approach more widespread in your courses.

Failing Better

Nearly every book or article you will read about failure cites, at some point or another, Samuel Beckett's oft-repeated maxim, "Ever tried. Ever failed. No matter. Try again. Fail again. Fail better."[90] Up until now I have resisted, but I'm afraid it's my turn, if for no other reason than I really like Beckett's writing. Beyond my personal predilections, though, the passage so nicely captures the essence of what I am arguing in this chapter. Beckett valorizes failing here rather than trying. For him, it is the quality of our failures that matters most. For our purposes, failing better suggests a kind of cycle where we continually fail and then learn from that failure in order to refine our understanding. There is no stopping point to the cycle because failure is not a negative. In many ways, Beckett is explaining that failure and learning are one and the same. This certainly holds true for our classrooms as well. Quite simply, students must (not should, but must) fail in order to learn. As teachers, it is our job to help them do so.

KEY TAKEAWAYS

· Students will arrive in our classrooms having experienced the stigma and negative associations of failure throughout their time in school. We must work to change this by providing opportunities for low-stakes failure so that students can take the risks necessary to enact deep learning.

· Our brains are adept at learning from failure, and in many ways they evolved for this purpose.

· Students may encounter failure in our courses for psychological, emotional, and cognitive reasons. Often a variety of these factors are in play when students are struggling to build understanding.

· A student whose basic needs—food, drink, sleep, shelter—are not met cannot learn as effectively as he or she might if these needs were fulfilled. Another way to think about this: A hungry brain cannot learn. A tired brain cannot think.

· In order to successfully learn from failure, students need to know how to cope with it psychologically. Working with them to cultivate growth mindsets, grit, agency, and other resiliency strategies will aid them in this process.

· Co-curricular initiatives at the institutional level can be beneficial here and augment work instructors are doing in their own classes. One example is the "Stop and Grow" program at Rice University, designed and facilitated by Sandra Parsons, which helps students to develop growth mindsets. See http://stopandgrowrice.wordpress.com for more information.

- Failure-based pedagogies help students to confront the limits of their knowledge and then provide tools for learning from these moments of difficulty in order to develop better understanding.

- Let's all agree to get rid of grades. What do you say? Not possible? Okay, then we'll need to find more ways to give feedback independent of grades so that our efforts to help students learn from failure will be more fruitful.

There and Back Again

The academy is not paradise. But learning is a place where paradise can be created. The classroom, with all its limitations, remains a location of possibility.

—bell hooks, *Teaching to Transgress*

Look at what a lot of things there are to learn.

—Merlyn, in T. H. White's *The Once and Future King*

I have recently had occasion to become a student again, albeit not in the traditional sense. As part of my work at our teaching center, I facilitate a practicum for graduate students where participants have the opportunity to design thirty-minute teaching demonstrations several times over the course of a semester and then get feedback on each of these from me and their peers. I really enjoy my work with this program, not least because I get the chance to work with talented folks from a wide range of disciplines. The topics for these demonstrations range from bioengineering to philosophy and everything in between. Most of the time I am conversant enough with the subject matter to follow along with the lesson and to engage with the material. Sometimes I am a bit more out of my element, and I need to ask a few questions to get up to speed (just like any other introductory-level student!). In one situation, though, I was completely clueless and felt as if I would only be able to comment on the teaching behaviors of the PhD student I was observing because I had absolutely no idea what was going on with respect to the content. The subject? Calculus. This is the story of how one talented teacher took me from frustration to a basic understanding of functions and limits.

As a preface to this tale, you should know that I have not studied calculus in over twenty years. I took AP Calculus in high school and, despite the fact that I received an A in the course, I scored a two on the AP test. Even at the ripe old age of 18, I could tell that there was a bit of a disconnect between those two outcomes. Looking back, I realize that I had figured out how to solve basic problems and work my way through an equation or two, but I could not apply these skills to problems I had never seen before. Also, I didn't have a clear sense of the purpose of calculus. Combine these two issues together and you have yourself a pretty common learning dilemma. My state of mathematical confusion continued unabated until the spring of 2017, when Emily Hendryx—a PhD student in computational and applied mathematics at Rice—helped me comprehend a foundational concept in calculus.

Emily's goal over the course of her three demonstrations was to teach us about the importance of functions and the concept of limits. To achieve her aims, she started us off slowly, providing us with examples of functions and then we were asked to sketch some basic functions. This was a very welcome entrée, considering I was starting from a point where I said, "Wait a minute, $f(x)$ and y are the same thing?" In subsequent lessons, Emily asked us to brainstorm our own definitions for what a limit might be before she explained the actual definition, she got us to conceptualize limits by thinking about the speed of an orange an inch before it hits the ground after it has been dropped from a second-story window, and there was a lot of group problem solving. She circulated the room during the times that we were working and helped all of us, especially me, when we got stuck. I was still struggling a bit after the first two sessions, but everything clicked for this humanities guy when Emily opened her final demonstration by discussing the history of calculus and talked about Augustin-Louis Cauchy (1789–1857), who did some of the earliest work on limits. As Emily walked us through Cauchy's description of limits in "Lectures on the Infinitesimal Calculus" and showed us some of the diagrams Cauchy used to explain limits, I finally understood them. My performance on the final assessment Emily had written for that day was not perfect, but I felt I actually learned something in a field with which I had personally struggled.

I was reminded of Emily's pedagogical success when I attended a recent conference and the keynote speaker spoke about the importance of wonder in learning. Emily worked hard to help everyone in the room discover a sense of wonder as we found the limits of functions. That's monumental in itself, but she paired this with a variety of strategies designed to tackle learning from a number of different angles. Emily's approach to teaching is directly in line with what I have been arguing over the course of this book. I see learning as an expansive terrain that is difficult to map if we use only one method. Our natural systems for learning are deeply connected to our evolution as a species and to our development as individuals from infancy to adulthood. This is akin to what Susan Debra Blum has called "learning in the wild," a category she sets in opposition to "learning in school."[1] Blum is one of the few researchers to acknowledge that an interdisciplinary approach to human development, anthropology, and cognition can lead to greater understanding about education, and her exploration of the subject has parallels with my own. Blum, however, believes that it would take a "revolution" to redesign our educational systems to account for the fundamental ways in which people learn.[2] Here is where I disagree with her. I don't think we actually need a revolution. We can help our students make tremendous gains simply by shifting our pedagogical practices in ways that reflect this research. We do not have to dismantle and rebuild our universities from the ground up just yet. Let's first try relying more on teaching techniques that situate our students in the broader context of human learning. It is true that some of these strategies are more complex than others, but the changes can be incremental and still be effective. The brain often responds quickly and powerfully to practices designed to meet it on its own terms.

I think the best news of all is this: each and every person who teaches college students can use this knowledge about the ways in which human beings learn to determine what will and will not work in our classrooms. We can avoid the educational fads that come and go and shun the buzzwords that can sometimes shape the discourse about these matters. After all, it turns out that effective teaching has been around for millennia.

NOTES

—

INTRODUCTION: HOW HUMAN BEINGS LEARN

1. Recent works include B. Carey, *How We Learn*; and P. Brown, Roediger III, and McDaniel, *Make It Stick*. Carey even suggests that "learning science" and "the study of memory" mean the same thing (193).

2. Outstanding examples of this approach include Bransford, et al., *How People Learn*; and Ambrose, et al., *How Learning Works*.

3. For one example, see Frensch and Rünger, "Implicit Learning," 13–18.

4. Qtd. in North, "Dangers."

5. See Willingham, *Why Don't Students*, 113–29.

6. Willingham, *Why Don't Students*, 113.

7. Gómez, *Apes, Monkeys, Children,* ix.

8. Love, "Conceptual Change," 1.

9. S. Carey, *Origin of Concepts*, 461–62.

10. Gopnik, "Scientist as Child," 490.

11. Gopnik, Meltzoff, and Kuhl, *Scientist in the Crib*, 155.

12. Izard, et al., "Newborn Infants," 10382–85.

13. G. Miller, "Brain Evolution," 288.

14. Zuk, *Paleofantasy*, 57.

15. Zuk, *Paleofantasy*, see especially 44–66.

16. P. Brown, Roediger III, and McDaniel, *Make It Stick*, 8.

17. Tokuhama-Espinosa, *New Science*.

18. If you do see a medievalist working in a physics lab, please let me know. I'd like to see what is going on.

CHAPTER 1. CURIOSITY

1. I first tackled the issue of the red cups in a blog post: "Active Learning is Not Our Enemy," *A Lifetime's Training.*

2. Kang, et al., "Wick in the Candle," 963.

3. Loewenstein, "Psychology of Curiosity," 75.

4. Voss and Keller, *Curiosity and Exploration,* ix; 127–37.

5. Loewenstein, "Psychology of Curiosity," 77.

6. Berlyne, *Conflict.*

7. Loewenstein, "Psychology of Curiosity," 87.

8. Leslie, *Curious,* 34–41; and Jirout and Klahr, "Children's Scientific Curiosity," 127ff.

9. Grossnickle, "Disentangling," 26.

10. Bardo, Donohew, and Harrington, "Psychobiology of Novelty Seeking," 26.

11. fMRI stands for functional magnetic resonance imaging. As a former athlete, I've had my share of MRIs for various injuries, but no one was asking me trivia questions while they were happening. I count this as a good thing. An fMRI, on the other hand, is typically used to collect data about brain activity for experimental purposes.

12. Kang, et al., "Wick in the Candle," 971.

13. Gruber, Gelman, and Ranganath, "States of Curiosity," 493.

14. As I was embarking on revisions for this book, a new study on curiosity—penned by acclaimed science writer Mario Livio—was published. Livio also cites the work of both Kang and Gruber as he builds up to his argument regarding the purpose of curiosity: "Modern research in psychology and neuroscience suggests that curiosity (at least the epistemic kind) is a mental decision process that aims at maximizing learning. To achieve this goal, it assigns values to competing alternatives based on their perceived potential to answer questions the individual finds intriguing. In essence, therefore, curiosity is really an engine of discovery." See *Why,* 105 and 117.

15. Grossnickle, "Disentangling," 27.
16. For more exploration regarding the definitions of curiosity, see the first chapter of Susan Engel's fantastic book *The Hungry Mind*. She even adds her own definition, which I really like: "Curiosity, in other words, can be understood as the human impulse to resolve uncertainty" (10).
17. de Arsuaga, *Neanderthal's Necklace*, 7.
18. Falk, *Braindance*, 83.
19. Jerison, *Evolution of the Brain*, 25.
20. Jerison, *Evolution of the Brain*, 5.
21. Jerison, *Evolution of the Brain*, 61–62.
22. Falk, *Braindance*, 51.
23. Finlay, "E Pluribus Unum," 294.
24. Gibson, "Epigenesis," 34.
25. August 20, 2015.
26. Gräslund, *Early Humans*, 86.
27. Gould, *Ontogeny and Phylogeny*, 357.
28. Gould, *Ontogeny and Phylogeny*, 357.
29. Gould, *Ontogeny and Phylogeny*, 386.
30. Tizard and Hughes, *Young Children Learning*, 13.
31. *Scientist in the Crib*, 86.
32. See Day, *Baby Meets World*, esp. 11–86.
33. Stahl and Feigenson, "Observing the Unexpected," 94.
34. Bonawitz, et al., "Double-Edged Sword," 325.
35. Bonawitz, et al., "Double-Edged Sword," 325.
36. Bonawitz, et al., "Double-Edged Sword," 326.
37. I discuss the Bonawitz article in more detail in a blog post "Lessons from a Toy," *A Lifetime's Training*.
38. Piaget, *Origin of Intelligence*, 275.
39. Piaget, *Origin of Intelligence*, 276.
40. Piaget, *Origin of Intelligence*, 280.
41. Voss and Keller, *Curiosity and Exploration*, 96.

42. I must acknowledge Engel's *The Hungry Mind* for pointing me toward Chouinard's important work.

43. Chouinard, "Children's Questions," 47.

44. Chouinard, "Children's Questions," 49. Interestingly, Chouinard found that there is a spike in explanatory questions between three years and six months of age and three years and eleven months in all of the groups that she studied. By age four, the number of explanatory questions realigns with levels seen at slightly earlier ages and then plateaus. Chouinard calls this the "A-ha spike" and suggests that this momentary increase indicates an important point in a child's cognitive development (50). What is happening here? Is this the moment when children are pulling together cognitive resources to make sense of the world in a new way? I am only able to speculate, but I think it would be valuable to attempt a replication of Chouinard's work.

45. Chouinard, "Children's Questions," viii.

46. Chouinard, "Children's Questions," 4.

47. Chouinard, "Children's Questions," 5.

48. Chouinard, "Children's Questions," 5.

49. Chouinard, "Children's Questions," 36.

50. Shernoff and Csikszentmihalyi, "Flow in Schools," 131.

51. Berger, in *A More Beautiful Question*, describes some of the schools that are using inquiry-based strategies in an attempt to combat waning curiosity (50ff).

52. Engel, *Hungry Mind*, 88.

53. Engel, *Hungry Mind*, 89.

54. Engel, *Hungry Mind*, 18.

55. Berger, *A More Beautiful Question*, 44.

56. Bain, *Best College Teachers*, 34.

57. Deresiewicz, *Excellent Sheep*, 41–48.

58. Voss and Keller, *Curiosity and Exploration*, 145–46.

59. Peters, "Effects," 389.

60. Peters, "Effects," 392.
61. Engel, *Hungry Mind*, 77.
62. Fink, *Significant Learning Experiences*, 25.
63. Wiggins and McTighe, *Understanding by Design*, 105.
64. Wiggins and McTighe, *Understanding by Design*, 107.
65. Shortly after drafting this chapter, I was fortunate that Robin Paige wrote a blog post about metaquestions and course design called "The Metaquestion."
66. Howard, *Discussion*, 6.
67. Brookfield and Preskill, *Discussion as a Way*, 21–22.
68. Howard, *Discussion*, 45.
69. Lang, *On Course*, 96.
70. Brookfield and Preskill, *Discussion as a Way*, 85.
71. Private communication, August 24, 2015.
72. Dewey, *How We Think*, 40.
73. Harter, "Challenge of Framing," 94.
74. Rothstein and Santana, *Make Just One Change*, 20.
75. For more information, see the original blog post where Newbury discusses this activity: "You Don't Have to Wait for the Clock to Strike to Start Teaching," *Science Edventures*. Newbury credits Annie Fetter of The Math Forum at Drexel University for inspiring the structure of this activity.
76. Bain, *Best College Teachers*, 31.
77. Fosnot, *Constructivism*, 29.
78. Fosnot, *Constructivism*, 30.
79. Howes, *Connecting Girls and Science*, 13.
80. Kirschner, Sweller, and Clark, "Minimal Guidance," 75–86.
81. It is perhaps worth recalling here the Bonawitz, et al., experiments with the toy and the warnings against too much direct instruction by teachers.
82. My phone interview with Saari took place on October 15, 2015.
83. Bain, *Best College Teachers*, 102–03.

84. Bain, *Best College Teachers*, 106.

85. Interviews with Hutchinson and Tran Lu took place on October 20, 2015, and February 18, 2016.

86. Hutchinson, *Concept Development Studies*, 1.

87. Hutchinson, *Concept Development Studies*, 5–6.

88. I am grateful to both John and Lesa for their patience in explaining these concepts to someone who has not studied chemistry since he was sixteen.

89. For a description and analysis of this activity as it was used during a lab section rather than a class session, please see Cloonan, Nichol, and Hutchinson, "Understanding Chemical Reaction Kinetics," 1400–03.

90. Damrosch, *The Buried Book*, 222.

91. Kawashima, "Sources and Redaction," 52.

92. Occasionally, a group would argue for Genesis being a source, largely due (as they indicated) to their religious beliefs. Such instances certainly bring up important and interesting issues regarding the teaching of religious texts in literature courses, but I do not have the space to address those here.

93. von Stumm, Hell, and Chamorro-Premuzic, "Intellectual Curiosity," 574–88.

94. Bain, *Best College Students*, 199–220.

CHAPTER 2. SOCIALITY

1. "Introduction to *A Class Divided*," *Frontline* (January 1, 2003): n.p. http://www.pbs.org/wgbh/frontline/article/introduction-2/

2. Naomi Eisenberger has done a lot of work in this area. For one example, see Eisenberger, Lieberman, and Williams, "Does Rejection Hurt," 290–92.

3. Caspi, et al., "Socially Isolated Children," 805–11.

4. At a late stage in my research process, I was fortunate to discover Louis Cozolino's wonderful book *The Social Neuroscience of*

Education: Optimizing Attachment in and Learning in the Classroom. I cite Cozolino's work several times in this chapter, but I also think it is important to point out that the two of us tread similar terrain, although we ultimately go in different directions— more deeply into neuroscience (him) and pedagogical strategies (me).

5. Gamble, Gowlett, and Dunbar, *Thinking Big*, 39.

6. Dunbar and Shultz, "Evolution in the Social Brain," 1346.

7. For details, see e.g., Knauft, et al., "Violence and Sociality," 397; Sanderson, *Evolution of Human Sociality*, 47–48; and Chapais, "Deep Structure of Human Society," 21–22. Robin Dunbar has theorized that extended social networks in both ancient and modern human populations would be limited to 150 individuals due to logistics of communication and relationship management. This has been called the "Dunbar number" and is not without its critics. The foundational essay is Dunbar, "Coevolution of Neocortical Size," 681–735.

8. Nowak, Tarnita, and Wilson, "Evolution of Eusociality," 1057.

9. Nowak, Tarnita, and Wilson, "Evolution of Eusociality," 1060.

10. Nowak, Tarnita, and Wilson, "Evolution of Eusociality," 1060.

11. Iacoboni, "Neurobiology of Imitation," 661.

12. Iacoboni, "Neurobiology of Imitation," 662.

13. Iacoboni, "Neurobiology of Imitation," 662.

14. Hickok, *Myth of Mirror Neurons*, esp. 229. See also, Borg, "If Mirror Neurons," 5–19.

15. Arbib, "From Monkey-like Action Recognition," 115.

16. Arbib, "From Monkey-like Action Recognition," 115.

17. King, *Dynamic Dance*, 209ff; and Tattersall, "Paleoanthropology and Language," 130.

18. McNeill, *Hand and Mind*, 245.

19. Dor, Knight, and Lewis, "Social Perspective," 3.

20. Dunbar, *Grooming, Gossip.*

21. Falk, *Finding Our Tongues.*
22. Falk, *Finding Our Tongues*, x.
23. See Bekoff, *Minding Animals*, 131; and Burghardt, "On the Origins of Play," 8.
24. Burghardt, "On the Origins of Play," 6.
25. S. Brown with Vaughan, *Play*, 32.
26. Carlsson-Paige, McLaughlin, and Almon, "Reading Instruction in Kindergarten," 2 and 4.
27. S. Brown with Vaughan, *Play*, 32–33.
28. An important foundational work here is Caro and Hauser, "Teaching in Nonhuman Animals," 151–74.
29. Thornton and Raihani, "Evolution of Teaching," 1824.
30. Thornton and Raihani, "Evolution of Teaching," 1824.
31. Csibra and Gergely, "Natural Pedagogy," 149.
32. Csibra and Gergely, "Natural Pedagogy," 148.
33. Csibra and Gergely, "Natural Pedagogy," 149.
34. Csibra and Gergely, "Natural Pedagogy," 152.
35. Skerry, Lambert, Powell, and McAuliffe, "Origins of Pedagogy," 550.
36. Skerry, Lambert, Powell, and McAuliffe, "Origins of Pedagogy," 553 and 566.
37. Cozolino, *Social Neuroscience of Education*, 187.
38. B. Boyd, *On the Origin of Stories*, 163.
39. Willingham, *Why Don't Students*, 66–67.
40. Willingham, *Why Don't Students*, 67.
41. Sanderson, *Evolution of Human Sociality*, 148.
42. Dron and Anderson, *Teaching Crowds*, 46.
43. Montessori, *Absorbent Mind*, 232–43.
44. Montessori, *Absorbent Mind*, 242.
45. Bandura, *Social Learning Theory*, 39.
46. Bandura, *Social Learning Theory*, 46–47.
47. Much of what follows was included in an earlier blog post called "More Than Mindsets."

48. Vygotsky, *Mind in Society*, 84.

49. For a good example of this research, see Doolittle, "Vygotsky's Zone of Proximal Development," 83–103.

50. Cozolino, *Social Neuroscience of Education*, 17.

51. Bass and Elmendorf, "Designing for Difficulty," n.p.

52. Bass and Elmendorf, "Designing for Difficulty," n.p.

53. I tackle the thorny subject of authenticity in chapter 4.

54. Cohen and Garcia, "Educational Theory, Practice, and Policy," 17.

55. Yeager and Walton, "Social-Psychological Interventions in Education," 267–301.

56. Walton and Cohen, "Question of Belonging," 82.

57. See Walton and Cohen, "Brief Social-Belonging Intervention," 1447–51.

58. Walton and Cohen, "Question of Belonging," 87.

59. Walton and Cohen, "Question of Belonging," 87.

60. Walton and Cohen, "Question of Belonging," 88.

61. Walton and Cohen, "Question of Belonging," 91–92.

62. Yeager and Walton, "Social-Psychological Interventions in Education," 287. For a very helpful synthesis of the research on social belonging, see Strayhorn, *College Students' Sense of Belonging*.

63. Jennings and Greenberg, "Prosocial Classroom," 506.

64. Solomon, et al., "Creating Classrooms," 744. Although this study focused on fourth graders, I don't find it hard to make the leap to college students. Clearly, though, more research is needed in this area.

65. Goldin-Meadow, "How Gesture Works," 5.

66. See esp., Macedonia and von Kriegstein, "Gestures Enhance Foreign Language Learning," 393–416.

67. This observation took place on October 19, 2015. An earlier version of these comments appeared in the blog post Jo. Eyler, "Active Learning is Not Our Enemy," *A Lifetime's Training*.

68. Barkley, Cross, and Major, *Collaborative Learning Techniques*, 3.

69. Barkley, Cross, and Major, *Collaborative Learning Techniques*, 44 and 44.

70. Barkley, Cross, and Major, *Collaborative Learning Techniques*, 9–10.

71. K. Smith, Sheppard, Johnson, and Johnson, "Pedagogies of Engagement," 91. See also the oft-cited Springer, Stanne, and Donovan, "Effects of Small-Group Learning," 21–51. For perspectives on collaborative learning and the humanities, one classic place to start is Bruffee, "Collaborative Learning," 635–52.

72. Colbeck, Campbell, and Bjorklund, "Grouping in the Dark," 61.

73. Colbeck, Campbell, and Bjorklund, "Grouping in the Dark," 79.

74. Mazur, "Farewell," 50–51. The Force Concept Inventory is an instrument comprised of twenty-nine validated conceptual questions related to Newton's laws. It was developed by David Hestenes, Malcom Wells, and Gregg Swackhammer at Arizona State University in the early 1990s. See Hestenes, Wells, and Swackhammer, "Force Concept Inventory," 141–58.

75. Although you do sacrifice the anonymity of a classroom response system when you opt to use something like notecards.

76. Crouch and Mazur, "Peer Instruction," 971.

77. M. Smith, et al., "Why Peer Instruction Improves," 122.

78. Smith, et al., "Why Peer Instruction Improves," 124.

79. Crouch and Mazur, "Peer Instruction," 970.

80. This sample question originally appeared in an email I sent to the POD Network listserv on October 20, 2015.

81. Desmond, *Evicted*.

82. Bergen, "Play as Learning," 415–16.

83. Froebel, *Pedagogics of the Kindergarten*, esp. 62–69.

84. Bergen, "Play as Learning," 421.

85. Major, Harris, and Zakrajsek, *Teaching for Learning*, 124.

86. Major, Harris, and Zakrajsek, *Teaching for Learning*, 125–26.

87. Gee, *Video Games*, 13.

88. Carnes discusses his reasons for creating Reacting to the Past games in chapter 1 of his book *Minds on Fire*, 17–36.

89. P. Lazarus and McKay, "Reacting to the Past Pedagogy," 351–63.

90. My observations and interview took place in 2014 on September 23 and 25.

91. See https://reacting.barnard.edu/node/2607 for lists of published games and games in development.

92. Higbee, "Reacting to the Past Games," 41–74.

93. Stroessner, Beckerman, and Whittaker, "All the World's a Stage," 605–20.

94. Stroessner, Beckerman, and Whittaker, "All the World's a Stage," 618.

95. Carnes, *Minds on Fire*, esp. 40–62.

96. S. Brown with Vaughan, *Play*, 34.

97. For important discussions of the use of social media in higher education, see Joosten, *Social Media for Educators*; and Bowen, *Teaching Naked*, esp. 27–50. Anecdotal accounts—like that of Lang, "Orwell and Twitter," n.p.—are helpful here as well.

98. Blended learning, where face-to-face instruction is combined with interactions facilitated by technology, is something else entirely. There is burgeoning support in the research for this kind of combined methodology.

99. Allen and Seaman, with Pouline and Straut, "2015 Online Report Card," 12.

100. M. Miller, *Minds Online*, esp. 19–41.

101. Bettinger and Loeb, "Promises and Pitfalls," 2.

102. Bettinger and Loeb, "Promises and Pitfalls," 2–3.

103. Bettinger and Loeb, "Promises and Pitfalls," 3.

104. See Cottom, *Lower Ed*.

105. Hart, Friedmann, and Hill, "Online Course-taking and Student Outcomes," 47.

106. Hart, Friedmann, and Hill, "Online Course-taking and Student Outcomes," 56.

107. Hart, Friedmann, and Hill, "Online Course-taking and Student Outcomes," 67.

108. Rovai, "Classroom Community," 198.

109. Dron and Anderson, *Teaching Crowds*, 65.

110. Wei, Chen, and Kinshuk, "Model of Social Presence," 530.

111. M. Miller, *Minds Online*, 29.

112. See Looser, "Why I Teach Online," n.p. Looser argues that online teaching is a "matter of social justice and feminist practice" for the flexibility it allows.

CHAPTER 3. EMOTION

1. Oatley and Jenkins, *Understanding Emotions*, 63.

2. Cavanagh, *Spark of Learning*, 15.

3. Tarlow, "Archaeology of Emotion and Affect," 171.

4. Ortony and Turner, "What's Basic about Basic Emotions," 315.

5. Darwin, Ekman, and Prodger, *Emotions in Man and Animals*.

6. Jane Goodall's famous work with chimpanzees comes to mind here, but I would also like to call attention to studies like King's *How Animals Grieve*.

7. Panksepp and Biven, *Archaeology of Mind*, 4.

8. Pessoa, "Relationship between Emotion and Cognition," 148.

9. Pessoa, "Relationship between Emotion and Cognition," 148.

10. Oatley and Jenkins, *Understanding Emotions*, 82.

11. Turner, *Origins of Human Emotions*, 19–20.

12. For context, Zajonc's initial paper, "Feeling and Thinking," appeared in 1980. R. Lazarus responded in 1982 and another round of responses followed in 1984. A valuable summary of the debate appears in R. Lazarus, "Cognition-Emotion Debate," 3–20.

13. Immordino-Yang, *Emotions, Learning, and the Brain*, 33.

14. Pessoa, "Relationship between Emotion and Cognition," 148.

15. Fuller, *Wonder*, 139–40.

16. Immordino-Yang, *Emotions, Learning, and the Brain*, 37.

17. Blair, et al., "Modulation of Emotion by Cognition," 437. See also, Gray, Braver, and Raichle, "Integration of Emotion and Cognition," 4115–120.

18. Holodynski and Friedlmeier, *Development of Emotions*, 1.

19. Holodynski and Friedlmeier, *Development of Emotions*, 91.

20. Holodynski and Friedlmeier, *Development of Emotions*, 91.

21. Lewis, Alessandri, and Sullivan, "Violation of Expectancy," 748.

22. Immordino-Yang, *Emotions, Learning, and the Brain*, 100.

23. Linnenbrink, "Role of Affect," 117.

24. Cavanagh, *Spark of Learning*, 36–43.

25. Respondek, Seufert, Stupinsky, and Nett, "Perceived Academic Control."

26. Immordino-Yang, *Emotions, Learning, and the Brain*, 101. See also, Cavanagh, *Spark of Learning*, 36.

27. For a useful overview of the subject, see S. Hughes, "Delight."

28. Scoffham and Barnes, "Happiness Matters," 545.

29. Scoffham and Barnes, "Happiness Matters," 547.

30. Noddings, *Happiness and Education*, 3.

31. Berk, "Using Humor in College Teaching," 72.

32. Cavanagh, *Spark of Learning*, 75.

33. Berk, "Using Humor in College Teaching," 83–87.

34. C. Bergin and D. Bergin put it succinctly: "To be effective, teachers must connect with and care for children with warmth, respect, and trust." For a review of important research in this area, see the article from which this quote is taken: "Attachment in the Classroom," 141–70. The quotation can be found on page 150. See also, Velasquez, West, Graham, and Osguthorpe, "Developing Caring Relationships in Schools," 162–90, and Chambliss and Takacs, *How College Works*, 112 and 132.

35. Hawk and Lyons, "Don't Give Up on Me," 324.

36. Hult Jr., "On Pedagogical Caring," 238.

37. Hult Jr., "On Pedagogical Caring," 238.

38. Noddings, *Caring.*

39. Noddings, *Caring,* 185.

40. Noddings, *Caring,* 186.

41. Noddings, *Caring,* 186.

42. Goldstein, "Relational Zone," 647–73.

43. Goldstein, "Relational Zone," 664.

44. Hawk and Lyons, "Don't Give Up on Me," 334.

45. Hawk and Lyons, "Don't Give Up on Me," 334.

46. C. Bergin and D. Bergin, "Attachment in the Classroom," 158.

47. Cavanagh, *Spark of Learning,* 100–01.

48. My observation and interview took place on October 19, 2016.

49. Eynde, de Corte, and Verschaffel, "Students' Emotions," 202.

50. C. Bergin and D. Bergin, "Attachment in the Classroom," 148.

51. LeDoux, "Emotion," 214.

52. Phelps, "Emotion and Cognition," 29.

53. Phelps and LeDoux, "Contributions of the Amygdala," 176.

54. Zull, *Art,* 74–75.

55. I want to be respectful here, though. There are those with anxiety disorders, PTSD, and other conditions who deal with fear on a much larger scale than the rest of us.

56. K. MacDonald and T. MacDonald, "Peptide that Binds," 1.

57. Feldman, "Oxytocin and Social Affiliation," 380–91.

58. Kirsch, et al., "Oxytocin Modulates Neural Circuitry," 11489ff. See also, Domes, et al., "Oxytocin Attenuates Amygdala Responses," 1187–190.

59. K. MacDonald and T. MacDonald, "Peptide that Binds," 3.

60. Hembree, "Correlates, Causes, Effects, and Treatment," 73.

61. For one of many examples, see Phelps, "Emotion and Cognition," 40–43.

62. Purvis, Cross, and Sunshine, *The Connected Child,* 48.

63. Purvis, Cross, and Sunshine, *The Connected Child,* 49.

64. Purvis and Cross, "Amygdala and a Hard Place."

65. I will discuss prior knowledge in more depth in the chapter on failure.

66. Cavanagh, "Caring Isn't Coddling," n.p.

67. See, for example, D. E. Elliott, et al., "Trauma-Informed or Trauma-Denied," 461–77.

68. Denial, "On Being Triggered."

69. Coyne, "Life is 'Triggering'," n.p.

70. Hanlon, "My Students Need Trigger Warnings," n.p.

71. Hanlon, "My Students Need Trigger Warnings," n.p.

72. For what it's worth, there have been some attempts to collect this kind of data. See, for example, D. M. Elliott, "Traumatic Events," 811–20.

73. I am grateful to Betsy Barre for outlining this perspective for me.

74. Ahmed, "Against Students."

75. Cavanagh, *Spark of Learning*, 206.

CHAPTER 4. AUTHENTICITY

1. Both my observation and interview of Boyd took place on September 30, 2015.

2. Petraglia, *Reality by Design*, 13.

3. Grabinger and Dunlap, "Rich Environments for Active Learning," 20–21.

4. A. Herrington and J. Herrington, "What is an Authentic Learning Environment," 69–70.

5. J. Brown, Collins, and Duguid, "Situated Cognition," 34.

6. Grabinger and Dunlap, "Rich Environments for Active Learning," 7.

7. J. Herrington, Reeves, and Oliver, "Immersive Learning Technologies," 80.

8. J. Herrington, Reeves, and Oliver, "Immersive Learning Technologies," 81.

9. Morgan-Short, Finger, Grey, and Ullman, "Second Language Processing," 14.

10. Kolb, *Experiential Learning*, 38.

11. Kolb, *Experiential Learning*, 42.

12. Roberts, *Experiential Education*, 24.

13. Roberts, *Experiential Education*, 41–42.

14. Ja. Eyler, "Linking Service and Learning," 517.

15. Conway, Amel, and Gerwien, "Teaching and Learning in Social Context," 237–38.

16. Russell, Hancock, and McCullough, "Benefits of Undergraduate Research Experiences," 548.

17. Hunter, Laursen, and Seymour, "Becoming a Scientist," 47–49.

18. Ishiyama, "Early Participation," 380–86.

19. My interview with McNabb took place on September 30, 2016.

20. By "short," I mean ten to fifteen minutes. I discuss this timeframe in more detail later in the chapter. Although they are sometimes valuable or—one could argue—necessary, even short lectures lack authenticity.

21. Bligh, *Use of Lectures*, 10.

22. Bruff recently explicated the term "continuous exposition" in "In Defense of Continuous Exposition."

23. Bligh, *Use of Lectures*, 6.

24. Persons, "Introductory Course in Economics," 96–97. The restrained, yet pointed, rhetoric of the last two sentences is something to behold.

25. Freeman, et al., "Active Learning Increases Student Performance," 8412.

26. Freeman, et al., "Active Learning Increases Student Performance," 8412. By "examination performance," they are referring to "the scores on identical or formally equivalent examinations, concept inventories, or other assessments" (8410).

27. Svinivki and McKeachie, *McKeachie's Teaching Tips*, 64. The ten- to fifteen-minute range was derived from an assessment of multiple studies and was codified in an earlier edition of *McKeachie's*

Teaching Tips, which is a highly respected handbook for research on teaching.

28. See esp. Wilson and Korn, "Attention During Lectures," 85–89.

29. With this in mind, Middendorf and Kalish have advocated for a "change up" during lectures, where instructors shift to a new strategy every fifteen to twenty minutes in order to "restart the attention clock," so to speak, and to maximize students' attention spans. See "The 'Change-Up' in Lectures," 1–5.

30. See, for example: Haak, HilleRisLambers, Pitre, and Freeman, "Increased Structure and Active Learning," 1213–16; Nagda, et al., "Undergraduate Student-Faculty Research Partnerships," 55–72; and Preszler, "Replacing Lecture," 182–92. These citations merely scratch the surface of what has become a robust research area. Most of the studies I read on the effectiveness of undergraduate research made sure to comment on the success of such initiatives for underrepresented populations of students.

31. Lorenzo, Crouch, and Mazur, "Reducing the Gender Gap," 118–22. Although this paper focuses primarily on strategies affecting the academic performance of women, the findings are consistent with research on other populations of students as well.

CHAPTER 5. FAILURE

1. Livio, *Brilliant Blunders*, 124.

2. Livio, *Brilliant Blunders*, 138.

3. I include Rosalind Franklin as a key player in this narrative because her story—including her essential contributions to the findings of Watson and Crick—is too often untold.

4. Firestein, *Failure*, 41.

5. Lahey, *Gift of Failure*, xx.

6. Schulz, *Being Wrong*, 117–18.

7. Kahneman, *Thinking, Fast and Slow*, 8.

8. Kahneman, *Thinking, Fast and Slow*, 21.

9. Kahneman, *Thinking, Fast and Slow*, 81.

10. Kahneman, *Thinking, Fast and Slow*, 78.

11. Kahneman, *Thinking, Fast and Slow*, 76; emphasis in original.

12. Kahneman, *Thinking, Fast and Slow*, 199.

13. Kahneman, *Thinking, Fast and Slow*, 204–05.

14. Moser, et al., "Mind Your Errors," 1485.

15. Wiersema, van der Meere, and Roeyers, "Developmental Changes in Error Monitoring," 1650.

16. G. Hughes and Yeung, "Dissociable Correlates of Response," 405.

17. Hester, et al., "Neural Mechanisms," 602.

18. There is some debate about the role of the ERN in processing errors. Early work suggested that it was much more involved in attending to errors after they have been made. Current studies, however, argue the ERN's activity is much narrower in scope. See Moser, et al., "Mind Your Errors"; and G. Hughes and Yeung, "Dissociable Correlates of Response."

19. Wiersema, van der Meere, and Roeyers, "Developmental Changes in Error Monitoring," 1654.

20. Piaget, *The Construction of Reality in the Child*, 50ff.

21. L. Smith, Thelen, Titzer, and McLin, "Context of Acting," 235–60.

22. Fagen, Morrongiello, Rovee-Collier, and Gekoski, "Expectancies and Memory Retrieval," 936–43.

23. Schulz, *Being Wrong*, 291.

24. Maslow, "Theory of Human Motivation," 370–96.

25. Maslow, "Theory of Human Motivation," 384.

26. Goldrick-Rab, Broton, and Eisenberg, *Hungry to Learn*. See also the op-ed called "Hungry, Homeless, and in College" by Goldrick-Rab and Broton. This essay opens with an account of Brooke Evans, a student at the University of Wisconsin-Madison, who lived in her car for some of her time at the university. Evans was later featured in a powerful story in *Glamour* by Liz Brody called "I Didn't Even Have an Address."

27. Doyle and Zakrajsek devote an entire chapter to the importance of sleep for college students in their book *New Science of Learning*, 15–34.

28. Lahey, *Gift of Failure*, xi.

29. Teevan and McGhee, "Fear of Failure Motivation," 345–48.

30. P. Brown, Roediger III, and McDaniel, *Make It Stick*, 91.

31. Tough, *How Children Succeed*, 18.

32. Beilock, *Choke*, 5–6.

33. Beilock, *Choke*, 32.

34. Beilock, *Choke*, 32.

35. Beilock, *Choke*, 71.

36. Schulz, *Being Wrong*, 144.

37. Schulz, *Being Wrong*, 143–44.

38. Steele, *Whistling Vivaldi*, 40.

39. Steele, *Whistling Vivaldi*, 61.

40. In a 2011 article, V. Taylor and Walton sought to demonstrate that stereotype threat had negative consequences on student learning itself in addition to performance as measured by test scores. Their findings were consistent with the previous literature and showed a clear, detrimental effect on learning. See "Stereotype Threat Undermines Academic Learning," 1055–67.

41. Goldrick-Rab, "Basic Needs."

42. Bain, *Best College Teachers*, 27.

43. Zull, *Art*, 99.

44. Zull, *Art*, 101.

45. The Force Concept Inventory, mentioned in chapter 2, is perhaps the most well-known of these instruments.

46. Bain, *Best College Teachers*, 27–28.

47. Schulz, 194.

48. Bain, *Best College Teachers*, 28.

49. van Merriënboer and Sweller, "Cognitive Load Theory," 150.

50. van Merriënboer and Sweller, "Cognitive Load Theory," 149. See also Ambrose, et al., *How Learning Works*, 103–07.

51. van Merriënboer and Sweller, "Cognitive Load Theory," 150.

52. Ambrose, et al., *How Learning Works*, 108 and 109.

53. Kiesel, et al., "Control and Interference in Task Switching," 849–74.

54. Boaler, *Mathematical Mindsets*, 12.

55. Bain, *Best College Students*, 118.

56. Dweck, *Mindset*, 6.

57. Dweck, *Mindset*, 7.

58. See Moser, et al., "Mind Your Errors"; and Mangels, et al., "Why do Beliefs," 75–86.

59. Here is a survey developed by Dweck herself: http://mindsetonline. com/testyourmindset/step2.php.

60. Research is beginning to suggest, for example, that talking to younger students in science classes about the struggles of famous scientists improved achievement in those courses. See Lin-Siegler, et al., "Even Einstein Struggled," 314–28.

61. Duckworth, *Grit*, 3–14.

62. Duckworth, *Grit*, 10.

63. Credé, Tynan, and Harms, "Much Ado about Grit," 494.

64. Kamenetz, "Angela Duckworth Responds."

65. Duckworth, *Grit*, 17.

66. Kundu, "Grit, Overemphasized; Agency, Overlooked," 80.

67. These and other suggestions are outlined in a blog post entitled, "Addressing a 'Threat in the Air.'"

68. Lahey, *Gift of Failure*, 218.

69. Schmidt and R. Bjork, "New Conceptualizations of Practice," 207–17.

70. E. Bjork and R. Bjork, "Making Things Hard on Yourself," 58.

71. E. Bjork and R. Bjork, "Making Things Hard on Yourself," 60.

72. For a more detailed discussion of some of these strategies, particularly as they apply to pedagogy in higher education, see Lang's

recent book *Small Teaching*, especially the chapters "Interleaving" and "Practicing."

73. Kapur, "Examining Productive Failure," 289–90.

74. Kapur, "Examining Productive Failure," 295–96.

75. Kapur, "Examining Productive Failure," 293.

76. I'm grateful to the HyperPhysics website at Georgia State University for some quick tutorials on Newtonian physics.

77. Yerushalmi and Polingher, "Guiding Students," 533.

78. Boaler, *Mathematical Mindsets*, 17.

79. Much of the material in this section was included in my earlier blog post "What is the Error Climate of Your Course?"

80. Steuer and Dresel, "Constructive Error Climate," 263.

81. Steuer and Dresel, "Constructive Error Climate," 264.

82. Steuer and Dresel, "Constructive Error Climate," 272.

83. Steuer and Dresel, "Constructive Error Climate," 273.

84. At least one researcher has begun to study teachers' perceptions of error climate, but this work has focused primarily on K–12 classrooms. See O'Dell, "Classroom Error Climate".

85. As part of my work on this book, I have designed an "Error Climate Inventory for College Instructors" that draws heavily from the research of Steuer and Dresel. The purpose of the inventory is to help college instructors assess the error climate of their courses. Please feel free to use this instrument and to share it: http://qeasttrial.c01.qualtrics.com/jfe/form/SV_4NGkrVrTdoU9Ac5

86. Patricia sent this to me during an online conversation regarding error climate.

87. This includes an extended observation on March 12, 2015.

88. Walvoord and Anderson, *Effective Grading*, 1.

89. Nilson, *Specifications Grading*, 128.

90. The line originally appears in Beckett's short prose piece "Worstward Ho," which was first published in 1983. The most readily available version of the piece can now be found in *Nohow On*.

EPILOGUE: THERE AND BACK AGAIN

1. Blum, *I Love Learning*, 190–213.
2. Blum, *I Love Learning*, 233–35.

BIBLIOGRAPHY

—

Ahmed, Sara. "Against Students." *feministkilljoys* (blog). June 25, 2015.
https://feministkilljoys.com/2015/06/25/against-students/

Allen, I. Elaine, and Jeff Seaman, with Russell Pouline and Terri Taylor
Straut. "2015 Online Report Card: Tracking Online Education in
the United States." Babson Survey Research Group (February 2016):
1–57.

Ambrose, Susan A., et al. *How Learning Works: Seven Research-Based
Principles for Smart Teaching*. San Francisco: Jossey-Bass, 2010.

Arbib, Michael A. "From Monkey-like Action Recognition to Human
Language: An Evolutionary Framework for Neurolinguistics."
Behavioral and Brain Sciences 28 (2005): 105–67.

Bain, Ken. *What the Best College Students Do*. Cambridge, MA: Harvard
University Press, 2012.

———. *What the Best College Teachers Do*. Cambridge, MA: Harvard
University Press, 2004.

Bajak, Aleszu. "Lectures Aren't Just Boring, They're Ineffective, Too,
Study Finds." *Science News*. May 12, 2014. http://www.sciencemag.
org/news/2014/05/lectures-arent-just-boring-theyre-ineffective-too-
study-finds

Bandura, Albert. *Social Learning Theory*. Englewood Cliffs, NJ:
Prentice-Hall, 1977.

Bardo, M. T., R. L. Donohew, and N. G. Harrington. "Psychobiology of
Novelty Seeking and Drug Seeking Behavior." *Behavioural Brain
Research* 77.1–2 (1996): 23–43.

Barkley, Elizabeth, K. Patricia Cross, and Claire Howell Major. *Collaborative Learning Techniques: A Handbook for College Faculty*. San
Francisco: Jossey-Bass, 2005.

Bass, Randy, and Heidi Elmendorf. "Designing for Difficulty: Social Pedagogies as a Framework for Course Design." Teagle Foundation White Paper (2011): n.p. https://blogs.commons.georgetown.edu/bassr/social-pedagogies/

Beckett, Samuel. *Nohow On: Company, Ill Seen Ill Said, and Worstward Ho*. New York: Grove, 2014.

Beilock, Sian. *Choke: What the Secrets of the Brain Reveal about Getting It Right When You Have To*. New York: Free Press, 2010.

Bekoff, Marc. *Minding Animals: Awareness, Emotions, and Heart*. Oxford: Oxford University Press, 2002.

Bergen, Doris. "Play as the Learning Medium for Future Scientists, Mathematicians, and Engineers." *American Journal of Play* 1 (2009): 413–28.

Berger, Warren. *A More Beautiful Question*. New York: Bloomsbury, 2014.

Bergin, Christi, and David Bergin. "Attachment in the Classroom." *Educational Psychology Review* 21 (2009): 141–70.

Berlyne, D. E. *Conflict, Arousal, and Curiosity*. New York: McGraw-Hill, 1960.

Berk, Ronald A. "Student Ratings of 10 Strategies for Using Humor in College Teaching." *Journal on Excellence in College Teaching* 7.3 (1996): 71–92.

Bettinger, Eric, and Susanna Loeb. "Promises and Pitfalls of Online Education: Executive Summary." Evidence Speaks Reports 2.15 (Brookings Institute, June 9, 2017): 1–4.

Bjork, Elizabeth L., and Robert Bjork. "Making Things Hard on Yourself, but in a Good Way: Creating Desirable Difficulties to Enhance Learning." In *Psychology and the Real World: Essays Illustrating Fundamental Contributions to Society*. Eds. Morton Ann Gernsbacher, Richard W. Pew, Leaetta M. Hough, and James R. Pomerantz. New York: Worth, 2011. 56–64.

Blair, K. S., et al. "Modulation of Emotion by Cognition and Cognition by Emotion," *Neuroimage* 35 (2007): 430–40.

Bligh, Donald. *What's the Use of Lectures*, 5th ed. Exeter, UK: Intellect, 1998.

Blum, Susan Debra. *"I Love Learning; I Hate School": An Anthropology of College.* Ithaca, NY: Cornell University Press, 2016.

Boaler, Jo. *Mathematical Mindsets: Unleashing Students' Potential through Creative Math, Inspiring Messages, and Innovative Teaching.* San Francisco: Jossey-Bass, 2016.

Bonawitz, Elizabeth, et al. "The Double-Edged Sword of Pedagogy: Instruction Limits Spontaneous Exploration and Discovery." *Cognition* 120.3 (2011): 322–30.

Borg, Emma. "If Mirror Neurons Are the Answer, What Was the Question?" *Journal of Consciousness Studies* 14.8 (2007): 5–19.

Bowen, José Antonio. *Teaching Naked: How Moving Technology Out of Your College Classroom Will Improve Student Learning.* San Francisco: Jossey-Bass, 2012.

Boyd, Brian. *On the Origin of Stories: Evolution, Cognition, and Fiction.* Cambridge, MA: Belknap Press of Harvard University Press, 2009.

Boyd, Donna. Classroom observation and personal interview. September 30, 2015.

Bransford, John D., et al., *How People Learn: Brain, Mind, Experience, and School.* Expanded ed. Washington, DC: National Academies Press, 2000.

Brody, Liz. "I Didn't Even Have an Address." *Glamour* (August 9, 2016): n.p. http://www.glamour.com/story/i-didnt-even-have-an-address

Brookfield, Stephen D., and Stephen Preskill. *Discussion as a Way of Teaching: Tools and Techniques for Democratic Classrooms.* 2nd ed. San Francisco: Jossey-Bass, 2012.

Brown, John Seely, Allan Collins, and Paul Duguid. "Situated Cognition and the Culture of Learning." *Educational Researcher* 18 (1989): 32–42.

Brown, Peter C., Henry L. Roediger III, and Mark A. McDaniel. *Make It Stick: The Science of Successful Learning.* Cambridge, MA: Harvard University Press, 2014.

Brown, Stuart, with Christopher Vaughan. *Play: How It Shapes the Brain, Opens the Imagination, and Invigorates the Soul.* New York: Avery, 2009.

Bruff, Derek. "In Defense of Continuous Exposition by the Teacher." *Agile Learning* (blog). September 15, 2015.

Bruffee, Kenneth A. "Collaborative Learning and the 'Conversation of Mankind.'" *College English* 46 (1984): 635–52.

Burghardt, Gordon M. "On the Origins of Play." In *Play in Animals and Humans.* Ed. Peter K. Smith. Oxford: Basil Blackwell, 1984. 5–42.

Carey, Benedict. *How We Learn: The Surprising Truth About When, Where, and Why It Happens.* New York: Random House, 2014.

Carey, Susan. *The Origin of Concepts.* Oxford: Oxford University Press, 2009.

Carlsson-Paige, Nancy, Geralyn Bywater McLaughlin, and Joan Wolfsheimer Almon. "Reading Instruction in Kindergarten: Little to Gain and Much to Lose." Report for the Defending the Early Years Project. Boston: Alliance for Childhood, 2015. https://deyproject.files.wordpress.com/2015/01/readinginkindergarten_online-1.pdf

Carnes, Mark C. *Minds on Fire: How Role-Immersion Games Transform College.* Cambridge, MA: Harvard University Press, 2014.

Caro, T. M., and M. D. Hauser. "Is There Teaching in Nonhuman Animals?" *Quarterly Review of Biology* 67 (1992): 151–74.

Caspi, Avshalom, et al. "Socially Isolated Children 20 Years Later." *Archives of Pediatrics and Adolescent Medicine* 160 (August 2006): 805–11.

Cavanagh, Sarah Rose. "Caring Isn't Coddling." *Chronicle Vitae* (November 22, 2016): n.p. https://chroniclevitae.com/news/1621-caring-isn-t-coddling

———. *The Spark of Learning: Energizing the College Classroom with the Science of Emotion*. Morgantown: West Virginia University Press, 2016.

Chambliss, Daniel F., and Christopher G. Takacs. *How College Works*. Cambridge, MA: Harvard University Press, 2014.

Chapais, Bernard. "The Deep Structure of Human Society: Primate Origins and Evolution." In *Mind the Gap: Tracing the Origins of Human Universals*. Eds. Peter M. Kappeler and Joan B. Silk. Berlin: Springer, 2010. 19–51.

Chouinard, Michelle M. "Children's Questions: A Mechanism for Cognitive Development." *Monographs of the Society for Research in Child Development* 72 (2007): i-129.

Cloonan, Carrie A., Carolyn A. Nichol, and John S. Hutchinson. "Understanding Chemical Reaction Kinetics and Equilibrium with Interlocking Building Blocks." *Journal of Chemical Education* 88 (2011): 1400–03.

Cohen, Geoffrey L., and Julio Garcia. "Educational Theory, Practice, and Policy and the Wisdom of Social Psychology." *Policy Insights from the Behavioral and Brain Sciences* 1 (2014): 13–20.

Colbeck, Carol L., Susan E. Campbell, and Stefani A. Bjorklund. "Grouping in the Dark: What College Students Learn from Group Projects." *The Journal of Higher Education* 71 (2000): 60–83.

Conway, James M., Elise L. Amel, and Daniel P. Gerwien. "Teaching and Learning in the Social Context: A Meta-Analysis of Service Learning's Effects on Academic, Personal, Social, and Citizenship Outcomes." *Teaching of Psychology* 37 (2009): 233–45.

Cottom, Tressie McMillan. *Lower Ed: The Troubling Rise of For-Profit Colleges in the New Economy*. New York: The New Press, 2017.

Coyne, Jerry A. "Life is 'Triggering.' The Best Literature Should Be, Too." *The New Republic* (May 14, 2015): n.p. https://newrepublic.com/article/121790/life-triggering-best-literature-should-be-too

Cozolino, Louis. *The Social Neuroscience of Education: Optimizing Attachment in and Learning in the Classroom*. New York: Norton, 2013.

Credé, Marcus, Michael C. Tynan, and Peter D. Harms. "Much Ado about Grit: A Meta-Analytic Synthesis of the Grit Literature." *Journal of Personality and Social Psychology* 113.3 (2017): 492–511.

Crouch, Catherine H., and Eric Mazur. "Peer Instruction: Ten Years of Experience and Results." *American Journal of Physics* 69 (2001): 970–77.

Csibra, Gergely, and György Gergely. "Natural Pedagogy." *Trends in Cognitive Sciences* 13.4 (2009): 148–53.

Damrosch, David. *The Buried Book: The Loss and Rediscovery of the Great Epic of Gilgamesh*. New York: Henry Holt, 2006.

Darwin, Charles, Paul Ekman, and Phillip Prodger. *Expression of the Emotions in Man and Animals*, 3rd ed. London: HarperCollins Publishers, 1998.

Day, Nicholas. *Baby Meets World: Suck, Smile, Touch, Toddle: A Journey Through Infancy*. New York: Macmillan, 2013.

de Arsuaga, Juan Luis. *The Neanderthal's Necklace: In Search of the First Thinkers*. Trans. Andy Klatt. New York: Four Walls Eight Windows, 2002.

Denial, Catherine J. "On Being Triggered." *Cate Denial* (blog). March 9, 2017. http://catherinedenial.org/blog/uncategorized/on-being-triggered/

Deresiewicz, William. *Excellent Sheep: The Miseducation of the American Elite and the Way to a Meaningful Life*. New York: Free Press, 2015.

Desmond, Matthew. *Evicted: Poverty and Profit in the American City*. New York: Penguin Random House, 2016.

Dewey, John. *How We Think, a Restatement of the Relation of Reflective Thinking to the Educative Process.* Boston: D.C. Heath and Company, 1933.

Domes, Gregor, et al. "Oxytocin Attenuates Amygdala Responses to Emotional Faces Regardless of Valence." *Biological Psychiatry* 62 (2007): 1187–190.

Doolittle, Peter E. "Vygotsky's Zone of Proximal Development as a Theoretical Foundation for Cooperative Learning." *Journal on Excellence in College Teaching* 8 (1997): 83–103.

Dor, Daniel, Chris Knight, and Jerome Lewis. "Introduction: A Social Perspective on How Language Began." In *The Social Origins of Language.* Eds. Daniel Dor, Chris Knight, and Jerome Lewis. Oxford: Oxford University Press, 2014. 1–12.

Doyle, Terry, and Todd Zakrajsek. *The New Science of Learning: How to Learn in Harmony with Your Brain.* Sterling, VA: Stylus, 2013.

Dron, Jon, and Terry Anderson. *Teaching Crowds: Learning and Social Media.* Athabasca, AB: Athabasca University Press, 2014.

Duckworth, Angela. *Grit: The Power of Passion and Perseverance.* New York: Scribner, 2016.

Dunbar, R. I. M. "Coevolution of Neocortical Size, Group Size and Language in Humans." *Behavioral and Brain Sciences* 16 (1993): 681–735.

Dunbar, R. I. M., and Susanne Shultz. "Evolution in the Social Brain." *Science* 317 (September 2007): 1344–47.

Dunbar, Robin. *Grooming, Gossip, and the Evolution of Language.* Cambridge, MA: Harvard University Press, 1996.

Dweck, Carol. *Mindset: The New Psychology of Success.* New York: Ballantine, 2006.

Eisenberger, Naomi I., Matthew D. Lieberman, and Kipling D. Williams. "Does Rejection Hurt? An fMRI Study of Social Exclusion." *Science* 302 (2003): 290–92.

Elliott, Denise E., et al. "Trauma-Informed or Trauma-Denied: Principles and Implementation of Trauma-Informed Services for Women." *Journal of Community Psychology* 33 (2005): 461–77.

Elliott, Diana M. "Traumatic Events: Prevalence and Delayed Recall in the General Population." *Journal of Consulting and Clinical Psychology* 65 (1997): 811–20.

Engel, Susan. *The Hungry Mind*. Cambridge, MA: Harvard University Press, 2015.

———. Personal interview. August 24, 2015.

Eyler, Janet. "Reflection: Linking Service and Learning—Linking Students and Communities." *Journal of Social Issues* 58 (2002): 517–34.

Eyler, Joshua R. "Active Learning is Not Our Enemy: A Response to Molly Worthen." *A Lifetime's Training* (blog). October 20, 2015. https://josheyler.wordpress.com/2015/10/20/active-learning-is-not-our-enemy-a-response-to-molly-worthen/

———. "Lessons from a Toy: New (to me) Research on Pedagogy and Cognition." *A Lifetime's Training* (blog). July 3, 2014. https://josheyler.wordpress.com/2014/07/03/lessons-from-a-toy-new-to-me-research-on-pedagogy-and-cognition/

———. "Error Climate Inventory for College Instructors." http://qeasttrial.c01.qualtrics.com/jfe/form/SV_4NGkrVrTdoU9Ac5

———. "More Than Mindsets: Why Vygotsky Still Matters." *Reflections on Teaching and Learning: The CTE Blog* (blog). July 14, 2015. http://cte.rice.edu/blogarchive/2015/07/14/morethanmindsets?rq=Vygotsky

———. Personal email to the POD Network listserv. October 20, 2015.

———. "What I Have Learned about Teaching from My Daughter." *A Lifetime's Training* (blog). December 10, 2012. https://josheyler.wordpress.com/2012/12/10/what-i-have-learned-about-teaching-from-my-daughter/

———. "What is the Error Climate of Your Course?" *Reflections on Teaching and Learning: The CTE Blog* (blog). July 6, 2016. http://cte.rice.edu/blogarchive/2016/7/6/what-is-the-error-climate-of-your-course

Fagen, Jeffrey W., Barbara A. Morrongiello, Carolyn Rovee-Collier, and Marcy J. Gekoski. "Expectancies and Memory Retrieval in Three-Month-Old Infants." *Child Development* 55 (1984): 936–43.

Falk, Dean. *Braindance: New Discoveries about Human Origins and Brain Evolution.* Gainesville: University Press of Florida, 2004.

———. *Finding Our Tongues: Mothers, Infants, and the Origins of Language.* New York: Basic Books, 2009.

Feldman, Ruth. "Oxytocin and Social Affiliation in Humans." *Hormones and Behavior* 61 (2012): 380–91.

Fink, L. Dee. *Creating Significant Learning Experiences: An Integrated Approach to Designing College Courses.* San Francisco: Jossey-Bass, 2003.

Finlay, Barbara L. "E Pluribus Unum: Too Many Unique Human Capacities and Too Many Theories." In *The Evolution of Mind: Fundamental Questions and Controversies.* Eds. Steven W. Gangestad and Jeffry A. Simpson. New York: Guilford Press, 2007. 294–301.

Firestein, Stuart. *Failure: Why Science Is So Successful.* Oxford: Oxford University Press, 2016.

Fosnot, Catherine Twomey. *Constructivism: Theory, Perspectives, and Practice.* New York: Teachers College Press, 1996.

Freeman, Scott, et al. "Active Learning Increases Student Performance in Science, Engineering, and Mathematics." *Proceedings of the National Academy of Sciences* 111 (June 10, 2014): 8410–15.

Freire, Paulo. *Pedagogy of the Oppressed.* Trans. Myra Bergman Ramos. 20th Anniversary Ed. New York: Continuum, 1995.

Frensch, Peter A., and Dennis Rünger, "Implicit Learning." *Current Directions in Psychological Studies* 12.1 (2003): 13–18.

Froebel, Friedrich. *Friedrich Froebel's Pedagogics of the Kindergarten; or, His Ideas Concerning the Play and Playthings of the Child.* Trans. Josephine Jarvis. New York: D. Appleton, 1914.

Fuller, Robert C. *Wonder: From Emotion to Spirituality.* Chapel Hill: University of North Carolina Press, 2006.

Gamble, Clive, John Gowlett, and Robin Dunbar. *Thinking Big: How the Evolution of Social Life Shaped the Human Mind.* London: Thames & Hudson, 2014.

Gee, James Paul. *What Video Games Have to Teach Us about Learning and Literacy.* New York: Palgrave Macmillan, 2003.

Gibson, Kathleen R. "Epigenesis, Brain Plasticity, and Behavioral Versatility: Alternatives to Standard Evolutionary Psychology Models." In *Complexities: Beyond Nature and Nurture.* Eds. Susan McKinnon and Sydel Silverman. Chicago: University of Chicago Press, 2005. 23–42.

———. Personal interview. August 20, 2015

Goldin-Meadow, Susan. "How Gesture Works to Change Our Minds." *Trends in Neuroscience and Education* 3 (2014): 4–6.

Goldrick-Rab, Sara. "Basic Needs Security and the Syllabus." Medium.com. August 7, 2017. https://medium.com/@saragoldrickrab/basic-needs-security-and-the-syllabus-d24cc7afe8c9

Goldrick-Rab, Sara, and Katharine Broton. "Hungry, Homeless, and in College." *New York Times* (December 4, 2015): n.p. https://www.nytimes.com/2015/12/04/opinion/hungry-homeless-and-in-college.html

Goldrick-Rab, Sara, Katharine Broton, and Daniel Eisenberg. *Hungry to Learn: Addressing Food & Housing Insecurity among Undergraduates.* Madison, WI: Wisconsin HOPE Lab, December 2015.

Goldstein, Lisa S. "The Relational Zone: The Role of Caring Relationships in the Co-Construction of Mind." *American Educational Research Journal* 36 (1999): 647–73.

Gómez, Juan Carlos. *Apes, Monkeys, Children, and the Growth of Mind.* Cambridge, MA: Harvard University Press, 2004.

Gopnik, Alison. "The Scientist as Child." *Philosophy of Science* 63 (1996): 485–514.

Gopnik, Alison, Andrew N. Meltzoff, and Patricia K. Kuhl. *The Scientist in the Crib.* New York: Perennial, 1999.

Gould, Stephen Jay. *Ontogeny and Phylogeny.* Cambridge, MA: Belknap Press of Harvard University Press, 1977.

Grabinger, R. Scott, and Joanna C. Dunlap. "Rich Environments for Active Learning: A Definition." *Research in Learning Technology* 3.2 (1995): 5–34.

Gräslund, Bo. *Early Humans and Their World.* London: Routledge, 2005.

Gray, Jeremy R., Todd S. Braver, and Marcus E. Raichle. "Integration of Emotion and Cognition in the Lateral Prefrontal Cortex." *Proceedings of the National Academy of Sciences* 99.6 (2002): 4115–120.

Grossnickle, Emily M. "Disentangling Curiosity: Dimensionality, Definitions, and Distinctions from Interest in Educational Contexts." *Educational Psychology Review* 28.1 (2016): 23–60.

Gruber, Matthias, J., Bernard D. Gelman, and Charan Ranganath. "States of Curiosity Modulate Hippocampus-Dependent Learning via the Dopaminergic Circuit." *Neuron* 84.2 (2014): 486–96.

Haak, David C., Janneke HilleRisLambers, Emile Pitre, and Scott Freeman. "Increased Structure and Active Learning Reduce the Achievement Gap in Introductory Biology." *Science* 332 (June 3, 2011): 1213–16.

Hanlon, Aaron R. "My Students Need Trigger Warnings—and Professors Do, Too." *The New Republic* (May 17, 2015): n.p. https://newrepublic.com/article/121820/my-students-need-trigger-warnings-and-professors-do-too

Hart, Cassandra M.D., Elizabeth Friedmann, and Michael Hill. "Online Course-taking and Student Outcomes in California Community Colleges." *Education Finance and Policy* 13.1 (2018): 42–71.

Harter, Susan. "The Challenge of Framing a Problem: What Is Your Burning Question?" In *The SAGE Handbook for Research in Education: Pursuing Ideas as the Keystone of Exemplary Inquiry*, 2nd ed. Eds. Clifton F. Conrad and Ronald C. Serlin. Los Angeles: SAGE, 2011. 93–110.

Hawk, Thomas F., and Paul R. Lyons. "Please Don't Give Up on Me: When Faculty Fail to Care." *Journal of Management Education* 32 (2008): 316–38.

Hembree, Ray. "Correlates, Causes, Effects, and Treatment of Test Anxiety." *Review of Educational Research* 58 (1988): 47–77.

Herrington, Anthony J., and Janice A. Herrington. "What is an Authentic Learning Environment?" In *Online and Distance Learning: Concepts, Methodologies, Tools, and Applications*. Ed. L. A. Tomei. Hershey, PA: Information Science Reference, 2007. 68–77.

Herrington, Jan, Thomas C. Reeves, and Ron Oliver. "Immersive Learning Technologies: Realism and Online Authentic Learning." *Journal of Computing in Higher Education* 19 (2007): 80–99.

Hestenes, David, Malcolm Wells, and Gregg Swackhammer. "Force Concept Inventory." *The Physics Teacher* 30 (1992): 141–58.

Hester, Robert, et al. "Neural Mechanisms Involved in Error Processing: A Comparison of Errors Made with and without Awareness." *NeuroImage* 27 (2005): 602–08.

Hickok, Gregory. *The Myth of Mirror Neurons: The Real Neuroscience of Communication and Cognition*. New York: Norton, 2014.

Higbee, Mark D. "How Reacting to the Past Games 'Made Me Want to Come to Class and Learn': An Assessment of the Reacting Pedagogy at EMU, 2007–2008." *The Scholarship of Teaching and Learning at EMU* 2.4 (2008): 41–74.

Holodynski, Manfred, and Wolfgang Friedlmeier. *Development of Emotions and Emotion Regulation*. Trans. Jonathan Harrow. New York: Springer, 2006.

hooks, bell. *Teaching to Transgress: Education as the Practice of Freedom.* New York: Routledge, 1994.

Howard, Jay R. *Discussion in the College Classroom: Getting Your Students Engaged and Participating in Person and Online.* San Francisco: Jossey-Bass, 2015.

Howes, Elaine V. *Connecting Girls and Science: Constructivism, Feminism, and Science Education Reform.* New York: Teachers College Press, 2002.

Hughes, Gethin, and Nick Yeung. "Dissociable Correlates of Response Conflict and Error Awareness in Error-Related Brain Activity." *Neuropsychologia* 49 (2011): 405–15.

Hughes, Scott Frederick. "Romancing Children into Delight: Promoting Children's Happiness in the Early Primary Grades." PhD diss., Queen's University, 2013.

Hult Jr., Richard E. "On Pedagogical Caring." *Educational Theory* 29.3 (1979): 237–43.

Hunter, Anne-Barrie, Sandra L. Laursen, and Elaine Seymour. "Becoming a Scientist: The Role of Undergraduate Research in Students' Cognitive, Personal, and Professional Development." *Science Education* 91 (2007): 36–74.

Huston, Dennis. Classroom observation. October 19, 2015.

Hutchinson, John S. *Concept Development Studies in Chemistry.* Rev. ed. Houston: Connexions, 2012. http://cnx.org/content/c0110264/1.5/

Hutchinson, John S., and Lesa Tran Lu. Personal interviews. October 20, 2015, and February 18, 2016.

Iacoboni, Marco. "Neurobiology of Imitation." *Current Opinion in Neurobiology* 19 (2009): 661–65.

Immordino-Yang, Mary Helen. *Emotions, Learning, and the Brain: Exploring the Educational Implications of Affective Neuroscience.* New York: Norton, 2016.

"Introduction to *A Class Divided*." *Frontline* (January 1, 2003): n.p. http://www.pbs.org/wgbh/frontline/article/introduction-2/

Ishiyama, John. "Does Early Participation in Undergraduate Research
    Benefit Social Science and Humanities Students?" *College Student
    Journal* 36 (2002): 380–86.

Izard, Véronique, et al. "Newborn Infants Perceive Abstract Numbers."
    Proceedings of the National Academy of Sciences 106 (2009):
    10382–85.

Jennings, Patricia A., and Mark T. Greenberg. "The Prosocial Classroom:
    Teacher Social and Emotional Competence in Relation to Student
    and Classroom Outcomes." *Review of Educational Research* 79
    (2009): 491–525.

Jerison, Harry J. *Evolution of the Brain and Intelligence.* New York:
    Academic Press, 1973.

Jirout, Jamie and David Klahr. "Children's Scientific Curiosity: In Search
    of an Operational Definition of an Elusive Concept." *Developmental
    Review* 32.2 (2012): 125–60.

Joosten, Tanya. *Social Media for Educators.* San Francisco: Jossey-Bass,
    2012.

Kahneman, Daniel. *Thinking, Fast and Slow.* New York: Farrar, Straus
    and Giroux, 2011.

Kamenetz, Anya. "MacArthur 'Genius' Angela Duckworth Responds to
    a New Critique of Grit." npr.org. May 25, 2016.

Kang, Min Jeong, et al. "The Wick in the Candle of Learning: Epistemic
    Curiosity Activates Reward Circuitry and Enhances Memory."
    Psychological Science 20.8 (2009): 963–73.

Kapur, Manu. "Examining Productive Failure, Productive Success,
    Unproductive Failure, and Unproductive Success in Learning."
    Educational Psychologist 51 (2016): 289–99.

Kawashima, Robert S. "Sources and Redaction." In *Reading Genesis: Ten
    Methods.* Ed. Ronald Hendel. Cambridge: Cambridge University
    Press, 2010. 47–70.

Kiesel, Andrea, et al. "Control and Interference in Task Switching—A
    Review." *Psychological Bulletin* 136 (2010): 849–74.

King, Barbara J. *The Dynamic Dance: Nonvocal Communication in African Great Apes*. Cambridge, MA: Harvard University Press, 2004.

———. *How Animals Grieve*. Chicago: University of Chicago Press, 2013.

Kirsch, Peter, et al. "Oxytocin Modulates Neural Circuitry for Social Cognition and Fear in Humans." *The Journal of Neuroscience* 25 (2005): 11489–493.

Kirschner, Paul A., John Sweller, and Richard E. Clark. "Why Minimal Guidance During Instruction Does Not Work: An Analysis of the Failure of Constructivist, Discovery, Problem-Based, Experiential, and Inquiry-Based Teaching." *Educational Psychologist* 41.2 (2006): 75–86.

Kiser, Barbara. "Learning Through Doing." *Nature* 523 (July 16, 2015): 286–89.

Knauft, Bruce M., et al. "Violence and Sociality in Human Evolution." *Current Anthropology* 32.4 (1991): 391–428.

Kolb, David A. *Experiential Learning: Experience as the Source of Learning and Development*, 2nd ed. New York: Pearson, 2014.

Kundu, Anindya. "Backtalk: Grit, Overemphasized; Agency, Over-looked." *The Phi Delta Kappan* 96 (2014): 80.

Lahey, Jessica. *The Gift of Failure*. New York: HarperCollins, 2015.

Lang, James. "How Orwell and Twitter Revitalized My Course." *Chronicle of Higher Education* (October 28, 2013): n.p. http://www.chronicle.com/article/How—OrwellTwitter/142617

———. *On Course: A Week-by-Week Guide to Your First Semester of College Teaching*. Cambridge, MA: Harvard University Press, 2010.

———. *Small Teaching: Everyday Lessons from the Science of Learning*. San Francisco: Jossey-Bass, 2016.

Lazarus, Paula Kay, and Gretchen Kreahling McKay. "The Reacting to the Past Pedagogy and Engaging the First-Year Student." *To Improve the Academy* 32 (2013): 351–63.

Lazarus, Richard S. "The Cognition-Emotion Debate: A Bit of History." In *Handbook of Cognition and Emotion.* Eds. Tim Dalgleish and Mick J. Power. Chichester: John Wiley & Sons, 1999. 3–20.

———. "Thoughts on the Relations between Emotion and Cognition." *American Psychologist* 37.9 (1982): 1019–24.

LeDoux, Joseph E. "Emotion: Clues from the Brain." *Annual Review of Psychology* 46 (1995): 209–35.

Leslie, Ian. *Curious: The Desire to Know and Why Your Future Depends on It.* New York: Basic Books, 2014.

Lewis, Michael, Steven M. Alessandri, and Margaret Wolan Sullivan. "Violation of Expectancy, Loss of Control, and Anger Expressions in Young Infants." *Developmental Psychology* 26.5 (1990): 745–51.

Lin-Siegler, Xiaodong, et al. "Even Einstein Struggled: Effects of Learning about Great Scientists' Struggles on High School Students' Motivation to Learn Science." *Journal of Educational Psychology* 108 (2016): 314–28.

Linnenbrink, Elizabeth A. "The Role of Affect in Student Learning: A Multi-Dimensional Approach to Considering the Interaction of Affect, Motivation, and Engagement." In *Emotion in Education.* Eds. Paul A. Schutz and Reinhard Pekrun. Burlington, MA: Academic Press, 2007. 107–24.

Livio, Mario. *Brilliant Blunders: From Darwin to Einstein—Colossal Mistakes by Great Scientists That Changed Our Understanding of Life and the Universe.* New York: Simon & Schuster, 2013.

———. *Why? What Makes Us Curious.* New York: Simon & Schuster, 2017.

Loewenstein, George. "The Psychology of Curiosity: A Review and Reinterpretation." *Psychological Bulletin* 116.1 (1994): 75–98.

Looser, Devoney. "Why I Teach Online." *Chronicle of Higher Education* (March 20, 2017):n.p.http://www.chronicle.com/article/Why-I-Teach-Online/239509

Lorenzo, Mercedes, Catherine H. Crouch, and Eric Mazur. "Reducing the Gender Gap in the Physics Classroom." *American Journal of Physics* 74 (2006): 118–22.

Love, Alan C. "Conceptual Change and Evolutionary Developmental Biology." In *Conceptual Change in Biology: Scientific and Philosophical Perspectives on Evolution and Development.* Ed. Alan C. Love. New York: Springer, 2015. 1–54.

MacDonald, Kai, and Tina Marie MacDonald. "The Peptide that Binds: A Systematic Review of Oxytocin and its Prosocial Effects in Humans." *Harvard Review of Psychiatry* 18 (2010): 1–21.

Macedonia, Manuela, and Katharina von Kriegstein. "Gestures Enhance Foreign Language Learning." *Biolinguistics* 6.3–4 (2012): 393–416.

Major, Claire Howell, Michael S. Harris, and Todd Zakrajsek. *Teaching for Learning: 101 Intentionally Designed Educational Activities to Put Students on the Path to Success.* New York: Routledge, 2016.

Mangels, Jennifer A., et al. "Why do Beliefs about Intelligence Influence Learning Success? A Social Cognitive Neuroscience Model." *Social Cognitive and Affective Neuroscience* 1.2 (2006): 75–86.

Maslow, Abraham H. "A Theory of Human Motivation." *Psychological Review* 50 (1943): 370–96.

Mazur, Eric. "Farewell, Lecture?" *Science* 323 (January 2, 2009): 50–51.

McKay, Gretchen Kreahling. Classroom observation and personal interview. September 23 and 25, 2014.

McNabb, Cameron Hunt. Personal Interview. September 30, 2016.

McNeill, David. *Hand and Mind: What Gestures Reveal about Thought.* Chicago: University of Chicago Press, 1992.

Middendorf, Joan, and Alan Kalish. "The 'Change-Up' in Lectures." *National Teaching and Learning Forum* 5.2 (1996): 1–5.

Miller, Geoffrey. "Brain Evolution." In *The Evolution of Mind: Fundamental Questions and Controversies.* Eds. Steven W. Gangestad and Jeffry A. Simpson. New York: Guilford Press, 2007. 287–93.

Miller, Michelle D. *Minds Online: Teaching Effectively with Technology*. Cambridge, MA: Harvard University Press, 2014.

Montessori, Maria. *The Absorbent Mind*. Trans. Claude A. Claremont. New York: Holt, Rinehart, and Winston, 1967.

Morgan-Short, Kara, Ingrid Finger, Sarah Grey, and Michael T. Ullman. "Second Language Processing Shows Increased Native-Like Responses after Months of No Exposure." *PLoS ONE* 7.3 (2012): 1–18.

Moser, Jason S., et al. "Mind Your Errors: Evidence for a Neural Mechanism Linking Growth Mind-Set to Adaptive Posterror Adjustments." *Psychological Science* 22 (2011): 1484–89.

Nagda, Biren, et al. "Undergraduate Student-Faculty Research Partnerships Affect Student Retention." *The Review of Higher Education* 22 (1998): 55–72.

Nave, C. R. "HyperPhysics." Georgia State University. http://hyperphysics.phy-astr.gsu.edu/hbase/hph.html

Newbury, Peter. "You Don't Have to Wait for the Clock to Strike to Start Teaching." *Science Edventures* (blog). August 23, 2013. http://www.peternewbury.org/2013/08/you-dont-have-to-wait-for-the-clock-to-strike-to-start-teaching/

Nilson, Linda B. *Specifications Grading: Restoring Rigor, Motivating Students, and Saving Faculty Time*. Sterling, VA: Stylus, 2015.

Noddings, Nel. *Caring: A Relational Approach to Ethics and Moral Education*, 2nd ed. Berkeley: University of California Press, 2013.

———. *Happiness and Education*. Cambridge: Cambridge University Press, 2003.

North, Anna. "The Dangers of 'Brain'-Speak." *Op-Talk* (blog). June 5, 2014. https://op-talk.blogs.nytimes.com/2014/06/05/the-dangers-of-brain-speak/

Nowak, Martin A., Corina E. Tarnita, and Edward O. Wilson. "The Evolution of Eusociality." *Nature* 466 (August 26, 2010): 1057–62.

Oatley, Keith, and Jennifer M. Jenkins. *Understanding Emotions.* Cambridge, MA: Blackwell, 1996.

O'Dell, Sean M. "Classroom Error Climate: Teacher Professional Development to Improve Student Motivation." Doctoral dissertation, University of Central Florida, 2015.

Op 't Eynde, Peter, Erik de Corte, and Lieven Verschaffel. "Students' Emotions: A Key Component of Self-Regulated Learning?" In *Emotion in Education.* Eds. Paul A. Schutz and Reinhard Pekrun. Burlington, MA: Academic Press, 2007. 185–204.

Ortony, Andrew, and Terence J. Turner. "What's Basic about Basic Emotions?" *Psychological Review* 97.3 (1990): 315–31.

Paige, Robin. "Addressing a 'Threat in the Air': How Stereotypes Affect Our Students and What We Can Do about It." *Reflections on Teaching and Learning: The CTE Blog* (blog). June 6, 2016. http://cte.rice.edu/blogarchive/2016/5/19/addressing-stereotype-threat-creating-an-inclusive-environment-in-the-college-classroom

———. "The Metaquestion: A Different Approach to Course Design." *Reflections on Teaching and Learning: The CTE Blog* (blog). March 9, 2016. http://cte.rice.edu/blogarchive/2016/03/09/metaquestions

Panksepp, Jaak, and Lucy Biven. *The Archaeology of Mind: Neuroevolutionary Origins of Human Emotions.* New York: Norton, 2012.

Persons, Charles E. "Teaching the Introductory Course in Economics." *The Quarterly Journal of Economics* 31 (1916): 86–107.

Pessoa, Luiz. "On the Relationship between Emotion and Cognition." *Nature Reviews—Neuroscience* 9.2 (2008): 148–58.

Peters, Ruth A. "Effects of Anxiety, Curiosity, and Perceived Instructor Threat on Student Verbal Behavior in the College Classroom." *Journal of Educational Psychology* 70.3 (1978): 388–95.

Petraglia, Joseph. *Reality by Design: The Rhetoric and Technology of Authenticity in Education.* Mahwah, NJ: Lawrence Erlbaum, 1998.

Phelps, Elizabeth A. "Emotion and Cognition: Insights from Studies of the Human Amygdala." *Annual Review of Psychology* 57 (2006): 27–53.

Phelps, Elizabeth A., and Joseph E. LeDoux. "Contributions of the Amygdala to Emotion Processing: from Animal Models to Human Behavior." *Neuron* 48 (2005): 175–87.

Piaget, Jean. *The Construction of Reality in the Child*. Abingdon, UK: Routledge, 2000. First published 1954 by Routledge and Kegan Paul Ltd.

———. *The Origin of Intelligence in the Child*. Trans. Margaret Cook. New York: Routledge, 1997. First published 1953 by Routledge.

Preszler, Ralph W. "Replacing Lecture with Peer-Led Workshops Improves Student Learning." *CBE—Life Sciences Education* 8 (2009): 182–92.

Purvis, Karyn B., and David R. Cross. "Caught between the Amygdala and a Hard Place." *Fostering Families Today* (November/December 2006): n.p.

Purvis, Karyn B., David R. Cross, and Wendy L. Sunshine. *The Connected Child*. New York: McGraw-Hill, 2007.

"Reacting to the Past: Curriculum." https://reacting.barnard.edu/node/2607

Respondek, Lisa, Tina Seufert, Robert Stupinsky, and Ulrike E. Nett. "Perceived Academic Control and Academic Emotions Predict Undergraduate University Student Success: Examining Effects on Dropout Intention and Achievement." *Frontiers in Psychology* 8 (2017): n.p. http://journal.frontiersin.org/article/10.3389/fpsyg.2017.00243/full

Roberts, Jay W. *Experiential Education in the College Context: What It Is, How It Works, and Why It Matters*. New York: Routledge, 2016.

Rothstein, Dan, and Luz Santana. *Make Just One Change: Teach Students to Ask Their Own Questions*. Cambridge, MA: Harvard Education Press, 2011.

Rovai, Alfred P. "Development of an Instrument to Measure Classroom Community." *The Internet and Higher Education* 5 (2002): 197–211.

Russell, Susan H., Mary P. Hancock, and James McCullough. "Benefits of Undergraduate Research Experiences." *Science* 316 (April 27, 2007): 548–49.

Saari, Donald. Personal interview. October 15, 2015.

Sanderson, Stephen K. *The Evolution of Human Sociality: A Darwinian Conflict Perspective.* Lanham, MD: Rowman & Littlefield, 2001.

Saterbak, Ann, and Matthew Wettergreen. Personal interviews. March 12, 2015.

Schmidt, Richard A., and Robert A. Bjork. "New Conceptualizations of Practice: Common Principles in Three Paradigms Suggest New Concepts for Training." *Psychological Science* 3 (1992): 207–17.

Schulz, Kathryn. *Being Wrong: Adventures in the Margin of Error.* New York: Ecco, 2010.

Scoffham, Stephen, and Jonathan Barnes. "Happiness Matters: Towards a Pedagogy of Happiness and Well-Being," *The Curriculum Journal* 22 (2011): 535–48.

Shaw, Kimberly. Classroom observation and personal interview. October 19, 2016.

Shernoff, David J., and Mihaly Csikszentmihalyi. "Flow in Schools: Cultivating Engaged Learners and Optimal Learning Environments." In *Handbook of Positive Psychology in Schools.* Eds. Rich Gilman, E. Scott Huebner, and Michael J. Furlong. New York: Routledge, 2009. 131–45.

Skerry, Amy E., Enoch Lambert, Lindsey J. Powell, and Katherine McAuliffe. "The Origins of Pedagogy: Developmental and Evolutionary Perspectives." *Evolutionary Psychology* 11 (2013): 550–72.

Smith, Karl A., Sheri D. Sheppard, David W. Johnson, and Roger T. Johnson. "Pedagogies of Engagement: Classroom-Based Practices." *Journal of Engineering Education* 94 (2005): 87–101.

Smith, Linda B., Esther Thelen, Robert Titzer, and Dewey McLin. "Knowing in the Context of Acting: The Task Dynamics of the A-Not-B Error." *Psychological Review* 106 (1999): 235–60.

Smith, Michelle K., et al. "Why Peer Instruction Improves Student
    Performance on In-Class Concept Questions." *Science* 323 (January
    2, 2009): 122–24.

Solomon, Daniel, et al. "Creating Classrooms that Students Experience
    as Communities." *American Journal of Community Psychology* 24
    (1996): 719–48.

Springer, Leonard, Mary Elizabeth Stanne, and Samuel S. Donovan.
    "Effects of Small-Group Learning on Undergraduates in Science,
    Mathematics, Engineering, and Technology." *Review of Educational
    Research* 69 (1999): 21–51.

Stahl, Aimee E., and Lisa Feigenson. "Observing the Unexpected
    Enhances Infants' Learning and Exploration." *Science* 348 (April 3,
    2015): 91–94.

Steele, Claude M. *Whistling Vivaldi: How Stereotypes Affect Us and
    What We Can Do*. New York: Norton, 2010.

Steuer, Gabrielle, and Markus Dresel. "A Constructive Error Climate as
    an Element of Effective Learning Environments." *Psychological Test
    and Assessment Modeling* 57 (2015): 262–75.

Strayhorn, Terrell L. *College Students' Sense of Belonging: A Key to
    Educational Success for All Students*. New York: Routledge, 2012.

Stroessner, Steven J., Laurie Susser Beckerman, and Alexis Whittaker.
    "All the World's a Stage? Consequences of a Role-Playing Pedagogy
    on Psychological Factors and Writing and Rhetorical Skill in
    College Undergraduates." *Journal of Educational Psychology* 101
    (2009): 605–20.

Svinicki, Marilla, and Wilbert J. McKeachie. *McKeachie's Teaching Tips:
    Strategies, Research, and Theory for College and University
    Teachers*, 13th ed. Belmont, CA: Wadsworth, 2011.

Tarlow, Sarah. "The Archaeology of Emotion and Affect." *Annual Review
    of Anthropology* 41 (2012): 169–85.

Tattersall, Ian. "Paleoanthropology and Language." In *New Perspectives
    on the Origins of Language*. Eds. Claire Lefebvre, Bernard Comrie,

and Henri Cohen. Amsterdam: John Benjamins Publishing, 2013. 129–46.

Taylor, Patricia R. Personal communication. July 6, 2016.

Taylor, Valerie Jones, and Gregory M. Walton. "Stereotype Threat Undermines Academic Learning." *Personality and Social Psychology Bulletin* 37.8 (2011): 1055–67.

Teevan, Richard C., and Paul E. McGhee. "Childhood Development of Fear of Failure Motivation." *Journal of Personality and Social Psychology* 21 (1972): 345–48.

Thornton, Alex, and Nichola J. Raihani. "The Evolution of Teaching." *Animal Behaviour* 75 (2008): 1823–36.

Tizard, Barbara, and Martin Hughes. *Young Children Learning.* Cambridge, MA: Harvard University Press, 1984.

Tokuhama-Espinosa, Tracey. *The New Science of Teaching and Learning: Using the Best of Mind, Brain, and Education Science in the Classroom.* New York: Teachers College Press, 2009.

Tough, Paul. *How Children Succeed: Grit, Curiosity, and the Hidden Power of Character.* Boston: Houghton Mifflin Harcourt, 2012.

Turner, Jonathan. *On the Origins of Human Emotions: A Sociological Inquiry into the Evolution of Human Affect.* Palo Alto, CA: Stanford University Press, 2000.

van Merriënboer, Jeroen J. G., and John Sweller. "Cognitive Load Theory and Complex Learning: Recent Developments and Future Directions." *Educational Psychology Review* 17.2 (2005): 147–77.

Velasquez, Andrea, Richard West, Charles Graham, and Richard Osguthorpe. "Developing Caring Relationships in Schools: A Review of the Research on Caring and Nurturing Pedagogies." *Review of Education* 1.2 (2013): 162–90.

von Stumm, Sophie, Benedikt Hell, and Tomas Chamorro-Premuzic. "The Hungry Mind: Intellectual Curiosity Is the Third Pillar of Academic Performance." *Perspectives on Psychological Science* 6 (2011): 574–88.

Voss, Hans-Georg, and Heidi Keller. *Curiosity and Exploration: Theories and Results*. New York: Academic Press, 1983.

Vygotsky, L. S. *Mind in Society: Development of Higher Psychological Processes*. Eds. Michael Cole, Vera John-Steiner, Sylvia Scribner, and Ellen Souberman. Cambridge, MA: Harvard University Press, 1980.

———. *Thought and Language*. Eds. and Trans. Eugenia Hanfmann, Gertrude Vakar, and Alex Kozulin. Revised and expanded ed. (Cambridge, MA: MIT Press, 2012).

Walton, Gregory M., and Geoffrey Cohen. "A Brief Social-Belonging Intervention Improves Academic and Health Outcomes of Minority Students." *Science* 331 (March 18, 2011): 1447–51.

———. "A Question of Belonging: Race, Social Fit, and Achievement." *Journal of Personality and Social Psychology* 92 (2007): 82–96.

Walvoord, Barbara E., and Virginia Johnson Anderson. *Effective Grading: A Tool for Learning and Assessment*. San Francisco: Jossey-Bass, 1998.

Wei, Chun-Wang, Nian-Shing Chen, and Kinshuk. "A Model of Social Presence in Online Classrooms." *Educational Technology Research and Development* 60 (2012): 529–45.

White, T. H. *The Once and Future King*. New York: Ace Books, 1987.

Wiersema, Jan R., Jacob J. van der Meere, and Herbert Roeyers. "Developmental Changes in Error Monitoring: An Event-Related Potential Study." *Neuropsychologia* 45 (2007): 1649–57.

Wiggins, Grant, and Jay McTighe. *Understanding by Design,* Expanded 2nd ed. Alexandria, VA: Association for Supervision and Curriculum Development, 2005.

Willingham, Daniel T. *Why Don't Students Like School?* San Francisco: Jossey-Bass, 2009.

Wilson, Karen, and James H. Korn. "Attention During Lectures: Beyond Ten Minutes." *Teaching of Psychology* 34.2 (2007): 85–89.

Yeager, David S., and Gregory M. Walton. "Social-Psychological Interventions in Education: They're Not Magic." *Review of Educational Research* 81 (2011): 267–301.

Yerushalmi, Edit, and Corina Polingher. "Guiding Students to Learn from Mistakes." *Physics Education* 41 (2006): 532–38.

Zajonc, Robert. "Feeling and Thinking: Preferences Need No Inferences." *American Psychologist* 35.2 (1980): 151–75.

Zuk, M. Marlene. *Paleofantasy: What Evolution Really Tells Us about Sex, Diet, and How We Live.* New York: Norton, 2013.

Zull, James E. *The Art of Changing the Brain: Enriching the Practice of Teaching by Exploring the Biology of Learning.* Sterling, VA: Stylus, 2002.

INDEX

—

evolutionary developmental
  biology, 8
  community, 67
  emphasis on continuity, 8
Excellent Sheep, 38
experiential learning, 3, 158–60
Eyler, Janet, 159

failure, 12, 22, 171–217
  as default, 172
  choking (as in, under pressure),
    183
  correcting faulty assumptions or
    hypotheses, 27
  desirable difficulties, 202–203
  learning from, 171–72, 196–97,
    216
  opportunities to fail with low
    stakes, 173, 197, 216
  prioritizing correctness, 173
  productive, 205
Falk, Dean, 24, 71
Fee, Chris, 2–3, 7, 15, 163
Feigenson, Lisa, 30
Fink, L. Dee, 42
Finlay, Barbara L., 26
Fosnot, Catherine Twomey, 51
framework
  complex conceptual, 24, 155
  developing new, 32
  for thinking, 106–107

of knowledge, 7
of learning, 78, 180
Freeman, Scott et al., 166
Friedlmeier, Wolfgang, 123

Gamble, Clive, 67
Gelman, Bernard D., 22
Gergely, György, 75–76
Gibson, Kathleen, 26–27
Goldin-Meadow, Susan, 89
Goldrick-Rab, Sara, 181, 188
Goldstein, Lisa, 132
Gómez, Juan Carlos, 8
Gopnik, Alison, 1, 8–9, 30
Gowlett, John, 67
grades, 183, 212–14, 217
  correctness, 173–74
  inhibiting novelty, 39–40
  online education, 108–109
Gräslund, Bo, 27
Greenberg, Mark, 86–87
grit, 198–200
Grossnickle, Emily M., 21, 23
Gruber, Matthias J., 22

Hanlon, Aaron, 143–44
Happiness and Education, 113
Harms, Peter D., 198–99
Harris, Michael, 100–101
Harter, Susan, 49